DREAMS AND MAGIC

THE unXPLAINED

DREAMS
AND MAGIC

p

First published in 2000 by Parragon

Parragon
Queen Street House
4 Queen Street
Bath BA1 1HE, UK

Produced by Magpie Books, an imprint of
Constable Robinson Ltd, London

Copyright © Parragon 2000

ARPT WKCC

ISBN 0-75253-595-1

Illustrations courtesy of Fortean Picture Library and Popperfoto

Page design by Sandie Boccacci

A copy of the British Library Cataloguing-in-Publication Data
is available from the British Library

Printed and bound in the EC

Contents

• •

Contents ·

PART THREE: Powers of Healing
SIMON TOMLIN

PART FOUR: Witches and Witchcraft
JOULES TAYLOR

PART FIVE: The Magical Arts

KEN TAYLOR

PART SIX: Dreams and Dreaming

JOULES TAYLOR

Introduction

●●●●●●●●●●●●●●●●●●●●●●●●●●●●●●●●●●●●●

Another thousand years has passed in the history of humankind, and as we celebrate the dawning of the third millennium we can justifiably take pride in our achievements. Comfortably insulated in our centrally-heated, double-glazed homes, with plentiful food in the fridge and within easy reach of medical services undreamed of even fifty years ago, we may well feel that we have our world neatly organized and under control. But is it? And do we?

Just glance up at the stars on a frosty winter's night, catch sight of the cold, pale moon gliding through the dark heavens and what do you feel? A sense of wonder, perhaps even a shiver of unease? Of course, we know all about the planets – we've even sent men to the moon – but there's more to it than that, isn't there? There's something about the scene that touches us deep inside – just as it must have touched our ancestors, who knew nothing about astronomy or even what was beyond the horizon. We may insulate ourselves from nature, but it is still there, waiting, just beyond our reach, and its secret mysteries are as fascinating to us today as they have been since time began. And what about those less tangible forces – the unseen influences and deep, disturbing feelings which our ancestors recognized and valued, but which are today dismissed and derided by those who pride themselves on their rational, scientific view of the universe. (The same people who, of course, never walk under ladders and always wear their "lucky" tie or necklace to important meetings or job interviews!) Then there are dreams, those bizarre, alien innerscapes over which we have no control and which baffle us with their strange, lucid visions.

All these strands are brought together in **Dreams and Magic**, a study of the beliefs, traditions, history and practice of the magical arts, healing, the mysterious world of dreams, secret sects and the old religions – Wicca or witchcraft and the worship of the Earth itself.

Our ancestors, of course, worshipped nature, so dependent were they on the seasons, the weather, for their very survival. Their lives were intricately linked to the rhythms of the natural world, the spirit of Mother Earth herself, source of all goodness. The four natural elements – Earth, Air, Fire and Water – were attuned in perfect harmony, and all life depended on living in accordance with natural laws, respecting the Earth and its gods, taking only what was needed and not damaging or despoiling the creations of the world. In **Earth Energies** Ken Taylor outlines these central beliefs and discusses the renewed interest today in such facets as crystallography, sacred sites and feng shui. Wicca or witchcraft, the craft of the wise, also celebrates the Earth, the Mother Goddess, giver of birth, death and rebirth. Time is seen as a great wheel, rolling onwards on its endless journey, and each individual's lifepath is inextricably intertwined with this natural cycle, as celebrated in Wicca festivals and rites of passage. Learn more about the history and contemporary practice of this fascinating belief system in Joules Taylor's **Witches and Witchcraft**.

Long and cruelly-persecuted, Wicca was driven underground for hundreds of years, its adherents forced to practise their gentle, creative faith in secret. Many other religious practices have, however, actively endorsed secrecy as vital to their function, and underground sects have flourished all over the world for centuries – such as the extraordinary twelfth-century Islamic Assassins, whose ability to gain access to the most heavily-guarded enemy to kill or leave a deadly warning defies belief; the rich and powerful crusading Templars; and the followers of Jim Jones and the People's Temple, who committed mass suicide in the South American jungle in 1978. In his chapter on **Ancient and Modern Secret Sects**, Jamie Stokes examines ten of the most famous sects from the past thousand years; he shows how they became powerful and the ways in which they maintain their commanding, all-pervasive hold over their followers.

The founders and leaders of secret sects have much in common with the great practitioners of the magical arts; they exert a profound impression upon all those around them and they are driven by an obsession which influences every aspect of their lives. The great medieval magicians and alchemists are often seen as being more akin to the devil than to the gods, but this impression can sometimes be misleading. Ken Taylor, in his chapter on **The Magical Arts**, shows how the practice of magic has sometimes become debased and devalued by human greed and desire. For the true magician was (and is today) searching for ways to help humankind, for the universal truths, although many were sidetracked into other paths which they thought

3

would lead to wealth and glory for themselves. These men took advantage of their skills and personal magnetism to deceive and cheat, in much the same way as we find tricksters and charlatans today who dupe and defraud vulnerable people.

Many sceptics would cast healers in that mould. However, the extraordinary and incontrovertible achievements of the laying-on of hands to heal and cure become even more amazing when we consider the phenomenon of distance healing, when the healer may be hundreds, if not thousands, of miles away from their patients. Simon Tomlin, in **Powers of Healing** takes a balanced view of the practice, and looks at other alternative forms such as hypnosis, herbalism, colour and sound therapy, and even the placebo effect.

"It's all in the mind" scoff the sceptics – and perhaps some of it is, but the fact remains that we know very little about how our brains work. Who can explain, satisfactorily, why we dream, for instance? The body, in its dreaming state, is practically paralysed, yet somewhere in our heads we have passed into another world, a world where all normal precepts and realities are inverted and invalidated; what, in everyday life, would be irrational and absurd, becomes normal and acceptable. Dreamworlds create their own powerful magic, yet they vanish almost instantly the moment we wake. The importance of this strange phenomenon is only now being realized – scientific studies show that dream-deprivation has serious effects on our physical, emotional and mental well-being. Joules Taylor, in **Dreams and Dreaming**, discusses the latest scientific findings on the physiology of dreams and shows how dreaming has fascinated psychologists from Freud and Jung onwards.

The strange dreamworlds we inhabit in our sleep have, so far, defied scientists who are unable to define and categorize the phenomenon according to their principles. But so have the magical arts in general, for in our twentieth-century dependence on science we have sometimes lost touch with our other powerful, non-rational abilities, the intuitive, sensitive aspects of human nature. Fortunately, a recent revival of interest in alternative methods of healing and non-main-stream religions, and a renewed respect for the Earth and its natural laws, have encouraged many millions of people to open their minds and hearts to these non-intellectual, emotional aspects of our human character. Let's not lose sight of these valuable insights, but use them to help us gain even greater and more lasting achievements for the benefit of us all in the next thousand years.

PART ONE

Ancient and Modern Secret Sects

●●●●●●●●●●●●●●●●●●●●●●●●●●●●●●●●●●●●●●

The Assassins

One of the most significant global developments of the second half of the twentieth century was the resurgence of Islamic culture. Centuries of slow decline had seen the old Turkish Ottoman empire slip from its position as one of the world's greatest and most enlightened cultures, to a corrupt and decaying regime held together by little more than greed and inertia. The two World Wars marked the final end of a culture that had become an empty shell of the great religious and political movement that had swept the Middle East and northern Africa after the death of the Moslem prophet Mohammed in 632 AD. Freed from its corrupt political structure the Islamic faith was reborn all across the region, and provided the motivating force behind a series of revolts against imperial rule by western European powers. In the decades that followed, the world came to know and fear the shadowy fundamentalist sects that carried out their holy wars against the unwanted cultural imperialism of the West. A new and terrifying term entered our vocabulary: "Islamic terrorism".

In the Western nations, where religion had largely become a cultural backwater, people struggled to understand what drove fundamentalists to carry out hand-grenade attacks at European airports packed with holidaymakers or to bring down an airliner full of "innocent" people with a bomb. Most terrifying of all was not the randomness of the violence but the total devotion of its perpetrators, who apparently thought nothing of driving a truck packed with explosives into a foreign embassy compound to meet their own certain death.

The terrorist activity of this period was not only a reaction to contemporary circumstances, but those who carried out these attacks that so shocked the world were also acting in accordance with a long tradition of fundamentalist terrorism. The roots of this tradition can be traced back to the eleventh century and the foundation of the legendary order of assassins. The assassins were the world's first true terrorists. They acted on the orders of a charismatic leader, they carried out political acts motivated by their religious beliefs and their devotion to their cause was utterly fanatical. Then, as now, they were lionized in their own lands and regarded with awe and fear by their enemies.

The origin of the movement that was to become the assassins can be traced back to the years immediately following the death of Mohammed in the seventh century. The prophet died without clearly indicating a successor and, as seems to be inevitable in all matters of belief, his followers soon split into two camps and stood behind different leaders. These two camps came to be known as the Sunni and the Shi'a respectively, and there was intense and bloody rivalry between them for centuries. The distinction still exists today, although in practice their faiths differ on only a few minor points of theology. The long and bitter war between Iran and Iraq in the 1980s can be traced, at least in part, to this divide.

In the years that followed the initial split the Shi'a also broke into two factions when the seventh Imam, the spiritual and political head, was passed over in favour of his younger brother. Those who held true to the seventh Imam, named Ismail, became known as the Ismailis and these were the spiritual ancestors of the assassins. By the middle of the eleventh century the Ismailis had become the dominant force in the Islamic world. Combining religious fervour with a devotion to learning and military training they swept aside the decadent Sunni regime. Suddenly the appearance of a new political force, the Turks, shifted the balance in favour of the Sunnis and the Ismailis were forced onto the defensive.

It was into this tumult that the Ismailis' greatest leader was born; Hasan bin Sabbah, the man who was to found the assassins sect and almost overturn the political order of the region. Hasan was born an orthodox Shi'a and only became a convert to the Ismailis after a serious illness almost cost him his life in 1072. After a two-year journey Hasan arrived in Cairo, a new city built as the seat of the Ismaili caliph. Although he became a favourite at the court, his extreme views often got him into trouble and eventually led to his being sentenced to death. Shortly before his execution was due to take place, one of the city's tallest and strongest towers collapsed, and this was taken as an omen that the fiery young Hasan should be allowed to live. Shortly afterwards, he took to the road to live the life of a wandering preacher for Ismailism.

There are numerous stories describing Hasan's journeys, many of which are similar to stories told about countless other prophets and holy men. On one occasion Hasan was on board a ship that was caught in a violent storm. Alone among the passengers Hasan remained calm and unafraid. He was confident that his god would not allow him to die until he had carried out his mission and restored the power of the Ismailis. When the storm miraculously passed and the vessel was able to continue on its journey, Hasan was hailed as a prophet and gained many followers.

Hasan clearly had a persuasive knack of collecting converts to his cause, especially in his homeland – the region around modern Tehran – and it was here that he established his stronghold. Above all he appealed to the people's hatred of Turkish rule, but he certainly also had the gift of inspiring religious devotion in his growing band of followers. Hasan knew that he could not rely on the Cairo caliph for support, enemies at the court had already tried to have him killed once, so he set about establishing a stronghold for himself. His first step was to acquire a fortress, an objective that he carried out in a manner that was to become typical.

First, Hasan sent preachers to the villages surrounding the castle and converted many of them to his cause. Then the military garrison and the servants at the castle itself were targeted. One day, the unfortunate owner of the castle woke up to find that virtually all his soldiers and staff had a new master and that the castle was no longer his. Hasan moved in and made the fortress, known as Alamut, or the Eagle's Nest, his home and base of operations for the next thirty-five years. His successes earned him the fear and respect of the whole region and also the nickname "Old Man of the Mountain", a title which still applied to his descendants two hundred years later when the Venetian explorer Marco Polo passed through the area.

Hasan's followers quickly took other strongholds in the region and Hasan himself gradually expanded his power to encompass all the surrounding villages. The Turks attempted full-scale military assaults against Alamut and other Ismaili castles, but Hasan had chosen his ground well and had the support of the local population. All the assaults failed and the Turks were forced to leave him to consolidate his power. Although the offensives against him were unsuccessful, Hasan knew that he could never defeat the vast Turkish armies in all-out war. He reasoned that, since he could not destroy his enemy's armies, he would destroy his enemies one by one by murder. The weapon in this new, personal, war was to be the assassins – the world's first dedicated terrorist organization.

By 1092 Hasan's most dangerous enemy was Nizam Al-Mulk, vizier of the Turkish sultan, Malik Shah. The sultan was young and Nizam had been vizier to his father for many years; he was the most powerful man in the empire and he was determined to put an end to Hasan and his annoying Persian uprisings. In October of 1092, during the feast of Ramadam, Nizam was being carried through the streets on a litter when he was approached by a holy man. The holy man, actually one of Hasan's agents in disguise, drew a knife and plunged it into the vizier's chest killing him instantly. The killer was immediately hacked to pieces by the vizier's guards, but it was too late, Nizam was dead and Hasan's reign of terror had begun.

Back at Alamut, Hasan was overjoyed by the news and the young man who had carried out the deed, Bu Tahir Arrani, was hailed as the first martyr of the assassins. Within a short time the sultan himself was dead, although historians are not sure if this was the work of the assassins, and two of his sons had also been stabbed. The shadowy and fanatical assassins' brotherhood seemed able to infiltrate any city and to reach any victim no matter how powerful. Invariably the assassin was struck down within a moment of carrying out his mission, but this didn't seem to deter others from stepping into his place. Where did these men come from and what drove them to act with such total disregard for their own lives?

There are many tales and legends about the initiation rites of the assassins, but almost all agree that initiates were willing to lay down their lives because they had already been given a glimpse of paradise after death. According to the ancient stories, initiates were given drugged wine that made them fall into a profound sleep. When they awoke, they found themselves in a beautiful and fragrant garden. The air was scented with blossom and filled with the gentle music of magnificent fountains, whose water splashed into pools filled with gemstones. Beautiful women draped with the finest silks played music, danced and satisfied the young men's every whim and desire. After a few days, they were drugged again and returned to the castle. When they awoke this time they were faced with the Old Man of the Mountain himself who told them that they had seen paradise and that to die in his service would transport them there instantly.

Life at the castle was very different from what the

initiates had seen in the garden of paradise. Meals were spartan and wine was absolutely forbidden in accordance with Muslim law. Legend has it that Hasan had one of his own sons executed for taking wine. The stark contrast between the pleasures of paradise and the soberness of life at Alamut impressed itself deeply on the minds of the assassins. At the centre of everything was Hasan, the man who held the key that would allow them to return to the garden, so it's little wonder they were so ready to die for him.

The word "assassin", which owes its English meaning to the activities of Hasan's political killers, comes from the Arabic word "hashshashin", which means "users of hashish". It has been claimed that the hashshashin were so named because they carried out their murders while under the influence of that drug, although it is more likely they were so named because they resembled crazed addicts without thought for their personal safety as they carried out their missions.

Some sources, including Marco Polo, maintain that the paradise garden was a real place that Hasan had built in a quiet valley near the castle. Others maintain that it was a paradise of the mind, a vision induced by a combination of powerful drugs, hypnosis and the influence of the stories the initiates had heard about the afterlife. Either way, the effect was undoubtedly profound. Hasan held the lives of his assassins in his hands. There are many stories of him ordering one of his followers to leap to his death from a window as a way of impressing a visitor. To be ordered to die by their master was the ultimate wish of any assassin, even if it did not involve a killing, because it was an invitation to paradise.

Hasan always chose his victims carefully to create

the greatest impact. The chaos in the Turkish court after the death of Sultan Malik Shah diverted attention from the Ismailis, and Hasan made sure that the conflict continued for as long as possible. He formed an uneasy alliance with one of the sultan's sons, Berkyaruq, and aided his bid for power by ordering his assassins to take out Berkyaruq's enemies. Once established in power Berkyaruq turned against Hasan, but the assassins had already infiltrated his army. Hasan ordered one of his men to leave a dagger stuck in the ground by the head of Berkyaruq's half-brother and military commander, Sanjar, as he slept. Later, Sanjar received a message reminding him the dagger could just have easily been in his chest.

No official at the court would leave his house without armour under his robes and there were constant rumours of plots and threatened assassinations. Despite his ability to strike almost anywhere at anytime, Hasan's bid to undermine the Turkish sultans eventually failed. The first blow came when the Shi'a caliph at Cairo was replaced by a man opposed to Hasan. Without even the nominal support of his own religious sect, Hasan found himself an old man and regarded as an enemy by almost the entire Islamic world. Many of Hasan's agents in Cairo were arrested and executed or exiled, and there seemed to be no hope of a comeback. The Old Man of the Mountain died in 1144 at the age of ninety, but it was not the end of the assassins.

By 1192 the assassins were deeply embroiled in the politics of the Third Crusade, the latest Christian holy war to take Jerusalem and Palestine. In that year, two assassins murdered the Crusader, Conrad of Montferrat, and Europe came to know of their existence for the first time. Their fanaticism and ruth-lessness became legendary in Europe through exagger-ated tales told in the chronicles of the time, and they passed into myth as the devious and insane Moslem of popular imagination. Their new master, the latest Old Man of the Mountain, was described as an evil and powerful sorcerer who could see all from his strong-hold and strike his enemies down at will.

The end came for the assassins when the armies of Ghengis Khan swept through Asia. By the time Marco Polo visited Alamut their power had all but disap-peared, although their legend would live on after them. Most of the assassins were killed by the Mongols. Some survived and their descendants live in Iran to this day; others fled as far afield as India where they may have met up with kindred spirits – the terrifying Thuggee.

The Templars

On the night of 12 October 1307, troops of the French King Philip I arrested more than 15,000 people who were members of the most powerful religious body in Europe, known as the Sacred Order of the Knights Templar. The subsequent execution of many of the Knights' leaders, and the dissolution of the order by Pope Clement V, signalled the end of a remarkable two-hundred-year story of adventure, war and politics. Since the destruction of their order the Templars have taken on a near legendary status; due in part to the allegations of heresy made against them by King Philip, they have been identified by various occult groups as holders of ancient wisdom and secrets who survive to this day as an underground movement.

The Templar story began in 1099, when the First Crusade against the Moslems succeeded in conquering the holy city of Jerusalem and much of Palestine. For the first time in centuries the way was open for Christian pilgrims to visit the lands they knew from the Bible. Unfortunately, the crusaders' victory over the Moslems had been less than complete and it remained a dangerous journey. Moslem raiders were keen on ambushing parties of pilgrims as they passed through the wild lands, and liberating any items of value they might have about them.

In 1118 one veteran of the First Crusade, a French knight named Hugh de Payens, decided that something had to be done and set out with a band of like-minded adventurers to curtail these raids. Initial successes brought them to the attention of the new Christian King of Jerusalem, Baldwin II, who gave them part of his royal palace near the ancient temple of Solomon, as their headquarters. Calling themselves the Poor Fellow-Soldiers of Christ and the Temple of Solomon, the small band of knights took oaths to defend pilgrims and to live a life of monastic simplicity and purity. They were essentially warrior monks.

In 1127 Hugh de Payens returned to Europe to seek funding for his rapidly-growing organization. He met St Bernard of Clairvaux, the founder of the Cistercian order of monks and one of the most influential churchmen in Europe. Bernard was greatly impressed by the new fighting order and wrote an open letter praising the Templars, as they were now known. Bernard praised the lifestyle of the knights as much as their mission, and noted that in an era when most supposedly Christian nobles were busy lining their pockets the Templars were true soldiers of God.

Although Bernard was probably genuinely impressed by the Templars, he also had an astute political mind and recognized the potential of a force of fighting men dedicated to the Christian church. Europe was a violent and dangerous place in the twelfth century, feudal lords hungry for power and wealth needed little excuse to start wars with their neighbours, and many openly flouted the spiritual authority of the church.

The church's best weapon against such men was excommunication, an order that prevented an individual from receiving the holy sacraments. Although considered a serious punishment in those days, it did little to prevent misconduct and diminished the church's available fighting force for the holy lands. The Templars, by contrast, had a policy of seeking out excommunicated knights and giving them a second chance in their order. Bernard saw a way of not only building a fanatical fighting force loyal to the pope alone, but also of turning the most dangerous hotheads of the age to a good purpose.

At the Council of Troyes, one of the defining moments in the history of the Roman Catholic Church, Hugh de Payens received official church sanctioning for the Templars. The Rule of the Temple, the code by which all Templars swore to live, was approved and its members were exempted from excommunication. With the approval of the highest authority in the church, money and other gifts flooded into the order's coffers. Kings, dukes, lords and other wealthy landowners from all over Europe gave them gifts, ranging from fine suits of armour and horses to entire estates and castles. The Templar Order quickly became one of the wealthiest landowners in Europe.

Within a few years, the church also granted them the right to have their own priests, so that previously excommunicated brothers could receive the sacrament, and exempted them from paying taxes.

The Second Crusade of 1146 to 1150 was intended to strengthen the Europeans' hold on the holy lands, but it met with disaster after disaster. The Templars fought bravely as they had promised, however, and gained even greater respect. To the pope it seemed that the Templars, although small in number, were the one force that had prevented the Crusade from ending in total defeat, and that they were all that stood between Jerusalem and a Moslem counter-attack. The truth of this belief was not to be tested until 1187 when the army of Saladin smashed a Christian army, including many Templars, at the Battle of the Horns of Hattin and went on to take the holy city itself.

In the thirty years between the end of the Second Crusade and their defeat at Hattin, the power of the Templars reached its peak. Later leaders of the order were often less dedicated to the cause than Hugh de Payens had been, and took advantage of the many opportunities to enrich themselves and their brothers. Much of their power was derived from the role they had taken on as the leading bankers of Europe and the Middle East. Many monarchs entrusted their funds to the Templars and fell under their sway by borrowing huge sums to pay for wars of their own.

Over the course of the twelfth century, things began to go badly wrong for the Crusader kingdoms. Jerusalem was retaken in 1228 but fell to Saladin in 1244, never to be recaptured. Stronghold after stronghold was overrun and, by 1290, the only Christian fort left in the region was the massive Templar castle at

Acre. It fell the following year and most of the Templars garrisoned there, including the then Grand Master of the order, died in the fighting. Despite having lost their foothold in the holy lands, and the very reason for their existence, the Templars were still strong, fabulously wealthy and not about to lie down and die. The head-quarters of the order was moved to Cyprus, where they continued to battle Moslem pirates in the Mediterranean.

Ever since their foundation the Templars had inspired not only admiration but also jealousy and resentment. Kings and lords, many of them in debt to the Templars, resented their exemption from taxes, while bishops and other powerful churchmen hated the fact that they answered to no authority other than the pope. When the order lost its last stronghold in the holy lands, its enemies saw their chance to strike. King Philip I of France, known as Philip the Fair, was the most powerful monarch in western Europe and one of the Templars' biggest debtors. He suggested that the Templars should be merged with another order of knights known as the Hospitallers, knowing that the idea would be furiously rejected by the order's then Grand Master, Jacques de Molay.

At about the same time, an ex-Templar who had been banned from the order for particularly blatant crimes, came to Philip and offered to give him infor-mation that could destroy the order. Philip was only too glad to hear it and listened to the revengeful knight's tale with interest. Esquiu de Florian told him that the Templars engaged in blasphemies and heresies of every imaginable kind, including spitting on the Cross, worshipping a false god called Baphomet and practising sexual perversions. Philip was

19

Armoiries accordées à
L'Ordre des Templiers par
le Pape Eugène III.

A Templar in his war outfit.

delighted; there had long been rumours that the order carried out weird and blasphemous rites during its secret initiation ceremonies and this was just the kind of detail that he needed to sway the opinion of the pope.

Pope Clement V was unimpressed by Philip's evidence, but he owed his position to the French king's military might and did not forbid him from taking action. The arrests of October 1307 included not just the knights of the order then in France, but virtually every kind of artisan and servant working on the order's many French estates. The Grand Master, Jacques de Molay, then in Paris, was among those arrested. Under torture administered by the feared Inquisition, most of the knights confessed to a range of charges. The details of their confessions, scrupulously copied down by Philip's agents, rarely corroborated one another. One of the commonest accusations was that the order worshipped a false god, and this was variously described by tortured knights as a skull encrusted with gems, a representation of the Moslem idol Baphomet, or the mummified corpse of a former Grand Master.

Those knights who repeated their confessions "voluntarily" three days after their interview with the Inquisition torturers were given penance and prison sentences. Those who refused to repeat their confessions were deemed to be heretics and handed over to the secular authorities for trial. After much vacillating the first trial got under way in April 1310. With the memory of their torture still burning in their minds, a number of Templars decided to go on the offensive. They recanted their confessions and vigorously asserted their innocence and the innocence of the order. Unfortunately Pope Clement had been almost entirely won over by Philip by this time and the strategy backfired badly. Sixty-seven knights were convicted of heresy and immediately burned at the stake.

Few knights attempted to defend themselves after that. In 1312 the pope formally dissolved the order and a large portion of its wealth was diverted into Philip's treasury. Jacques de Molay and three other of the order's most senior members were among those who recanted their original confessions, but they survived the mass burning of 1310. All four later re-confessed and were sentenced to life imprisonment but, as the sentence was being pronounced in front of a large crowd in Paris, Jacques de Molay shocked the authorities by withdrawing his confession once again.

> I confess that I am indeed guilty of the greatest infamy. But the infamy is that I have lied in admitting the disgusting charges laid against my order. I declare that the order is innocent. Its purity and saintliness have never been defiled. In truth, I had testified otherwise, but I did so from fear of terrible tortures. Life is offered to me but at the price of perfidy. At such a price life is not worth having.

There was uproar from the crowd, many of whom had been persuaded that the Templars were guilty of heresy. Philip was not pleased. The very next morning, 19 March 1314, all four men were burned at the stake. As the flames rose around him Jacques de Molay turned to the royal enclosure and cursed Philip, the pope and the king's minister, Nogaret.

Pope Clement, Chevalier Guillaume de Nogaret, King Philip, I summon you to the tribunal of Heaven before the year is ended, to receive your just punishment. I curse you and you will be cursed to the thirteenth generation of your lines.

The figurehead of the Templars died in agony, his words still ringing in the ears of his persecutors. Within a month, Clement V was dead; Philip the Fair was killed in a hunting accident seven months later and his first minister, Nogaret, died a few weeks after that. Jacques de Molay's curse seemed to have taken effect, which only added to suspicions about the true nature of the Templars.

Not all members of the order were arrested. In Spain and Cyprus many knights escaped persecution and went underground. In the centuries since the destruction of the Templar order, their name has been invoked by numerous secret sects and organizations who claimed them as ancestors for their own hidden powers.

It is difficult to imagine today the impact that the Crusades had on medieval society in Europe. The Middle East was seen as land of almost total mystery inhabited by people who were regarded as little more than human-like demons. Rumours about the magical and diabolical powers of the Moslems, or Saracens as they were then called, were rife. The Templars, as guardians of the holy lands, were suspected of having become involved in the dark, magical practices of the local inhabitants. Several factors contributed to these suspicions.

Firstly, the initiation rites of the order were secret. Even today historians do not know exactly what they involved, since no complete copies of the Rule of the Temple have survived. Initiation ceremonies took place in a locked and guarded chapel, and the initiated were warned to never to reveal their secrets to outsiders. Secondly, the Templars answered to no authority but their Grand Master and the pope. Neither church nor secular authorities had access to their internal affairs, fuelling speculation that much of what they got up to was "above the law" to say the least. Thirdly, the order was immensely wealthy. In an age when alchemy was openly practised and believed by many to be connected with satanic powers, it was easy to believe that the Templars' wealth was the result of a secret pact with the Devil, who had given them the secret of transmuting base metals into gold.

Almost all the evidence against the Templars was gained through confession. Under torture knights confessed to whatever crimes their tormentors mentioned – a familiar list that turns up again and again in medieval trials of heretics. The name of the alleged false god of the order, Baphomet, is a common medieval corruption of Mohammed, the prophet of Islam. No statues or images of this "idol" were found during searches of the Templars' forts. Most knights confessed to having spat on the cross as part of their initiation – again, a very common accusation levelled against supposed heretics, and one particularly popular with the church-going peasantry. Accusations of homosexuality, then considered an abomination, were also made. It is almost certain that in an order of 20,000 men, homosexual practices were widespread, just as they were in every monastic order and the church itself.

Since the eighteenth century the Templars have

been seen as representing a secret, underground religious tradition. It has been claimed that, during the early years of their formation in Jerusalem, they learned some truths about the life of Christ that did not fit with the New Testament version and which the Roman Catholic Church had to suppress to ensure its survival.

The most common suspicion is that the Templars learned that Christ did not die on the cross but survived and had children. It is claimed that the Templars' true mission was to defend the descendants of Christ, and to keep their identity secret until the time came for them to take their rightful place as rulers of the Earth. In this they are linked with a secret society known as the Priory of Sion, of which Leonardo da Vinci was said to be a prominent member. Some writers extend the story of the Templars into the present day, seeing their descendants as an underground organization of great power that controls governments and seeks world domination.

The Thuggee

When the British first began to arrive in India they found a land richer in unfamiliar beliefs than anything they had come across anywhere else in the world. The three major religions of the region, Islam, Hinduism and Buddhism, were supplemented by literally hundreds of sects, cults and movements, each one with its own distinct, and often distinctly strange, beliefs. In 1816 Robert Sherwood, a doctor stationed in Madras, wrote an article about one of the more terrifying cults of the region.

The article, entitled "On the Murderers Called Phansigers", described a group whose beliefs led them to see murder as a sacred act. The name "phansiger" is derived from a Hindustani word meaning "noose" and they earned it because of their habit of killing their victims by strangling them with a scarf. Also known as Thuggee, the cult caught the imagination of the British public and the word "thug" entered the English language meaning a mindless and brutal killer.

Sherwood's tale was certainly compelling. He had persuaded a group of Thuggee to tell him about their religious beliefs and practices. What struck Sherwood immediately was that, although the men were nominally Moslem, they actually worshipped a Hindu deity – Kali, the goddess of death. The Thuggee believed that they had been charged by Kali with the mission of killing demons that walked the Earth. At some point in the cult's history these demons had become identified with the thousands of pilgrims who travelled the roads of India every year during the pilgrimage season, which ran from November to December. Any goods that had belonged to the victims were seen as bounty from Kali and kept by the killers.

For most of the year the Thuggee lived as ordinary men in their villages. When pilgrimage season came around, however, they would set off in a band and travel for hundreds of miles in search of victims. After a few months on the road the band would return to its home village, richer from the results of their murders, and take up their ordinary lives again. It wasn't until 1829 when another Englishman, William Sleemen, published his own report on the Thuggee that the British realized the true extent of the cult. Sleemen, a British army captain, had studied Thuggee groups in the Nerbudda Valley and came to realize that the cult wasn't just a small local sect, but a nationwide phenomenon that was killing thousands of travellers every year.

India is a vast country and, at the beginning of the nineteenth century, its dangers were many and varied. Travellers who failed to return home after embarking on pilgrimages of hundreds of miles that might take many years, were simply assumed to have died or taken up residence somewhere else. Snakes, disease, starvation, natural disasters and bandits were just some of the more obvious causes of death that the hapless pilgrim could meet with, so the depredations of the Thuggee went virtually unnoticed. In any case the Thuggee were careful to conceal the evidence of their crimes.

Sleemen described their modus operandi in detail. Once they had travelled at least a hundred miles from home, to reduce the likelihood of being recognized, the Thuggee band would select its target. They preferred lone travellers who had obvious wealth, but could choose almost anyone. Once the victim had been chosen, a member of the band would befriend him on the road and offer to travel with him for safety. If the target was a larger group then several Thuggee would join them. Over a period of time other members of the band would join up with the travellers until they outnumbered the original group. Armed with total surprise and superior numbers the Thuggee would pounce.

The killing method was ritualized and highly effective. Three cultists would assault each victim simultaneously. One would grab his legs from behind and other would grab his arms, pulling him face down on the ground. The third killer then undid the length of cloth around his waist, slipped it around the victim's neck and swiftly strangled him. It was almost impossible for the victim to struggle or fight back and death was at least mercifully swift.

Once all the victims were dead their bodies were ritually mutilated and buried. To prevent identification of the victims their faces were stabbed and slashed repeatedly. Then, if there was time, the bodies would be dismembered and disembowelled to make decomposition swifter. Although these gruesome measures had a practical purpose the mutilations were seen as a part of the cultists' offering to Kali. The most important element of the ritual came once the bodies had been disposed of. The Thuggee erected a tent over the graves and held a sacred feast or Tuponee to honour their deity.

The leader of the Thuggee group first made an offering to Kali consisting of a pickaxe that had been used to bury the dead (considered their most sacred symbol), a piece of silver, some holy water and a little sugar or goor which the Thuggee regarded as holy food. This done, more goor would be distributed to those cultists who had proved themselves by strangling one of the victims. Those who hadn't killed were not allowed to take any of the sacred and sought-after food.

Although ruthless once they had selected their victims, the Thuggee had strict codes about who could be chosen – in fact they believed that their victims were pre-ordained by Kali and they did not "choose" them at all. Women were not killed, neither were craftsmen who worked in one of the trades protected by Kali; gold, iron and brass-workers, smiths, stonecutters, carpenters and cobblers were all protected, as were

28

blind or mutilated people, lepers and anyone leading a cow or a female goat. Violation of this code, whatever the temptation of rich spoils, was believed to lead to bad luck.

Not only did the cultists obey strict rules governing their murderous activities, but they often led lives of exemplary moral standards when at home and were highly regarded in their communities. One cultist served as many years as the trusted companion to the children of an English family living in Madras. Every year at the same time he was given leave to travel to his family's village to care for his mother – except that he actually went on a murderous spree across the countryside. Sleemen himself came to know many Thuggee and, although appalled by their beliefs, couldn't help but describe one leader he had met as "the best man I have ever known".

In 1830 the British authorities appointed Captain Sleemen to stamp out the threat of the Kali death cult. By this time the cult had actually become corrupt and lost many of its taboos. Many Thuggee gangs were little more than bandits, and didn't hesitate to kill women and children if it meant more loot. Some had also abandoned the strict rules about mutilating and burying the corpses of their victims. Coupled with the new and careful record-keeping of the British regime, this meant that more and more Thuggee were identified and arrested. Traditionalists of the cult were quick to point out that the suppression of their practices was clearly a punishment for having abandoned the old taboos, but it was too late by then.

By 1850 very few cultists remained and India's roads were much safer for pilgrims. Over four thousand members of the cult had been brought to trial. The

British, more concerned with stamping out the cult itself than individual retribution, gave pardons to those who turned informer. Fewer than five hundred of those convicted were executed, the rest were imprisoned for life or transported to other parts of the British empire.

Sleemen and others were fascinated by what drove such apparently gentle and moral men to commit such terrible acts of mass murder. One of the most famous of the Thuggee leaders, a man named Feringheea, was much admired by Sleemen who accepted that Feringheea saw the murders he carried out as sacred acts and not crimes. Sleemen successfully pleaded that Feringheea's death sentence should be commuted, even though he freely admitted that at the time of his arrest he had just returned from a journey during which he and his Thuggee band had killed more than a hundred men and women.

After his arrest Feringheea's testimony went some way to explaining his strange and dark calling:

> We all feel pity sometimes, but the goor of the Tuponee changes our nature. It would change the nature of a horse. Let any man taste of that goor, and he will be Thuggee though he know all the trades and have all the wealth in the world. I never wanted food; my mother's family was opulent, her relations high in office as I have been high in office myself. Yet I was always miserable when I was away from my brothers and obliged to return to the Thuggee. My father made me taste of that fatal goor when I was no more than a boy; and if I were to live a thousand years I shall never be able to follow any other trade.

It is clear from Feringheea's words that his devotion to the Kali cult was total, although not without its difficulties for his conscience. The religious ecstasy felt by the cultists as they partook of the sacred goor, in fact nothing more than coarse sugar, far outweighed any rational process. A sense of belonging and of being on an ordained mission also filled the cultists as it has the followers of many other, less deadly, religions.

The origins of the murderous Thuggee are something of a mystery. Many researchers have drawn parallels with the assassins of Persia and there is evidence that some Thuggee groups regarded the Ismaili Iman, leader of a breakaway Moslem movement, as their spiritual leader. Feringheea stated that representations of Thuggee rituals could be seen in the carvings of the Ellora temple complex. The caves and temples of Ellora in north-east Bombay are one of India's greatest treasures. Sculptures carved by Hindus, Jainists and Buddhists between the third and twelfth centuries line its walls. Feringheea claimed that the Thuggee had existed since the eighth century, at least two hundred years before the foundation of Persia's assassin brotherhood.

It is also notable that the methods of the assassins and the Thuggee are starkly different. Assassins famously had no concern for their personal safety and carried out their killings in public. The Thuggee on the other hand took great care to conceal their victims and to avoid detection – a practice that kept the true extent of their activities hidden for centuries. Some assassins certainly escaped into India when their own lands were overrun by Ghengis Khan in the thirteenth century, and it's entirely possible that they merged with already existing Thuggee clans, bringing their own beliefs and allegiances.

The Thuggee never really recovered from the onslaught of the British campaign against them in the mid-nineteenth century. Isolated murder sprees continued to occur right up until the 1940s and Kali has her followers even today, but the days when fanatical killers roamed the roads of India and killed in the name of their god are, thankfully, long gone.

The Khlysty

When Gregory Efimovich, a young carter from the little Siberian village of Pokrovskoe, agreed to take a theology student to the monastery at Verkhoture he little realized that it would change his life. On the journey, Gregory got talking to the student, whose name was Mileti Zaborovski, and impressed the young churchman with his knowledge of the Bible. Zaborovski was so impressed in fact that he invited his driver to spend some time studying at the monastery with him. Gregory readily agreed and ended up staying for four months. Verkhoture was no ordinary monastery; it was partly a prison and rehabilitation centre for members of a strange and heretical cult known as the Khlysty. Gregory was no ordinary man either; in later life he would come to be known as Rasputin and would hold the fate of all Russia in his hands.

Even as an adolescent the young Rasputin had a savage and dangerous streak. The little he had heard about the Khlysty's wild and orgiastic rites fascinated him and he was determined to find out more. Nobody knows for sure how much Rasputin found out about the Khlysty, although he was repeatedly accused in later life of being a secret member of the sect. It is fairly certain that he learned enough about their beliefs for it to affect his own views. His legendary taste for attractive women and wild living seems to suggest that he took at least some of them to heart.

The Khlysty emerged from a period of religious turmoil in Russia that had begun more than two hundred years before Rasputin's birth. In 1645, a wandering holy man, not unlike Rasputin himself, arrived in Moscow and became a favourite at the imperial court. The man's name was Nikon Mordvinov, a peasant who had turned to religion after the deaths of his three children. Within seven years Nikon had become the most powerful man in Russia after the tsar, and in 1652 he was appointed to run the country while the emperor was away campaigning. Nikon was obsessed with reforming the church although he seemed to have no clear ideas about how this should be done.

The reforms started with bizarre and arbitrary alterations to the standard prayer and service books of the Russian Orthodox Church. These included such theological masterstrokes as changing the spelling of Jesus and replacing the word "temple" with the word "church". Not only were the church authorities annoyed by these ridiculous and meaningless changes, they were also infuriated by Nikon's authoritarian, bullying approach. Nikon believed that the church should be the most powerful force in the country, and he encouraged priests to demand absolute obedience and respect from their parishioners. Failure to meet Nikon's standards could result in arrest, imprisonment and torture.

Those who resisted Nikon's reforms began to call themselves Old Believers and, for the first time in the history of Christianity in Russia, there was a religious divide. Eventually, Nikon incurred the disapproval of the tsar and was replaced. The Old Believers continued to resist the changes that the tsar had not bothered to abolish and a religious war was created out of nothing. Thousands of Old Believers were executed or exiled, thousands more committed mass suicide in an atmosphere of apocalyptic expectation. By the end of the century the largest concentrations of Old Believers had been eliminated. In fact small pockets persisted until well into the twentieth century. In the 1970s a family of Old Believers was discovered living in the remotest Siberian wastes, the patriarch still fuming over the policies of a tsar who had been dead for three hundred years – Russians have long memories.

Although the threat of the Old Believers was largely eliminated, an atmosphere of heightened religious feeling and chaos in the church encouraged a whole crop of bizarre and distinctly unorthodox sects to spring up. One of these was the Khlysty, which managed to survive for at least another two hundred years into the era of Rasputin and the last tsar of Russia. The essence of the Khlysty's beliefs was the idea that Christ is reincarnated in every new generation and suffers crucifixion in every new body – sometimes more than once. The Khlysty also believed that they alone could identify these incarnations, all of whom turn out to have been famous Russians.

One incarnation of Christ was believed to have been a man named Averzhan, who was crucified at the great Battle of Kulikovo in 1380. Another was a man named Yemeljan, who was executed by Ivan the Terrible. The most important was said to be Daniel Philipov, a peasant who had left his farm to support the Old Believers in the wars of the time of the reformer Nikon. The sites of Daniel's ministry were regarded by the Khlysty as the equivalent of Jerusalem or Mecca. His teachings were contained in a book known as the *Book of Doves* which instructed the faithful never to marry, drink, swear or produce children.

Given the somewhat strict, not to say suicidal, commandments of the Khlysty it is odd that they became known as wanton hedonists whose rituals included wild singing and all-night orgies. Nevertheless, that was the popular image and that was what attracted Rasputin. The root of this view can be traced to the sect's principle of the separation of the spirit and the flesh. The Khlysty believed the spirit to be good and the flesh to be evil. This led some groups down the extreme path, later followed by Rasputin, where spiritual good can only be achieved after passing through the evils of the flesh – in other words a person cannot be saved unless he or she has done something to be saved from.

Nineteenth-century descriptions of Khlysty ceremonies follow a familiar pattern. Like all suspected heretics they were accused of taking part in secret rituals, invariably held at night, that were based around unacceptable sexual licence.

> *The faithful used to assemble by night in a hut or forest clearing lit by hundreds of flaming torches. The purpose of these ceremonies was to create a religious ecstasy and an erotic frenzy. After magical invocations and hymns, the faithful formed a ring and began to sway in rhythm, then to whirl around*

and around, spinning faster and faster. As a state of dizziness was essential to the "divine flux" the master of ceremonies would whip any dancer who did not spin with sufficient vigour. The ceremony ended in a horrible orgy, with everyone rolling on the ground in ecstasy or in convulsions. They preached that he who is possessed by the spirit belongs not to himself but to the spirit that controls him and who is responsible for his actions and any sins he may commit. Finally the lights were extinguished and the worshippers coupled freely – the results frequently being incestuous.

Other accounts mention a sacred bowl of water which the Khlysty would dance around until it began to boil, and the faithful saw visions of a raven or a mother and child rising from the steam. The accuracy of such accounts is highly dubious; it has always been common practice to accuse unpopular, minority sects of sexual and spiritual perversion, and such accusations tend to reveal more about the accuser than they do about the truth. The real nature of Khlysty worship will probably never be known, but the practices of a group that grew out of the Khlysty are better documented.

The Skoptzy practised extreme self-mutilation where the Khlysty only went as far as whipping and scourging each other. In the 1760s a woman referred to by the Khlysty as "the mother of god" claimed to recognize a man named Kondrati Selivanov as the latest incarnation of Christ. Kondrati was to become the founder of the Skoptzy. A central precept of his teaching was that all men should be castrated and all women should have their breasts removed. Kondrati himself claimed to have castrated himself with a red-hot iron at the age of fourteen.

This was one of many periods of political turmoil in Russian history. The ineffectual Tsar Peter III had been ousted from his throne and later murdered by his wife, who ruled in his place as Catherine the Great. This rather unorthodox succession – there had never been a female ruler of Russia before – caused consternation in some circles and a number of adventurers and holy men saw a chance to grab power for themselves by claiming to be Peter, the true tsar. Among them was Kondrati Selivanov.

Catherine was a ruthless and clever leader and had little trouble putting down the contenders to her throne. Most ended up in exile or very dead at the hands of her zealous executioners. For example, a Cossack named Pugachev, who had claimed to be the true tsar, was brought to Moscow in an iron cage where he had his hands and feet cut off before being quartered alive. Kondrati was relatively lucky, perhaps because he posed no real threat. Catherine had him sent to a mental asylum and he was released in 1801 when Alexander I came to the throne.

Now well into his seventies Kondrati, who was known to his followers as Selivanov, found that his popularity seem to be growing rapidly. He continued to claim that he was Peter III and devotees carried an old coin with Peter's head on it as a symbol of their faith. Selivanov continued to preach his message of total abstinence and mutilation of the sexual organs. He was said to have carried out over a hundred "operations" himself. Although his followers were convinced that he was the true Messiah, few were willing to carry out his teachings to the letter. Sect members tended to carry out symbolic mutilations of their own bodies, for example it was considered acceptable for a woman to remove a nipple rather than a whole breast. In some quarters, however, the Skoptzy were zealous in sticking to the letter of the law, and men and women were subjected to horrendous mutilations that often resulted in infection and death. Children of sect members were taught to expect similar ministrations when they reached puberty and it was said that those who ran away were hunted down and ritually murdered.

Despite the rather obvious contradiction involved, the Skoptzy were accused of taking part in exactly the same kind of orgiastic rights as the Khlysty. It was claimed that members of a lower order of Skoptzy were "left whole" and used to replenish the numbers of the sect. Lower-order sect women were accused of being prostitutes whose job it was to earn money for the sect and find potential converts. Such practices, although unproven, are certainly possible. Very similar techniques were used by the sect known as the Children of God in the 1970s.

Selivanov himself died in 1830, reputedly well over a hundred years old. For decades, most Skoptzy refused to believe that he was dead and later generations came to expect his imminent reincarnation. According to Skoptzy doctrine, Selivanov will return to earth in the Irkutsk region of eastern Russia when the number of his followers who are perfect virgins reaches exactly 144,000. Like the Khlysty, the Skoptzy survived into recent times and in the chaos of modern Russia might be expected to make something of a comeback.

The Skoptzy and the Khlysty were not the only odd cults and sects found in Russia in the period before the

Bolshevik revolution. In much the same way as the original Old Believers, who used to commit mass suicide on giant bonfires, many of them had suicidal urges that echo some of the more disturbing cults of the late twentieth century. One of the most bizarre must surely be the so-called Ticklers, whose rites included mercilessly tickling selected sect members until they passed out or died of exhaustion.

Another suicide cult that used more direct methods was founded in the reign of Alexander II by a man named Shodkin. On the day appointed by their leader dozens of the faithful made their way to a cave and sealed themselves in to wait for death. When one woman decided that perhaps she didn't want to suffocate to death in a cave after all and broke out to alert the police, Shodkin ordered the rest of his followers to kill each other. Oddly, Shodkin and his right-hand man were the only two left alive when the authorities arrived.

The Anabaptists

The history of the Christian Church in Europe is notoriously steeped in blood, but few episodes in the long catalogue of man's inhumanity to man over the issue of religion can match the era that followed the coming of the great Reformation in the sixteenth century.

The basic story of the Reformation is well known. Several times in the history of the Roman Catholic Church, visionary reformers had tried to sweep away the abuses of power and the influence of worldly concerns that seemed to afflict the church so heavily. One of these periods of reform resulted in the creation of the great monastic movements of the ninth to the thirteenth centuries. Conceived by their founders as perfect communities living strictly according to Christ's teachings, these too had become largely corrupt and worldly institutions by the sixteenth century.

Other "heresies" arose out of peoples' discontent with the established church, such as the Albigensian sect, and were brutally persecuted by kings and popes alike. It wasn't until the emergence of a man named Martin Luther that a widespread and lasting schism was created in the Western Christian faith that offered people a real choice. Martin Luther famously nailed his complaints against the abuses of the Roman Catholic Church to a church door in Wittenberg. His actions, and the brilliance with which he defended his views in the face of the bitterest abuse, opened the floodgates for a Europe-wide revolution in religious thinking.

In the decades following Luther's opening salvo much of Europe was converted to his views and, although this was later to be largely reversed in a series of bitter and devastating wars, for a while at least, a cornucopia of new faiths and sects flourished. One of the most vociferous was the Anabaptist sect. Like other groups protesting against Roman Catholic traditions, the Anabaptists wanted a faith in which the individual was free to make up his or her own mind about what was a sin from reading the Bible. Until the Reformation, the Bible was reproduced only in Latin so that the vast majority of uneducated people had to rely on the interpretation of their priest. For the first time the Bible was made available in the languages spoken by ordinary people.

The Anabaptists received their name because they believed that the practice of baptizing infants was wrong and had no biblical justification. In fact the name was misleading. Coined by their critics it implied that the group believed in re-baptism; *ana* is from the Greek meaning "again". Their actual belief was that a person should not be baptized until they were old enough to fully understand the meaning of the faith they were committing themselves to. To the Roman Catholic Church understanding was unnecessary for faith; all that was required was that the individual live according to the laws handed down to him by the pope – God's representative on Earth.

The birth of the Anabaptist faith is often traced to 21 January 1525. On that day a group of leading protesters, or "Protestants" as they came to be known, in Zurich decided to baptize each other as a symbol of their new faith. Even though the city authorities of the time had a degree of sympathy for the Protestants' views the actions of the re-baptizers were a step too far. In a move typical of the cruelty and intolerance of the age an Anabaptist leader, Felix Manz, was executed by drowning – dubbed the "third baptism" – and his colleagues were burned as heretics. Another group was locked up in a tower and left to starve to death, until the stench of rotting bodies caused complaints from locals and the few wretched survivors were dispatched with the sword. Despite persecution of this kind the movement grew rapidly and developed a well-thought-out canon of beliefs.

Not surprisingly the Anabaptists were seen as a dire threat to society by governments and the church. In many ways these fears were to be proved absolutely right. Although professed pacifists, a streak of violent

Anabaptist beliefs and goals

1. The restoration of "original" Christianity; including the abolition of oaths to church or state and the ending of capital punishment.

2. The total authority of the scriptures as the only source of knowledge about God's will. No law or custom could be supported unless there was a precedent for it in the Bible.

3. The rejection of infant baptism as unsupported by scripture.

4. The creation of the kingdom of God on Earth; a totally new society in which wealth and privilege were to be eradicated and all goods and property were to be held in common.

radicalism characterized the movement and lead to a number of armed conflicts.

Thomas Münzer, a Protestant reformer from southern Germany, is seen as one of the founding fathers of the Anabaptists. Arriving in the city of Müllhausen in 1525 Münzer, and a fellow reformer named Pfeifer, attracted a huge following. Within a short time they had established themselves as the absolute rulers of the city and had begun to build an army to overthrow the feudal rulers of the region. Before their preparations were complete, however, several powerful nobles launched a combined attack against the city and destroyed Münzer's army at the Battle of Frankenhausen. Münzer and Pfeifer were both executed as heretics. Another uprising in southern Germany, known as the Peasants' War, was largely inspired by Anabaptist leaders, but it too was brutally suppressed. Both Protestant and Roman Catholic governments in the regions of Germany – then a collection of semi-independent states – attempted to stamp out the Anabaptists. In towns and cities across the region there were nightly burnings of members of the sect, often billed as popular entertainment. It looked as if the movement had stalled before it had really got started but the most startling developments were still to come.

Many persecuted sects found refuge in the Netherlands during this period. Then, as now, it was a tolerant state. Among them were the Anabaptists, who had found a place under the leadership of one Melchior Hoffman. Hoffman's followers continued to travel widely throughout Germany and, in 1533, a number of them arrived in the city of Münster in Westphalia.

Two of their leaders, John Matthys and John Bockold, made a dramatic entrance to the city when they turned up one day in the market square and announced that Münster was to become the new Jerusalem. Attired in rich, flowing robes and accompanied by his beautiful wife, an ex-nun, Matthys proceeded to read the tenets of the new faith to the startled townsfolk from two stone tablets. He called the citizens of Münster "God's chosen people" and very quickly gathered a huge following, particularly among the women of the city.

Within a month of their arrival the two men had gained total control of the city's governing body and set about creating the Kingdom of God on Earth. One of their first acts was to banish all those who refused to convert to Anabaptism. Dissenters were stripped of all their worldly goods, including their clothes, and thrown out of the city; their wealth was then redistributed among the remaining citizens in keeping with the Anabaptist principle of common ownership.

The local ruler, the Bishop of Münster, backed up by troops from neighbouring governments, reacted quickly and a large force soon laid siege to the city. Matthys proved to be more resilient than previous Anabaptist leaders and organized the defence of the city well. Unfortunately for him he was misled by a vision which convinced him that he could defeat the encircling army with just twenty men. Within minutes of riding forth to liberate the city, he and his tiny band were cut to pieces. John Bockold, also known as John of Leyden, announced that he was taking over as leader and appropriated Matthys's wife as his first act.

Bockold reorganized the city's government, appointing himself as king of the new Jerusalem, and twelve of his most trusted followers as a ruling council. New laws came thick and fast. All property was to be communal; divorce and polygamy were to be legal and the death penalty was introduced for blasphemers and women who refused to marry any man who chose them. Bockold himself eventually took sixteen wives and dressed them and himself in the finest silks. He had crown jewels made from gold melted down from the "common" treasury and medallions were struck bearing Bockold's head and the inscription "The Word Was Made Flesh" – a direct reference to the biblical description of Christ.

A proclamation was issued and read aloud from the street corners:

John Bockold of Leyden, the saint and prophet of God, must be king of the whole Earth. His authority will extend over emperors, kings and princes, and all the powers of the world, and none shall rise above him. He will occupy the throne of his father, David, and will carry the sceptre till the Lord reclaims it from him.

Religious fervour gripped the city. Every night gangs of devotees high on expectations of an imminent apocalypse would dance through the streets, speaking in tongues and proclaiming the majesty of their king. The women of the city especially, who were trained to take an active part in its defence, took the fervour to greater and greater heights. Outside the city walls the besiegers heard these riotous goings-on and imagined blasphemous rituals and wild orgies. The latter certainly took place and increasingly so as the siege dragged on and on into its twelfth month.

By the summer of 1535 the citizens of Münster were starving, and moral and social order had almost totally broken down. Bockold promised miracles but they never came, and there were growing voices of dissent. Eventually Bockold allowed those who wished to surrender to leave the city, although he warned them that they risked eternal damnation. Those who did leave found themselves in an even worse position. Able-bodied men were executed immediately while the rest were kept in the no man's land between the surrounding troops and the city walls. There they slowly starved to death under the taunts of their former brethren still inside the city.

Bockold, finally realizing that the end had come, made preparations to set fire to the city killing everyone inside and delivering them to paradise. Just as the act was about to be carried out, one of the exiles showed the soldiers a secret way into the city and troops crept in under cover of darkness. After a day of savage fighting the Anabaptists had been conquered. Bockold and a few of the other leaders were captured alive and paraded through Germany. Six months later they were taken back to Münster and tortured to death in the town square. Bockold's torn and battered body was put in an iron cage suspended from the church of St Lambert. The cage hangs there to this day.

It was the end of the Anabaptists' dream of creating a new social order. Hunted and persecuted by virtually every authority in Europe, members survived by renaming their churches or moving to new locations. The sect survived in a much milder form and thrives to this day – modern-day Mennonites are direct spiritual descendants of the sixteenth-century Anabaptists. Many of its members emigrated to England and later made their way to America where persecution and association with the excesses of Münster were less of a risk.

Ironically the Anabaptists were probably the most populist of all the major sects that emerged from the Reformation. Unlike the Lutherans they were as concerned with political reform as reform of the church, and this made them a focus for much of the dissatisfaction felt by the ordinary people of the era – hence their involvement in the Peasants' War and the uprising at Mühlhausen. Also, unlike other Protestant groups, their leaders tended to be simple tradesmen rather than highly educated priests, like Luther, who had decided to leave the church. Both these factors contributed to their downfall: they were simply too radical and became something of a scapegoat for both sides in the great religious struggle.

The Family

Born in Cincinnati in 1934, Charles Manson had the kind of nightmare childhood that could turn a child psychologist's hair white. His mother was a fifteen-year-old girl who had become pregnant by her seventeen-year-old boyfriend, and she clearly had very little interest in the child. Manson was passed around from relative to relative while his mother got drunk, indulged in endless short-term love affairs and eventually ended up in jail for armed robbery. When Manson was ten she tried, unsuccessfully, to have him taken into a foster home, and when he was twelve he was sent to an institution in Indiana.

Manson, feeling rejected and ignored, developed a hatred for institutions that was to remain with him. During frequent "escapes" Manson committed a series of burglaries and armed robberies and, aged thirteen, was sent to a reform school for young offenders. A parole officer, who knew Manson at the time, later described him as the most aggressive and violent young inmate he had ever met. He had a tremendous desire to dominate and compensated for his rather slight physical stature with displays of bravado and violence.

After his release, at the age of twenty, Manson married a seventeen-year-old and drove across the country with her to Los Angeles. In 1956 Manson's wife had a son; Manson himself was sent to prison for car theft – he had driven to California in a stolen car – and spent the next ten years in and out of jail for a series of offences. In 1967, now aged thirty-two, Manson drifted to San Francisco. The city had become the spiritual centre of the hippy movement in America; free love and experimentation with mind-altering drugs were widely advocated and practised. Manson liked to talk himself up and had soon acquired a retinue of awestruck fans.

Manson had a strong dislike of women and sex, but he enjoyed dominating his female admirers and built up a veritable harem of young girls who responded to his intense personality. Many of these girls had psychological problems of their own which Manson took full advantage of. Despite frequent beatings and threats of mutilation, Manson's women were utterly devoted to him. One girl, Susan Atkins, later described him as "the only man I have ever met . . . He will not take back-talk from a woman. He will not let a woman talk him into doing anything. He is a man".

By October 1967 Manson had begun to indoctrinate his small band of devotees, who he referred to as "The Family", into the belief that he was a Messiah. He was fond of pointing out that his name meant "son of man" and hinted that he had been Jesus in a previous life. Tiring of the city, Manson decided to take his Family into the wilderness. The hippy doctrines of freedom and revolution had allowed him to assemble a group who could be moulded to his will, but Manson's ultimate goals were far from peace and love. They drove to a ranch that one of the girls had told them was owned by a blind man named George Spahn, and persuaded him to let them stay for a few weeks.

Now numbering sixteen girls and four men, Manson's Family, isolated in remote Topanga Canyon and almost constantly high on LSD, were drawn deeper and deeper into their leader's weird belief system. He taught them to hate authority and the established social order and prophesized that a great racial war was coming in which the white race and the black race would battle for world supremecy. Amongst other things Manson thought of himself as a musical genius and believed that legendary pop group The Beatles were attempting to communicate with him through their songs.

In the song *Revolution 9*, Manson believed he could hear a voice whispering "Charlie, Charlie, send us a telegram". The title was significant to Manson because it was the number of his favourite chapter in the Book of Revelations. He often quoted its apocalyptic words to his Family.

> *Neither repented they of their murders, nor of their sorceries, nor of their fornications, nor of their thefts.*

The message was clear; any crime was acceptable for the Messiah or his followers. Another Beatles' hit, *Helter Skelter*, was to provide Manson with the codeword for the final conflict that he saw coming. Manson was violently racist but nevertheless believed that the blacks would triumph in the war. After that, Manson told his followers, they would realize that they were incapable of governing themselves and turn to him for help. The war would be global and result in nuclear holocaust but Manson reassured his followers that they would survive. Eventually he also came to believe that he himself would have to strike the first blow.

For a while it looked as though fame and fortune would step in and divert the coming tragedy of the Family. Manson sold a song to the Beach Boys and one of the band's members invited him and the Family to live in his luxury house for a while. Separate developments led to discussions about a twenty-thousand dollar record deal, but these came to nothing. If Manson had become suddenly wealthy and achieved his ambition of pop stardom it's likely that his need to be recognized and praised would have been satisfied, or at least channelled down less dangerous avenues. As it was, Manson's brief success came to nothing and he went back to brooding on his apocalyptic visions.

Meanwhile the Family continued its wandering existence. In October 1968 they drove into the Mohave desert's Death Valley and spent some time living in an abandoned ranch house. Manson's proclamations to the family became darker and his hatred of the establishment more marked. Manson's women were treated with ever-increasing brutality; they were expected to remain silent, to do all the daily chores and to submit to the sexual advances of any male member of the family at any time. Despite their treatment they remained devoted to their leader. One later commented, "I never wanted him to hit me, but I wanted to be made to see in a different way. And the only way Charlie knew how to make me see in a different way was to do that."

Whatever she was "made to see" it would have been increasingly obvious to an outside observer that the Family was heading for disaster. Back in Los Angeles Manson, now on a non-stop psychedelic trip, started to act out his violent compulsions. The family began to collect guns and knives and, in 1968, Manson shot a black drug dealer named Crowe. The man recovered in hospital and the police did not become involved. In July, Manson slashed and stabbed Gary Hinman with a sword when he refused to give up all his possessions and join the Family. He later died. Back at the Spahn ranch the group began to come under suspicion from the police, who connected them to a number of car and credit card thefts. Unfortunately the link was never made with the violent attacks that Manson had carried out in the city.

Then, early in August, Manson made the announcement the Family had been waiting for. The time for Helter Skelter had come. On the evening of 8 August four members of the family set off by car from the Spahn ranch. Tex Wilson, Linda Kasabian, Susan Atkins and Patricia Krenwinkel drove to 10050 Cielo Drive intending to murder everyone in the house. Manson knew the house from the days of his near-miss record contract and briefed the murder gang about its layout. The house was then being rented by Polish film director, Roman Polanski, and was occupied by Polanski's wife, movie actress Sharon Tate, and three dinner guests. Polanski himself was in London.

The gang arrived at the house late in the evening and cut the telephone wires before proceeding. A young man, Steven Parent, who had been visiting one of the house staff became their first victim. As he drove down the drive he stopped to ask the four what they were doing and was shot five times in the head. At the house, the gang broke in through a screen door and went into the living room where one guest was alseep on the settee. He was woken up and his hands were tied behind his back. Another man came downstairs, saw what was happening, and made a grab for the gun. He was shot through the chest. The other two guests were shot as thay tried to escape and then stabbed several times. Sharon Tate, who was heavily pregnant, was stabbed in the chest and left to bleed to death.

Outside, the gang stripped of their blood-soaked clothes and showered in a lawn sprinkler. An elderly resident noted the number of their car as they left, but did not report it to the police. Later that night, Manson himself visited the murder scene to make sure everybody was dead. The bodies were not found until the next morning when a housemaid turned up for work. By the afternoon the news was dominated by the brutal murders, the story made all the more sensational by the wealth and fame of the victims. Manson was delighted. His aim was to make people believe that the murders had been carried out by blacks, hoping that it would spark the race war he had predicted. To make sure, Manson decided to stage another attack.

The next evening Manson and six members of the Family set out for the city again. They chose a house at random and Manson broke in without trouble. Upstairs in the bedroom he found middle-aged couple Leno and Rosemary LeBianca. With a gun in his hand he ordered them to get up and then tied them both hand and foot. Manson then went back to the car and ordered two veterans of the previous night's murders, and another girl, to go into the house and kill the couple.

Between them the LeBiancas suffered sixty-seven stab wounds. Rosemary had been struck with such force that her spine was severed and somebody had carved the word "War" on her chest. Before they left, the killers calmly took a shower, helped themselves to a snack from the kitchen and fed the LeBiancas' two dogs – concerned that they might starve before their owners were discovered. Police found "Helter Skelter"drawn in blood on a bedroom wall. A second target that night was abandoned when Manson left two of his girls in an apartment block with orders to kill a movie producer. The girls deliberately knocked on the wrong door and reported back that the intended victim was not at home.

Back at their makeshift home the Family continued to come under police scrutiny for entirely unconnected crimes. Just six days after the murders, Manson and twenty-four Family members were arrested and the car used in both murders was seized. Four days later they were all released. At around the same time a ranch hand named Shorty O'Shea disappeared from the Spahn ranch. Many believe that he was murdered by the Family because he knew too much about their activities and because he had recently married a black woman. The case has never been proved conclusively because his body has never been found.

In September the Family moved back to Death Valley where they again attracted police attention after setting fire to a bulldozer. On 9 October police raided the Family's new home after a local mineworker said that they had attempted to kill him. Manson was not at the ranch at the time but police arrested most of the women on the premises. Three days later Manson nearly escaped a second raid when he hid in a tiny kitchen cupboard, but he was discovered at the last minute and taken into custody. The police had no idea that they already had the killers they were searching for in custody until Susan Atkins, in jail in Los Angeles under suspicion of involvement in the attack on Gary Hinman, confessed to the murder of Sharon Tate.

Manson and those directly involved with the killings were brought to trial. Other members of the Family were released and still others had never been arrested. Eight days into the trial the attorney assigned to defend the Family, Ronald Hughes, disappeared and his decomposed body was later found in the desert. Hughes had strongly opposed Manson's decision to plead not guilty and many people suspect that he was killed by Family members on their leader's orders. On 30 March, Charles Manson, Susan Atkins, Leslie Van Houten and Patricia Krenwinkle were sentenced to death. Tex Watson received the same sentence a year later. Although California had the death penalty at the time, executions were never carried out so the sentence effectively meant life imprisonment.

Manson and the accused Family members maintained their innocence all through the trial and long afterwards. When faced with overwhelming evidence of their guilt they insisted that the guilt lay with society and not with them. In the words of Manson's favourite biblical quotation "neither repented they of their murders . . . nor of their fornications".

Self-styled Messiah and leader of the Family, Charles Manson currently resides in a maximum security penitentiary in California. He has made a number of escape bids since his conviction, has applied for and been refused parole numerous times, and continues to maintain his innocence. For a brief period in the early 1970s he was regarded as the ultimate anti-hero by extremists of the hippy movement, who saw him as a man who had struck a real blow against authority. Ironically for a man so opposed to institutions he has spent all but a brief period of his adult life in one prison or another. Debates have raged about Manson as they have about other killers: is he mad or bad; should he have been executed; what drove the Family to follow him? Whatever the answers to these questions the story of his life was plainly that of a tragedy waiting to happen.

Jim Jones and the People's Temple

18 November 1978 became a defining moment in the world's perception of religious sects and cults. Over the course of several days, news emerged that on that date more than nine hundred people, all belonging to the People's Temple Christian Church, had committed mass suicide at their colony in Guyana. Among the dead was their charismatic leader, Jim Jones. The group had been living in the tiny South American country for about three years and, until their apoca-lyptic end, were almost completely unknown. Jim Jones took his place as one of the twentieth-century's icons of evil. His smiling, square-cut face staring out at millions of Americans from newspapers and television screens became a symbol of the modern mad Messiah.

James Warren Jones was born in 1931 in Crete, Indiana. Largely brought up by his mother, who taught him to distrust organized religion, and influenced by a friend of the family who belonged to the Christian Pentecostal movement, Jones developed strong spiritual beliefs at an early age and became fascinated by biblical descriptions of the end of the world. His career as a religious leader began in 1955 when he formed a breakaway sect with several members of the Assemblies of God Pentecostal Church. Jones had insisted that the church's congregation should contain

55

an even mix of black and white members – something virtually unheard of in 1950s Indiana. He named his new movement Wings of Deliverance, but later changing it to People's Temple to reflect its aim of ethnic diversity.

In 1960, Jones was ordained as a minister of the Christian church in the Disciples of Christ denomination, although his ministry retained complete autonomy from that organization. By 1965 ever increasing racial tensions persuaded Jones to move himself and his followers to Ukaih, California. Part of the reason for this choice of location was that Jones had read that it was a "safe zone" in case of nuclear war – a motivation that was later to prompt the move to Guyana.

In California Jones set about enlarging his church by recruiting from the more affluent strata of society and, up until the mid 1970s Temple membership grew steadily. Like all successful religious leaders Jones had his own, strongly held beliefs and the talent of convincing others that he held the key to the truth. By 1972 the Temple had established a second centre in San Francisco.

Jones had first visited South America in the mid 1960s when he spent some time in Brazil and made a brief visit to Guyana. In 1974 he obtained permission from the Guyanan government to develop and settle a remote strip of jungle in the interior. The colony, initially called The People's Temple Agricultural Mission, grew slowly at first – only about fifty members lived there by the beginning of 1977. In that year, the US government began an investigation into alleged tax evasion by the Temple. Jones began to urge people to relocate to Guyana and he also went to live there full-time. By the following year the site had been renamed

Jonestown, after Jones himself, and was home to the majority of the sect's nine hundred plus members.

Devotees who made the trip to the jungle were often shocked by what they found, but had no means of leaving. Colonists were required to work eleven hours a day, six days a week and eight hours on Sundays. Most of the labour went into working in the fields to provide food for the colony, but there was also a great deal of building to be done and jungle clearance. One of the few survivors later described Jonestown as more like a concentration camp than a religious community. Everything was done communally. Everybody slept in dormitories, where husbands and wives were given separate beds, everybody ate at the same time, attended meetings together that went on for half the night and listened to the voice of their leader broadcast from a system of loud speakers.

Soon after his arrival in Guyana, Jones had begun to use drugs on a massive scale. He would often keep his followers awake all night by playing music over the public address system and preaching his endless, incoherent sermons and apocalyptic visions. Jones himself lived apart from the rest of his flock in a house which he shared with a small number of hand-picked favourites and lovers. Unlike the ordinary members, they had access to imported foods, alcohol and plentiful drugs. The workers ate mainly beans and rice.

During this period of the organization's development, Jones required all new members to completely sever their links with the outside world, including their family and friends, and to give all their assets and wealth for "redistribution". Ex-members who had managed to escape Jones's powerful mind-control techniques, and the families of members who had essentially disappeared off the face of the Earth, came together to form a group opposed to the People's Temple. In 1978 this group succeeded in persuading Congress to address their concerns. Californian Congressman Leo Ryan was dispatched to Jonestown to investigate alleged human rights abuses.

Ryan arrived in Jonestown on 17 November of that year. The residents had been warned by Jones to put on a unified and happy face but, by the end of the first day, Ryan had assembled a group of sixteen who wanted to return to the States with him. Jones was furious. That night a senior Temple member attempted to kill Ryan by cutting his throat, but was prevented by members of his entourage, which included several newspaper and television journalists. The next day, 18 November, Ryan decided to cut his visit short, probably believing that Jones had ordered the attempt on his life.

The Congressman's party made their way to Port Kaituma airfield where two planes were waiting to transport them out of the jungle. As they were boarding, a truck loaded with Temple guards burst into the clearing. The guards opened fire, killing Ryan and four others and wounding several more. Back at Jonestown everybody was assembled in a building to hear Jones make a speech about the Congressman's visit. Instead of the congratulations they expected Jones told them that the end had come for the people of the Temple, and that "revolutionary suicide" was the only course left open to them.

A lethal concoction of potassium cyanide, valium and chloral hydrate had been mixed into a big vat of grape-flavoured fizzy-pop for the occasion. The people calmly formed lines and filed past the vat to receive their dose. Mothers brought their children forward first and then took a drink themselves. The poison would have acted quickly. By the end of the day 914 people were dead, 276 of them were children. Jones himself did not take the poison but died from a gunshot wound to the head. Nobody knows if it was suicide or not; there weren't any surviving witnesses.

News of the suicides was met with almost universal shock and disbelief. People simply could not believe that 900 people would willingly give up their lives just because one man told them to. Most believed that Jones must have had some kind of mental control over his people. In a sense this is true, but the dynamics of a community like Jonestown are more subtle and complex than a simple case of mass hypnotic control. The most important factor is isolation. The Temple members were Americans living in a harsh and foreign land thousands of miles away from home, and completely cut off from information about the outside world. This immediately creates a siege mentality and makes it easy to plant the suggestion that unseen forces are out to destroy the community. Jones used this to justify his retinue of armed Temple guards, who were there mainly to keep residents from leaving rather than to protect them from outsiders. Jones had been telling his followers for years that he expected a global war at any time and, isolated in the jungle, it was easy to believe that such an event was imminent.

The leadership also held regular drills known as "White Nights" in which the community was expected to prepare for attacks from unspecified "mercenaries". Sirens would wake the entire community in the middle of the night and everyone was expected to run to defence stations. During one of these White Night exercises Jones told the community that it was time to commit suicide. In a chilling dress rehearsal for the events of November 1978 everybody was instructed to drink from a vat of supposedly poisoned liquid. In fact the concotion was harmless, but Jones now knew that his people would be willing to die if he told them to.

In an atmosphere of impending doom and destruction the group formed intensely strong bonds of reliance on each other. Despite the hardships and the fear it became psychologically almost impossible to leave. If anybody began to form doubts, the selfless sacrifice of those around them soon put them back on track. Who could leave their comrades when they were struggling so hard to survive? Total communal living greatly strengthened these bonds. Even justice was meted out communally. Those who had broken the rules were tried before a mass assembly of the community, thereby adding the punishment of shame to whatever other penalty was imposed. A popular sentence was the "catharsis session" in which a transgressor was placed in a ring and expected to fight another, much bigger and stronger, member of the Temple.

Jones himself came to be regarded as something of a god by the community. Although it was he who had put them in the situation they were in, the community didn't see it that way. Jones was separate from the rest of them, they rarely saw him and he didn't suffer the hardships they did. For a group essentially struggling to survive Jones was a kind of Messiah who promised deliverance – and if that deliverance was to come from a poisoned cup then it was still better than nothing.

Since the mass suicide at Jonestown, a number of researchers and writers have speculated that there may have been something altogether darker and more sinister going on than a simple tragedy among a misled and isolated group of people. A popular theory has been that Jim Jones was actually a CIA operative and that Jonestown was an experiment in mass thought control. The American military and intelligence agencies are known to have carried out a number of bizarre and disturbing experiments into the possibility of controlling the opinions or actions of large groups of people. Where they have admitted these activities at all, these agencies have always explained them as attempts to create psychological warfare weapons.

If the conspiracy theorists are to be believed, the CIA was involved in the People's Temple movement from the very beginning. The 1960s and early 1970s were a time of political turmoil in the United States. The assassinations of President Kennedy and Martin Luther King, the mass protests against the war in Vietnam and the friction caused by the issue of civil rights, led many people to believe that the country could be on the brink of revolution or total social breakdown. It's not impossible to imagine national security forces becoming involved in experiments to take control of public opinion. The conspiricists say that they chose a small, unknown sect as a test bed for their techniques, because its disappearance could easily be explained away as the action of a lunatic fringe. What evidence is there that some kind of conspiracy lay behind the Jonestown deaths?

Evidence that Jones himself was a CIA operative comes from those who remember his trip to Brazil in the mid 1960s. Jones told Temple members that he spent his time there helping orphans, but his neighbours in Brazil remember him living the life of a rich man and boasting that he was being paid by the US government. Later, in Guyana, Jones frequently met with representatives of the Russian embassy – Guyana had a socialist government at the time – and his speeches often preached extreme forms of communism. The suggestion is that Jones was being used as some kind of double agent, posing as a dissatisfied American citizen and passing false information to the Soviets.

The official version of the events of 18 November have also been called into question. Why did Jones order the suicide so soon after the Congressman's visit and why did the Congressman decide to leave so soon after his arrival? It is suggested that Congressman Ryan discovered what was going on and hurried to get back to Washington so that he could expose the operation.

With such an immediate threat on their hands the CIA had no choice but to liquidate Ryan and terminate the project – which meant killing everyone in Jonestown. It has been noted that initial reports suggested that 500 had died; two days later, using figures supplied by the CIA, journalists were reporting 900 dead. Perhaps a significant number of Jonestown residents escaped the poisoning and had to be hunted down and executed later. The Guyanan coroner who investigated the deaths suggested that at least 700 bodies had shown signs of having been "forcibly killed".

Another issue that has bothered some people is the fact that Jones died from a gunshot wound rather than from taking the poison. Why would he shoot himself rather than taking the poison with his brethren, and if he didn't intend to die, as some have suggested, who did shoot him? The conspiricists say that the CIA had a man on the ground during the two days of the Congressman's visit. A number of people have come under suspicion but the suggestion is that he was probably a member of the Congressman's party. Once the hit on Ryan had been successfully carried out he simply returned to Jonestown, ordered Jones to initiate the suicide and then, when everyone was dead, shot Jones to tie up the last loose end.

A man called Larry Layton was one of the very few Jonestown residents who survived. As a Temple guard he was part of the team that killed Ryan and the others at the airport. At his trial he seemed barely able to speak and his own father said that he had become like a robot. Layton's father was in fact the biochemist in charge of chemical warfare at the US Army's Dugway test site in Utah. Layton's brother-in-law was a mercenary working for CIA-backed rebels in Angola. Large amounts of psychotropic drugs were found scattered around the Jonestown compound.

If Jonestown was a mind-control experiment, an attempt to reprogramme ordinary citizens to carry out the will of a superior power, how could it have worked? Most likely a combination of techniques would have been used. The religious background beliefs certainly would have helped, as would the isolated location and the psychological effects of hardship. On top of that a host of mind-altering drugs have been developed which can have the effect of putting individuals into highly suggestive states and even of turning them into instant psychopaths. Apart from drugs there are rumours of sonic and electromagnetic devices that could be used to create similar effects. There may even have been experiments with direct thought control through telepathy.

Whether Jonestown was a thought control experiment or not it certainly provided some valuable lessons for any agency interested in how to achieve such a thing. As for the unfortunate members of the People's Temple at least one aspect of their faith in their leader proved not to be misplaced: the apocalypse came for them just as he said it would.

Aum Shinri Kyo

Ever since the development of atomic and nuclear weapons, the world has lived in fear of an extremist group or "rogue nation" acquiring such a weapon and using it as the ultimate car bomb to take out a city district. In fact this has never been likely. The manufacture of such a weapon is an extremely complex and delicate operation. Without the right tools and skilled personnel it's almost impossible to build a working nuclear bomb. The raw materials needed, especially weapons grade plutonium or uranium, are extremely hard to come by and even harder to make from scratch. The failure of Saddam Hussein's regime to build a nuclear weapon, despite years of research and the enormous wealth of an oil-rich state, demonstrates just how hard it is. Unfortunately, there is a far simpler and cheaper alternative.

On 20 March 1995, the world was stunned to hear the news that a militant religious sect in Japan had launched a nerve gas attack on the Tokyo subway system. Ordinary citizens on their way to work during the morning rush hour were struck down by a weapon that even the nuclear super powers have agreed never to use. Twelve people died and more than 5000 were affected. Gas warfare experts later confessed that, had the attackers been better informed about methods of dispersing the gas, the death toll could have reached many thousands. Japanese society was deeply shocked. The questions on everybody's lips was who could have done such a thing, and why?

In fact the police knew immediately who the culprits were; it wasn't the first time a gas attack of this kind had happened. Two days later they swooped on the headquarters of an organization known as Aum Shinri Kyo, a religious sect that had been under suspicion on a number of accounts for several years. The leader of the group, Shoko Asahara, was eventually discovered in a secret room at the organization's headquarters in the town of Kamikuishiki. Asahara and 200 of his followers were arrested on suspicion of involvement in the subway attack.

Shoko Asahara was born Chizuo Matsumoto in 1955. His eyesight was very weak from birth and he attended a school for the blind until 1977 when he moved to Tokyo, hoping to enter the university there. After failing to make the necessary grades Asahara studied acupuncture and herbal medicine, and began to develop an interest in Buddhism and other religions. With his wife he ran a herbal remedy shop and taught yoga classes where he gained quite a following among his students. In 1986 Asahara made a pilgrimage to northern India and Tibet to learn more about the Buddhist faith. By the time he returned he had already begun to assemble a strange mixture of Christian and Buddhist beliefs centred on the Hindu god Shiva – the symbol of destruction and the apocalypse.

On his return to Japan, Asahara adopted his new name and called his small but expanding group Aum

Shinri Kyo. "Aum" being the Sanskrit symbol for destructive and creative power, and "Shinri Kyo" meaning "teaching of the supreme truth". The purpose of the group was to reveal to the world the true nature of destruction and creation in the universe.

Asahara believed that the end of the world was coming and that the only way to avert the catastrophe was to gather 30,000 true believers. Later, Asahara abandoned his original aims and turned the group into an isolationist sect concerned only with its own survival. He became convinced that the powers of evil in the world were too strong to be defeated and that the only hope for the future of civilization was for Asahara and his followers to survive the apocalypse that was already under way. Once he had decided on this new path, Asahara began to tell his followers that he had travelled forward in time to the year 2006 and met survivors of the apocalypse. He was happy to report that many Aum members were among them.

Asahara had always showed signs of paranoia and when the authorities began to take an interest in his group, it triggered the belief that the governments of the world were out to destroy him. In May 1989, with a membership now numbering several thousand, the Aum Shinri Kyo faced its first real challenge. As with many cults Aum required new members totally to sever links with their families and to give up all their wealth. In response, several families of cult members and former cult members hired lawyer Sakamoto Tsutsumi to bring charges against Asahara. As part of his case against Aum, Tsutsumi made the mistake of personally attacking the group's leader. Asahara had told his followers on several occasions that blood tests carried out on him at the University of Tokyo showed that he had a unique form of DNA. He promised those who followed his teachings to the letter that they too could achieve this special quality, and that it would confer enormous psychic powers on them. Tsutsumi proved that no such blood tests had ever been carried out.

In November of the same year Tsutsumi, his wife and his infant son, disappeared from their home. Police found bloodstains and an Aum member's badge but, without bodies, were unable to press charges. It was the first example of the kind of response that was to become typical for Asahara. The police and cult members' families had not realized what they were dealing with. Asahara already believed that he was engaged in a war for his own survival and the future of humanity, and would stop at nothing to protect both.

The bodies of Tsutsumi and his family were found six years later at three separate mountain locations, but by then it was too late to stop Asahara. Aum members have since confessed to the killings. According to their testimony they entered the Sakamoto household under cover of darkness and injected the family with lethal doses of potassium chloride before strangling them and then removing the bodies.

1989 also saw another perceived setback for Aum. Asahara had decided that if he could win political power he might be able to avert tragedy after all, and so he set up the Supreme Truth Party to contest elections. All twenty-five candidates put up by the party were soundly beaten at the polls, further convincing Asahara that the conspiracy against him was massive and powerful. He ordered followers to begin constructing survival bunkers that could protect them during the coming global war. Asahara outlined his

"Lotus Village" plan which envisaged small self-contained communities that could emerge from hiding once the conflict was over, and re-establish civilization according to the precepts of Supreme Truth. Part of this massive construction project included the assembly of laboratories capable of producing nerve and biological agents.

In 1993 a cult member named Tsuchiya Masami, who had a master's degree in chemistry, was put in charge of making sarin gas and devising methods of dispersion. Within a year, Asahara had the capability to strike with lethal force, and that's exactly what he did. On 27 June 1994, the town of Matsumoto in central Japan became the first target for an Aum gas attack. Clouds of sarin released by trucks driven through the streets killed seven and injured hundreds. It wasn't until after the Tokyo attack that police discovered that Aum had been responsible. The attack had actually been directed at three judges who were scheduled to hear a case against the group. All three were injured but survived.

The almost unbelievable carelessness of such an attack provides a chilling insight into the convictions of the Aum Shinri Kyo. Using nerve gas to attack three individuals in a populated area was likely to result in widespread death and injury. Clearly the fact that innocent bystanders would be affected did not even enter into consideration. For Asahara, the distinction between Aum and the rest of the world was clear. Anyone who was not part of the family was an enemy, and anyway he expected most of them to be dead within a short time when global war broke out.

The Matsumoto attack was essentially an assassination attempt on three judges; the motivation for the

Tokyo attack is much harder to pin down. On the morning of 20 March 1995, at the height of the rush hour, ten cult members boarded five different subway trains at various points in the city. Each one carried a plastic bag containing sarin gas wrapped in newspaper. At a predetermined time the cultists punctured their bags with the tips of their umbrellas and left their trains. Within seconds, those closest to the release of gas began to show signs of distress. The invisible, odourless gas produces dizziness and nausea as it attacks the nerve pathways that control breathing. Death is from suffocation.

It has been suggested that police and government offices were the main targets because the station that suffered the worst of the attack is located beneath the National Police Agency headquarters. Although this probably was a consideration, it seems more likely that the target was society as a whole, and that the aim was simply to kill as many people as possible. A month after the Tokyo attack 400 subway passengers in Yokohama were hospitalized with symptoms of sarin poisoning. Later, police found gas dispersion devices in two other subway stations, and one had a timer and a valve that mixed gases to form deadly cyanide fumes. All these attacks are believed to have been carried out by Aum members.

By the time of the terror campaign of 1995 Asahara had withdrawn totally from the outside world. He maintained control over his disciples by keeping them similarly isolated and convincing them that the government was out to kill them all. Initiation practices were extremely harsh and rigorous. Initiates were subjected to a variety of physical and mental tortures to "cleanse" them of the pollution of society.

Powerful and toxic drugs were also used to break down the initiates' sense of reality, until they would accept whatever they were told. It has been estimated that dozens of people were killed by these initiation rites. A senior member of the cult was later convicted of disposing of the body of one unlucky initiate who died hanging upside-down from a ceiling beam while under the influence of psychedelic drugs. His body was incinerated in a microwave device and buried in the mountains.

Asahara made extensive use of drugs and threats of violence to maintain control. Numerous senior cult members, including those who initiated the sarin production project, are believed to have been murdered on Asahara's orders because they became too powerful in the organization. Apart from those who died accidentally during initiation, Japanese authorities suspect that between fifty and sixty Aum members were secretly killed, and a dozen more were publicly executed for disobedience.

When police searched the Aum compound they found tons of chemicals stockpiled for future production of sarin and other gases, and the sarin production facility itself concealed within a temple. Another lab had been kitted out with equipment for producing biological agents, including botulinum toxin, which is thousands of times more deadly than sarin. Police also found a truck fitted with canisters and pumps that could have been used to spray huge quantities of either nerve or biological agents onto the city streets.

Asahara and 104 members of Aum Shinri Kyo have been on trial since 1995. The extreme complexity of the multiple indictments against them makes it unlikely that the trials will end before 2005. Some members have already been convicted of involvement in the group's many crimes. Kazuaki Okazaki, one of Aum's founding members, was convicted of the murder of the lawyer Tsutsumi and his family, and sentenced to death. Asahara himself is charged with two counts of multiple murder in relation to the Tokyo and Matsumoto gas attacks, involvement in the Sakamoto murders, kidnapping and the illegal manufacture of drugs. He maintains his innocence of all charges.

The Japanese government has been unable to disband or outlaw Aum Shinri Kyo because it is not a political organization. The group is currently led by Asahara's third daughter, Riko Matsumoto, whom cult members believe has inherited her father's supernatural powers. Membership has fallen considerably in Japan – there are now believed to be between 1–2000 active members – but the organization has branches in Russia where membership figures are totally unknown.

The Federation of Damanhur

Mention the word "cult" and a whole range of negative connotations are immediately brought to mind. Mind control, the disruption of families, mass suicides and mindless murders have become synonymous with the modern notion of a cult or sect.

We live in an era of extreme individualism: think for yourself, fend for yourself and speak for yourself are the commandments of our age. Although the existence of mass consumerism and mass culture such as that represented by television and the movies tends to put this often-stated belief into doubt, it is certainly true that Western culture is strongly opposed to the idea of people telling other people what to do. This is one of the most powerful reasons for our distrust of modern sects and cults; we are basically revolted by the idea of belonging to a group dominated by rules of behaviour and an inflexible set of beliefs. Even the old, established religions are regarded with a degree of suspicion by most people. The majority of the population of the United Kingdom profess to be "Christian", but very few attend churches. In religion, as in everything else, people see little reason to defer their own judgment to an established organization.

On the other hand, there are literally thousands of cults and sects in the world today. Most remain almost completely unknown, unless some tragedy happens and lives are lost. When this happens, as it has all too often in the past century, mistrust of religious sects receives another boost. The fact remains, however, that the vast majority of sects do no actual harm and may even provide new and exciting perspectives on life. One that fulfils these criteria is the Federation of Damanhur. The Federation of Damanhur, founded in 1977, has been accused of every crime under the sun. No doubt some of these accusations are true, its members are as human as anyone else, but there are far stranger and more interesting things going on among the people of the Temple of Mankind. Its 400 plus full-time members, like many other groups around the world, are engaged in a search for a new way of living. Among their achievements are a vast, underground temple and, they claim, the discovery of time travel.

Damanhur was founded by a group of philosophers led by Oberto Airaudi, who still lives with the community and is regarded by many members as their chief inspiration. The community as it exists today is virtually a self-contained nation. Residing in a beautiful valley in northern Italy they have their own democratic government, justice system, currency and calendar. Although separate from the outside world they are not insular, actively welcoming guests, tourists and buyers interested in their wide range of handmade glassware.

The Federation has a range of business interests; it owns farms, woodlands, laboratories and more than seventy buildings in the valley. Members are largely free to work in the way they feel they can best contribute to the community, but are encouraged to spend a few hours every month helping out with communal chores. New members often come from the ranks of the students who come to the valley to take courses in subjects as esoteric as "Past Life Research". Once accepted into the community they take on the name of a plant or animal that best describes their nature. Anyone is free to leave at any time and many members of the community are effectively "part time".

The most concrete achievement of the Damanhur is the vast, subterranean Temple of Mankind. Secretly carved out of the side of a mountain, largely by hand over a period of sixteen years, the temple is an architectural marvel to rival any ancient monument. Built over five storeys the temple includes seven great halls, each one dedicated to a magical symbol. The Earth hall is entered through two vast doors, the door of the sun and the door of the moon, decorated with gold and stunning stained glass. The Hall of Mirrors has a vast stained glass dome flooded with artificial light. Everywhere there are mosaics, paintings and hieroglyphs taken from ancient cultures of all kinds.

Since 1992 journalists and other visitors have been allowed to see inside parts of the temple and have been deeply impressed by the years of hard work and creativity that it represents. For the Damanhur, however, the temple is far more than a pretty tourist trap. According to their beliefs the whole complex is a kind of cosmic battery that concentrates energies running through the Earth and "transmits" them into the human race. The location of the temple was carefully chosen by Damanhur scientists who identified a seam of the rare element mylonite in the mountain. The valley itself is believed to lie on the junction of three vast energy-cords that wind their way around the globe. The mylonite attracts and focuses this energy, say the Damanhur, and a complex system of hidden water pipes and cables snake out from behind the temple's walls to tap into this creative power source.

Aside from the network of cables and ducts sucking Earth energies from the mountain the temple holds other secrets too. Why do the Damanhur need all this power? The answer: time travel. According to community members secret doors within the temple lead deeper into the mountain where experiments in time travel are carried out in a "time cabin". Driven by devices the Damanhur call "selfic spheres" the time cabin allows selected members of the community to travel through a multiverse of alternative universes. The selfic spheres themselves certainly exist, there is one on a mountainside near Loch Ness in Scotland, although their effectiveness remains in some doubt among sceptical outsiders.

The lucky few community members chosen to take

part in the time travel experiments are selected with as much care as NASA astronauts. One goes by the unlikely name of Gorilla Eucalypto. Reports of his many voyages of discovery are available for scrutiny and are found under equally unlikely titles such as "Plant Matter Brought Back by Gorilla" – filed after a trip to the year 2727 BC – and "Gorilla Meets Local People and Eats Blueberries" – filed after a jaunt back to 4719 BC. One fascinating report details Gorilla's journey to the year 61,000 BC where he encountered an advanced civilization carrying out similar experiments to his own. Other members of the community are said to be able to witness these expeditions by taking over the senses of animals in ancient times.

In an interview, one of Damanhur's time travellers, Gattopardo Tek, talked about his experiences.

My journey was one of the first ones. We wanted to see how many events we could stimulate by doing an action that was not foreseen in another time period. In this case it was to develop commerce between two villages. So we stole a little boat and put it in another village so the boatbuilder would build another one as a result of the theft. So I found myself on a riverbank in this area which, using the spheroselfs, we calculated at 6140 years ago . . . So I entered into the body of this primitive lady. As I did so, her head became dizzy and she fell down. She fainted for a while because she was so over-whelmed. This made it easy for me to take control of the body . . . . The sensation of putting on a body, as you might put on a dress, was incredible – it was like I was gaining her feelings as I got into her arms and legs.

Apparently the mission was a great success. The boat-builder built a new and improved boat and people from the other village also learned how to make boats.

Damanhur's philosophy and world view is extremely complex and rarely explained to outsiders. They consider their time travel experiments to be important work and are not willing to let just anyone in on the secret. Essentially they believe in something known as the "many worlds" hypothesis. Familiar to students of philosophy and physics, the many worlds hypothesis states that there are in fact an infinite number of universes rather than just one. These universes, or alternative realities, come into existence every time a decision is made. For example, there is an alternative universe in which I am wearing green socks instead of blue and there is one in which Hitler won World War II and one where life never even evolved on Earth. The Damanhur time travellers believe that they are able to "harmonize" with these alternatives and, by doing so, travel there at any point along their time lines.

Apart from pure curiosity the Damanhur have other motives for travelling in time. They claim that they are helping civilizations to evolve – retrospectively. The prime mission for the time travellers is to introduce technology to primitive civilizations. Amongst other things they claim to have introduced the rudder to early peoples to encourage trade and exploration. They believe that every time they make such a change the results are automatically incorporated into history without us noticing. We are nudged from an alternative universe in which, say, the Romans, didn't have rudders on their ships to one in which they did. It's an extraordinary thought that a small band of philosophers could be literally rewriting the history of our civilization under our noses.

It has been pointed out that the field of archaeology is littered with unexplained instances of anachronistic objects – things found in ancient cultures that have no right to be there. Classic examples include the Baghdad battery. In 1936 railway workers uncovered a tomb from the Parthian period near Baghdad. The wealth of finds inside the tomb allowed archaeologists to date it to about 200 AD. One object, a clay jar containing a copper tube around an iron bar and some crumbled bitumen, caused a great deal of perplexity until a physicist from London examined it. He showed quite clearly that if the copper tube were filled with an acid, such as vinegar, the whole thing acted like a battery and produced a measurable voltage. Other, similar, jars were later found suggesting that they may have been hooked up together to produce enough current to power a simple light or some other unknown apparatus.

No other reasonable explanation of what purpose the jars could have served has been offered. Could it be an example of Damanhur meddling with the past? Another mind boggling example of an "out-of-time" object was discovered in 1900, although its true nature was not realized until seventy years later. The object first came to light when a party of Greek fishermen discovered the wreck of an ancient ship off the island of Antikythera. Archaeologists were immediately excited by the large numbers of bronze and marble statues found in the vessel, which they estimated had gone down in the first century AD. Lying among the wreckage they also found a whole series of badly tarnished and corroded bronze gearwheels, several with Greek inscriptions. They were clearly parts of some complex machine but the experts disagreed on its purpose since nobody could fit the pieces together in a convincing way.

Half a century later, Professor Derek de Sola Price of Yale University, developed an interest in this over-looked artifact and spent the next twenty years trying to figure it out. Using X-rays he was able to discern the original shape of the fragments and eventually succeeded in showing how they fitted together to make a complex mechanical computer for calculating the positions of the sun and the moon and predicting the rising of the most important navigational stars. According to the accepted view of Mediterranean civi-lization of the era such a machine was impossible, but its date is beyond question. How could it have got there?

The Damanhur are rarely specific about what they have introduced into the past; to them there is little point. We simply have to take them at their word or dismiss them as cranks. It's very easy to flatly state that time travel is impossible and from that conclude that the Damanhur are a lunatic fringe – except that they are not. Members of the community are hard working, level headed and clearly inspired by a vision of the future of humanity that is not just about more and better gadgets to entertain us. One journalist who visited the Damanhur community commented that it was like a colony on another world, and speculated that it might be something like the kind of community that humans will have to create if we ever manage to escape our own planet and settle elsewhere. Such thoughts are a pleasant antidote to our usual image of sects and secret communities.

Heaven's Gate

Following the rather disappointing showing of Halley's comet in the Northern hemisphere, amateur astronomers and the general public alike were treated to an unexpected display of brilliance from the Hale-Bopp comet in the spring of 1997. As its million-mile-long tail showed night after night people marvelled at the wonders of the heavens and there was a lot of light-hearted talk about omens and the end of the millennium. One small group in San Diego, California, took the idea rather more seriously. For the thirty-nine members of Heaven's Gate the comet was a sign that it was time to evacuate the Earth.

Members of Heaven's Gate combined a fundamentalist, apocalyptic Christian vision with concepts and language culled from cult science fiction shows such as *Star Trek* and *The X-Files*. They believed that cloaked in the tail of the Hale-Bopp comet, was a fabulous spacecraft crewed by beings from the "Level Above Human". This was no fearful invasion force, however, it was coming just for them, a kind of intergalactic taxi sent to pick them up before the Earth was "recycled" out of existence. For twenty years the "away team" as they called themselves, had been training mentally and physically for this moment, they had all earned their "boarding passes" and were ready to put their "Earth Exit" strategy into operation.

Unlike Captain Kirk's away teams the Heaven's Gaters had no need for transportation beams or atmospheric shuttles; to exit the planet and hitch a ride on the comet ship all they had to do was exit their bodies. Particle beam transporters were considered passé; all you needed was a lethal dose of phenobar-

bital and a plastic bag over your head. With the cleanliness and care of a routine twenty-fifth-century space
mission, the operation was carried out over a three-
day period beginning on 23 March 1997. Fifteen died
on the first day, fifteen on the second and the last nine
on the third. Before the last two ended their own lives
they took the rubbish out for collection and tidied up
the multi-million dollar mansion that the group rented
as their training base.

Police officers who found the bodies after an
anonymous tip-off met with an eerie scene. Each of the
twenty-one women and eighteen men were dressed
identically in baggy, black trousers, loose shirts and
brand new Nike trainers. The cultists were all lying on
their backs on their own cots or bunks and were
draped with triangular purple shrouds. They each had
identification on them, presumably to help the police
and, most bizarre of all, they all had a five dollar bill
and some change in their pockets – perhaps to buy
snacks for the long trip ahead. It was clear that all
thirty-nine cultists had died willingly and police saw
no reason to launch a murder inquiry.

Two weeks after the discovery of the bodies in San
Diego, two former members of Heaven's Gate decided
to try and join their comrades. Wayne Cook and Chuck
Humphrey were found at a Holiday Inn four miles from
the cult's San Diego base. Both men were dressed in the
same manner as their fellow cultists and each had the
mysterious five dollar bill in his pocket. Only one of the
men died however, the other is still in a coma.

The bizarre fusion of doomsday cult and science
fiction fan club that was Heaven's Gate was centred
around two leaders, Marshall Herff Applewhite and
Bonnie Lu Nettles, known respectively as Do and Ti, or

Bo and Peep, or collectively as "The Two". Ti died of cancer in 1985 and was believed to have already ascended to the level above human. The Two had first met in Houston in 1972 shortly after Applewhite had been dismissed from his job as professor of music at St Thomas's University over an alleged affair with a male pupil. Applewhite checked into a psychiatric hospital where Nettles was a nurse to try and find a "cure" for his homosexual urges.

They formed an immediate and deep connection and were inseparable for the next thirteen years. Applewhite was essentially disgusted by his sexuality and he found in Nettles a partner he could love without the issue of physical passion ever arising. She introduced him to her interest in metaphysics and the teachings of Theosophy, and they both immersed themselves in a dream world of visions and contact with alien visitors.

In 1973, at a campsite in Oregon, Applewhite had a vision in which it was revealed to him that he and Nettles were the two prophets of the eleventh Book of Revelations. After 1260 days, he believed, they would be assassinated by satanic forces and then ascend to heaven in a spaceship. Filled with a sense of purpose the pair set out across the country to preach their message. For a while they called themselves Guinea and Pig, then settled on Bo and Peep, both names being an ironic recognition of how unlikely it was that anybody would believe them.

At a series of lectures and talks The Two gradually acquired a following of several hundred, then, in 1975, they issued instructions that the membership should be split into small cells and dispersed across the country. The Two disappeared for six months without a word of communication to their followers. Many members left during this period, but a few kept the faith and were finally rewarded when Bo and Peep reappeared and announced that those who remained were the true believers. At this point the 1260 day deadline was also abandoned.

Do and Ti, as they now called themselves, revealed that their deaths and subsequent ascension in the heavenly spacecraft had been postponed because their followers were not ready. They had been given a new mission: to prepare a dedicated group of "travellers" to join them on the spacecraft when the time came for the Earth to be destroyed. A new and much clearer doctrine emerged from The Two's six months in the wilderness.

Christ, they said, had been an emissary from a race of highly evolved beings from the "level above", or "heaven" as it came to be known. When this first missionary was killed, and later returned to his space-craft, the extraterrestrial decided to give humanity another two thousand years to evolve a bit and then sent two new emissaries – Ti and Do. It was their mission to gather as many enlightened followers as possible before the world was "recycled" because it was a threat to the moral health of the universe.

Moving to a forty-acre compound near Albuquerque, New Mexico, the group's fifty or so members set to work building "The Earthship" based of Ti and Do's knowledge of the layout of flying saucers. Total abstinence from alcohol, drugs and sex had always been a prime teaching and this was now reinforced with a strict regime of mental and physical exercise, meditation and study that would prepare the crew of the Earthship for their journey to the "next evolutionary level".

By the late 1980s Heaven's Gate had established a commercial wing dedicated to constructing low-cost websites for corporate clients. Named Higher Source it provided much of the income that was needed for construction of the Earthship and for the upkeep of the group's subsequent home in San Diego. With the expertise of this company Heaven's Gate constructed its own website to spread their views. Mirrors of the Heaven's Gate website are still available on the net – perhaps one of the first historical documents to have emerged from this medium.

> *The joy is that our Older Member in the Evolutionary Level Above Human [meaning Ti, who died in 1985] has made it clear to us that Hale-Bopp's approach is the "marker" we've been waiting for – the time for the arrival of the space-craft from the Level Above Human to take us home to "Their World" – in the literal heavens. Our twenty-two years of classroom here on planet Earth is finally coming to a conclusion – "graduation" from the Human Evolutionary Level. We are happily preparing to leave "this world" and go with Ti's crew.*

Videos advertised at the site feature Applewhite lecturing on the beliefs of Heaven's Gate against sci-fi type psychedelic backgrounds. Other sections include "Statement by an ET presently incarnate", "Last chance to advance beyond human" and "Our position against suicide" – ironically the group was strictly opposed to suicide for anyone other than the selected away team.

Wayne Cook, one of the men who attempted to join

the away team after it had left, sent an "exit statement" video to family members and CNN before taking his own life. On the tape he says how much he regretted not having the perseverance to stay with the group – Cook's wife was among those who died at San Diego – and that he was happy to be finally joining them.

Many other cults have ended in the tragedy of mass suicide but never has the demise of such a group been so well documented and, frankly, cheerful. The Heaven's Gate website was dubbed history's most sophisticated suicide note by *Time* magazine, which may well be true, but its most extraordinary aspect is its cheeriness and naïve "spaceships and aliens" wonderment. In videos shot by the away team shortly before their suicide the cultists appear extremely relaxed and in good humour.

Unlike other death cults there was no hysterical mania, no fear of imminent destruction and no resentment of the outside world. The members of Heaven's Gate lived lives of remarkable blandness. There was no drug abuse or sexual excess and they lived by a moral code of tolerance and moderation that the United Federation of Planets would have been proud of. Above all they had absolute faith that they were on their way to greater and better things in a fantasy of clean living and advanced technology among the stars.

PART TWO

Earth Energies

●●●●●●●●●●●●●●●●●●●●●●●●●●●●●●●●●●●

Our World – Mother Earth

Born from the swirling residue of a vastly ancient supernova, planet Earth is reckoned to be middle-aged. And, ask anyone into their middle years – life begins at forty! It might be tempting to point to the bizarre creatures that roamed, swam, and flew 65 million years ago, and imagine them to be the eccentricities of an extravagant adolescence, but that would be wrong. If the Earth is forty today, it was barely six months ago that a party-pooping meteorite put paid to the dinosaur ball. There is no doubt that our planet still has plenty of surprises in store for us all.

Although mercifully rare, cataclysmic events like asteroid impacts help us to realize what a mistake it would be to take our globe too much for granted. Even relatively minor disasters such as hurricanes, volcanoes, earthquakes, drought and flood, all remind us that living in denial is not a healthy option (in the words of the ancient – but usually truncated – adage: "live in hope, die in despair").

Not surprisingly, people throughout recorded history, and before, have sought to understand the forces that shape our world, especially those that bring sudden death to communities and even entire cultures. The legend of Atlantis, for example, tells of natural forces rising up to completely obliterate a corrupt continent.

Although myths about angry gods, or raging dragons shaking the earth and spurting fiery breath, are often dismissed as primitive fables, they usually contain at least a kernel of truth. And what of science, our modern creed? Not only does it openly admit to not knowing all the answers (what is ball lightning for example?), but it often gives only a very brief warning of impending catastrophe, if any at all. And, of course, there is still absolutely nothing science can do to stop these devastating calamities.

Significantly, when the unthinkable does happen, our emotional response to tragedy is usually identical to that of someone living millennia ago. Perhaps we feel punished, maybe unfairly, and need to know "why me?". Or maybe we feel guilt at surviving when a loved one is lost forever in the wreckage of elemental violence.

Happily though, most of the time, the Earth is a great place to be. It is a gem among planets, and we are admirably well adapted to life in its various climes. It is also an exciting place to explore, both physically and with our minds and emotions. Contemplate, if you will, the magnificence of the sunrise over water, the beauty of scented flowers, the peace of high summer cirrus clouds, the wonder of the rainbow, the awesome lightning flash . . .

We are not divorced from the world. We are part of it, and it is part of us. There are many ways of enjoying inner communion with our mother Earth. The occult tradition maintains that she holds many wondrous mysteries and marvels that she can reveal to, and share with, the open-hearted seeker. There are also many ways of trying to connect with the spirit of the Earth. These range from the oriental discipline of Feng Shui, to the ecstatic rites of seasonal fertility cults; from mind-boggling meditations on the Sun, Moon and Heavens, to simply communing with faeries and devas. In fact, there are as many ways to get in touch with the Earth as there are people seeking to understand their place in the grand scheme of things.

And what do we hope to gain from this contact with our mother world? Perhaps the most important is a sense of balance that will enable us to act wisely. Wisdom, then, and our fair share of vitality – enough energy to live life to the full.

Many people have begun their search for wisdom by seeking for the truth. However, even this simple-sounding quest is not so straightforward as it first appears. The proverb "seek and you will find" certainly encourages the beginner, but after a while its message can turn sour. How often, for example, does an adolescent "crush" end in disappointment – not because the object of desire is unattainable, but rather because the couple actually do get together. Once he or she is known intimately, all the prosaic and rather dull elements of day-to-day life can quickly cloud a rose-tinted perception. Examined close up for the first time, the idol is soon discovered to have feet of clay!

Many people suffer one disappointment after another, and this can start a vicious cycle that can spiral into profound depression, and even lead to a loss of interest in life itself.

Imagine if you could find something that could bring an instantaneous cure to such misery. It would be a miracle, giving relief from all nagging self-doubts, anxieties, stress and moral dilemmas (not to mention religious wars, etc). The whole world could start with a clean slate, free from making mistake after mistake, and suffering a perpetual round of false hopes followed by painful disillusionment.

Such was the goal of the alchemists. They sought the universal truth that would banish ignorance and mistrust forever. In the midst of the apparent chaos of life, they hoped to find a single absolute fact that nobody could deny, and nothing could ever contradict. They sought a secure and stable foundation stone for their lives and the key to turn life's heartache and dismay into love's perpetual brightness.

"Turning lead into gold" was the catchphrase of these seekers of spiritual certainty. Despite the claims of their detractors, whose limited vision couldn't see beyond their own greed for physical gold (mistaking, ironically, the metaphor for the truth), the alchemists cherished noble and worthy aspirations.

Their writings are full of references to attempts to manufacture the ever-elusive Lapis Philosophorum, the Philosopher's Stone. This was the name they gave to the touchstone they believed they could find. It was a stone (or the crystallization of all that is good and true in the world) whose merest touch could heal, illuminate and transmute anything base and sullied into something priceless and pure.

It was, they hoped, a magical seed that would blossom into a new Golden Age of enlightenment – heaven on earth.

It may be a mote of comfort to know that there are some who have still not abandoned the quest.

Crystal Power

For thousands of years stone has been prized and revered for its sheer solidity. Rock is the most permanent feature of our landscape, and its power to resist the forces of decay and dissolution embodies our own desire for immortality.

More highly prized than any other crystal, for its hardness and durability, the diamond has been hailed king of stones.

It is currently estimated that to produce one carat of gemstone-quality diamonds, fifty tons of rock need to be processed. Despite this awesome fact, there is actually a glut of these particular stones. Diamond producers habitually hoard the gems (rather than allowing their stocks to flood the market) in order to keep shop prices unnaturally high.

Because it is the hardest naturally-occurring mineral, diamond has a reputation for endurance. This quality has been exploited by clever commercial interests which, in advertising campaigns relating the diamond to love itself, claim that a diamond "is forever". Such claims are, however, greatly exaggerated, as even the best quality gemstones are gradually but inexorably degrading into pure graphite, itself one of the softest minerals on Earth. This feature of metamorphosis is, incidentally, an important but little-researched aspect of a diamond's mystical significance. It is also salutary to consider that the dawning science of nanotechnology will soon be able to make flawless crystals of any chemical make-up and far superior to those found in their natural state. Forecasters predict, for example, that diamond, whose strengths make it a wonderful material for engineers to cast into a myriad roles, will become as common as plastic! Until such times, however, diamonds will remain expensive and highly desirable.

Diamonds have been prized throughout the ages, of course, but the latter decades of the twentieth century have witnessed a widespread resurgence of interest in all kinds of minerals, especially crystals. Of these, the most popular has undoubtedly been the pure, clear quartz (also known as rock crystal). A single quartz crystal can be large enough to be carved into the form of a life-sized human skull (as evidenced by some sinister artifacts of reputedly Aztec and Mayan origins), but even finger-sized specimens are prized by collectors and crystal mystics the whole world over.

Much has been claimed for these simple crystals. Some believe that they carry stored messages from mythical Atlantis or even from other worlds, while others claim that the straight shafts, which are tipped by a hexagonal array of triangular facets, can channel and focus mental energy. The latter are known as lazers or wands, and feature in many rites of Shamanic magic, both ancient and modern.

Some quartz crystals have their pointed tips ground until they are perfectly smooth, and are used to give a relaxing, healing massage. Some are even immersed in water that is subsequently drunk, the theory being that the crystal imparts its "vibrations" to the liquid, which then becomes a general tonic for body and mind.

Whatever the virtues of these various practices, there is no doubting the beauty of some of these common crystals, especially those whose internal flaws reward close inspection with a spectacular, delicately-coloured light-show of "nebulous rainbows".

Perhaps the second most popular crystal is another

semi-precious quartz gem: amethyst. Amethyst has long been associated with love and lovers. Roman wives valued it in the belief that its influence would ensure their husband's fidelity. It is also reputed to draw the love of a worthy woman to a man. St Valentine is famed for wearing an amethyst ring engraved with the figure of Cupid. Cleopatra's favourite piece of jewellery was an amethyst ring engraved with the figure of the Persian sun god, Mithras.

Greek legend tells us that the god Bacchus was once so annoyed with the goddess Diana that he set his sacred tigers upon a maiden attending one of her shrines. To preserve the maiden, whose name was Amethyst, Diana petrified her as sparkling rock crystal. Lamenting this virgin's demise, Bacchus poured a libation over the transparent statue, which immediately became infused with the purple of the grape.

The Greek name amethyst loosely translates as "anti-intoxicant". Goblets carved from this crystal cast a glorious hue over their contents, enabling even pure water to appear like wine. In the Middle Ages it was used as a charm to sharpen one's wits and stay wide awake. Since the thirteenth century, popes have received an amethyst ring on their investiture, and early Arabian lore attests that amethyst protects the wearer from nightmares.

One of the most popular gems for jewellery is, however, shunned by modern crystal healers and magicians. Pearls are formed when certain shellfish secrete a smooth, lustrous coating to embalm an irritant. The reason that few healers or mystics participate in the pearl trade is simply that the extraction of a pearl from the shell almost invariably entails the violent death of the animal itself.

The pearl is, perhaps, the earliest of all known jewels: it was certainly one of the first gems to be recorded in Egyptian hieroglyphs. Cleopatra is reputed to have dissolved a particularly valuable specimen in wine at a banquet, and promptly drank the infusion as a toast to her lover, Mark Anthony.

This gem has a reputation, if not for virginity and chastity, then certainly for purity of feeling, refinement and sophistication. For example, the New Testament contains both a parable of a man's desire to own a certain specimen, despite it costing everything he owned (Matthew 13), and a description of a celestial city whose twelve portals were made from pearls (Revelation 21).

It should, in contrast, be noted that in pre-Christian times pearls were associated with the goddess of carnal love, Aphrodite. Indeed, in Syria, she was known as the "Lady of Pearls" and her priestesses were prostitutes. Pearls have often been linked with tears: Saxons reckoned them to be the tears of the goddess of love, Freya; Arabians called them "tears of the gods", supposing them to form when raindrops fell into open oyster shells. They have been used medicinally for 4000 years in China where tradition states that the semen from writhing Cloud Dragons falls into oysters waiting to produce the jewels.

Amber is an organic gem with a growing reputation. It is actually fossilised tree resin which oozed from a wound in the bark (usually from conifers around fifty million years ago). Before hardening, it often trapped seeds, insects, and even small lizards in its sticky mass. Recent speculation about the possibility of resurrecting dinosaurs from DNA preserved in this way has given amber a new and potent element in its already considerable mythology.

For comprehensive information on this fascinating subject, I would like to refer readers to "Crystals for Health, Home, & Personal Power" (co-authored by my wife, Joules, and myself) which catalogues a wide range of practical mineral uses, both contemporary and ancient.

The Four Elements – The Earth in Harmony

One of the most useful of all natural stones is magnetic iron (magnetite), which was the basic component of the magnetic compass. Legend has it that the properties of this iron-rich ore were discovered by the Chinese Yellow Emperor, who invented the compass around the year 2700 BC. The compass is still at the heart of the Chinese system of Feng Shui, a form of geomancy that helps people live in harmony with the world.

The four compass points are of tremendous importance in ancient ideas about the world and its mystical energies. The cross, equated with suffering and redemption since Christ's crucifixion, is actually a vastly ancient symbol of wholeness and harmony.

Joining the terminal points of the equal armed cross (like a plus sign, +) we form a square. Projecting this figure into three dimensions, we produce a cube. This shape is regarded as the supreme symbol of matter: physical, solid, dense, and inert. It is the shape of the throne of the Goat of Mendes, the traditional lord of the material world (as opposed to the spiritual planes).

The oriental mandala is also based on the shape of the cross. These colourful pictures deliberately attempt to balance the extreme perspectives of spirit verses matter. The mandala unites these opposites into an all-embracing, holistic vision of a universe whose mystery is larger than our minds alone can divine.

Magicians (the term includes both men and women) who are keen to follow the spiritual path to union with God, often embark on a series of rites designed to balance their minds and emotions. Achieving inner harmony is regarded as an essential precursor to discovering any divine mysteries. After all, no God-fearing angel is going to give miraculous powers to a fool who would squander the gift on selfish whims!

To achieve this personal balancing act, the magician studies the four elements of air, fire, water, and earth (some modern magicians introduce a fifth element, plasma, which corresponds to the ancient quintes-sence of spirit). S/he invokes each element in turn, before combining all four in equal proportions. When they are in harmony they form a solid base from which the magician can operate.

These four elements have long been considered the building blocks of the whole world. Aristotle, a Greek philosopher of the fourth century BC, endorsed this idea wholeheartedly, and turned it into the corner-stone of scientific thinking for more than two millennia. It does make reasonable common sense too.

We may consider the example of mercury. We are all familiar with it in its liquid state (in thermometers, for example), but if we cool it sufficiently it will freeze as solid as the rocks of the Earth. On the other hand, if we heat it enough, it will boil and evaporate into a gas. Air, fire, earth and water – magicians and mystics around the globe agree that each of the four elements is invested with a unique energy, and exercises complete power over a quadrant of our world. Understanding them is a key to understanding both our world and ourselves.

The East, Dawn and the Element of Air
The moment of daybreak can be a magnificent spectacle and is associated with the bright flourishing of spring. It is the epitome of the new beginning, the fresh start from which every hope and aspiration might be realized. Of course this is an idealized portrayal, and for anyone in the condemned cell awaiting execution, dawn can have quite different connotations!

At a more fundamental level, the coming of light following darkness is an ancient metaphor for spiritual enlightenment. As such, it is associated with ideas of illumination and mystical awareness. Because the sun rises from an easterly direction (best seen at the Spring Equinox), this compass point is traditionally regarded as the source and origin of these sublime gifts. The dawn itself is often used as a metaphor of spiritual enlightenment and, on a more practical level, for social change and improvement. The phrase "coming forth by day", for example, is enshrined in the ancient Egyptian Book of the Dead as describing the soul's resurrection into the afterlife. And one of the nineteenth-century quasi-religious movements which aimed to replace the existing world order with a new, improved version, actually called itself the Hermetic Order of the Golden Dawn.

Deprived of oxygen for just a few minutes we inevitably perish, yet our sensory experience of this vital element is only indirect. Air itself is invisible, and we can only observe the effect of its motion on leaves and clouds. It cannot be felt with the skin unless either it or we are moving. Although it carries sound it makes no noise itself unless it is moving other objects. It cannot be smelled unless it carries the scent of something else, and it can neither be tasted nor grasped.

It is not surprising that this invisible element, absolutely vital to sustaining life, has often been associated with those unfathomable supernatural and divine powers that have long been held to sustain all life on Earth. Moreover, as evidenced by the movement of clouds in the wind, this element stretches far up into the heavens themselves – the home of the sun, moon, stars and the gods.

Anyone wishing to get in touch with their own, inner airy nature could do a lot worse than to spend a while concentrating on a traditional set of images and associations. First, focus on your breath, its inward and outward flow. Allow your mind to pay attention to the way it comes into your body from, and then returns to, the great body of air that surrounds you. The same reservoir of air that mantles the entire planet . . .

Feel the motion of the wind in the atmosphere. Fly, if you like, on the wings of a bird or in the form of a sylph (a race of beautiful, airy creatures whose home is the atmosphere itself). Enjoy the freedom of the skies far above the ground. You may even experience, in the safety of your invulnerable spirit-form, the titanic forces of the hurricane, and the wonderful stillness in its terrible eye . . .

Settle, at last, on high moorlands that are still half-shrouded in the twilight of dawn. Watch as the clouds are set aflame with gold and the dazzling orb breaks free of the horizon. You are surrounded by the flowers of purple heather sprinkled with the bright yellow blossoms of gorse and broom. Bask awhile in the fresh, cool air and warming sunshine, and breathe deeply of all the perfumes of this invigorating spring morning.

Such traditional meditations are best performed at dawn, although this is not vital. It not only helps us to appreciate one of the wonders of nature, but energizes both mind and body. It is especially useful if you feel the need to be more active and wish your reactions to be quicker, and is particularly helpful when you have to be prompt and alert. Such is the energy of the Earth's precious air.

Being linked with the dawn and spring, the air's association with new beginnings extends to the idea of human birth. The vivacious freedom of the uninhibited child is very characteristic of elemental air. Emotional honesty, innocence, eagerness to learn and discover new things are all fitting attributes of the star signs that astrologers place under the influence of air: Gemini, Libra and Aquarius. The element of air is traditionally linked with the colours yellow and purple, and the crystal that is believed to most embody its qualities is diamond.

The South, Noon and the Element of Fire

South, as every tracker knows, is where the sun reaches its highest point in the sky during its daily voyage across the heavens. And, as every beach-loving sunbather also knows, this is where the risk of sunburn gets intense!

In line with its associations with heat, fire is also linked with the summer months and, to an extent, with drought. People who feel the need to energize themselves with a fierce and burning passion look to fire and try to infuse themselves with its radiance. It is notable that people born under Leo, the zodiac sign with a powerful link to elemental fire, tend to be the "life and soul of the party", the centre of interest, and the hub of activity. It is as if they are the candle flame to which others are drawn. The signs of Aries and Sagittarius also exhibit strong fiery natures.

To conjure the spirit of fire into your psyche, tradition suggests that you imagine yourself standing on a rocky outcrop of ash in the midst of a lava field, with a smouldering volcano behind you. You gaze to the noonday sun and absorb its energy into your body until you fill and begin to radiate light yourself. As you do so, imagine your shape changing to that of a salamander (the traditional creature associated with this element). Now impervious to the destructive qualities of heat you can race away with the speed of lightning, and even plumb the fiery heart of the volcano itself. An almost electrical tingling and even sweating might accompany this meditation, which should certainly leave you feeling filled with the drive and enthusiasm to overcome any minor obstacles in your life. It is never easier to get out of a rut than when you are filled with elemental fire!

There are a whole host of other luminous phenomena that can also be thought of as part of this element. Lightning, St Elmo's Fire, earthquake-related "earth lights", rainbows and parhelia, meteors, fireflies and glow-worms, and phosphorescent algae, all contribute to the body of lore which comes under the general heading "fire".

Fire – physical fire – has its practical uses too, of

course. The ability of our species to make and control fire, allowed our ancient forebears to populate areas of the world that would otherwise be too cold for us to survive. Even in temperate zones it provides not only very welcome warmth, but light at night and, of course, heat for cooking. Anyone who has participated in an evening around a campfire will appreciate the almost mysterious way that people are drawn into its pool of light, and freely share their thoughts and stories in a way that would be difficult under other circumstances. The ignition and ritual surrounding the Olympic torch is another reminder of the potent symbolism of fire as a uniting force.

Perpetual flames also afford a thought-provoking focal point. The fire burning under the Arc de Triomphe in Paris, for example, commemorates the Allied dead from two World Wars. It keeps alive the zealous spirit of humanity that burned within the breasts of those who gave their lives so that others might live in freedom. Perhaps the best known of all perpetual flames is that which was tended by the Vestal Virgins. Based in Rome, the ancient cult of Vesta was a cult of the hearth, which included the domestic cooking fire. Girls were brought into service between the ages of six and ten, and served for thirty years, after which they could leave the sanctuary and marry. Infidelity during service was punishable by death.

Candlelight too creates a distinct mood wherever it shines. Candles are still an important part of our ritual life, from the sacrosanct altar candles, the romantic candlelit dinner, to the spangled birthday cake. Candles are also a favourite focal point for meditation, perhaps because they encompass all four elemental realms: from the solidity of its waxen body, the hot liquid lake at the top, to the flammable gas that is released from the wick, and the incandescence itself.

Because of its association with the sun at the zenith, this element is linked with the period of physical maturity in men and women. It signifies people at the height of their powers, possessed of fierce and ready strength, people not only able, but keen to compete and prove their fitness to rise to the very pinnacles of achievement.

The crystal that best represents fire is the red gem, ruby. Throughout the ages ruby has been hailed as supreme, not only because of its rarity, but also because of its red colouring, a warning of the often bloody road to dominion.

Many a chivalrous Crusader wore it, shaped like a heart, in remembrance of his fierce zeal for war in the name of love and faith. Preferring their symbolism less convoluted, the Romans simply held ruby sacred to the war god, Mars. An Eastern tradition regards the ruby as being coloured by the very heart's blood of Mother Earth, and rubies were known as glowing stones or lamps. Brahmins believed that the gods dwelt in the light from rubies. One Chinese emperor reputedly had a ruby that shone in the night as bright as day. Marco Polo, sojourning on the island of Sri Lanka, then known as Ceylon, was privileged to see a ruby "glowing red like fire". Greek mythology records how a female stork rewarded Heraclea by placing a ruby in her lap that was capable of lighting her room all night.

It is, perhaps, notable that rubies actually fluoresce a striking red colour when exposed to invisible ultraviolet radiation. The ruby crystal was at the heart of one of the earliest lasers, developed in the 1960s.

The West, Dusk and the Element of Water

Water can fill a container of any shape, yet always stays almost perfectly flat and featureless on the surface. This peculiarity suggests an appealing poetic image of someone who hides their true feelings behind a sort of mask. But it is the ability of still water to produce a crystal-clear reflection that is the key to understanding its deeper symbolic power. After all, what would we see were we to discover the Holy Grail, and gaze into its mysterious contents? Everyone would see something different, because each of us would see ourselves.

Watching the sun set behind the clear rim of an ocean is a particularly moving experience. Heralded by an inexorably darkening sky, the final disappearance of the light marks a dramatic and sobering moment. The twilight of dusk is mirrored in the cooling of summer into the slow decline of autumn. These are also emblems of our own descent from a peak of full physical fitness into the gradual enfeeblement of old age. It is, perhaps, the idea of "settling down" that most links these times with the element of water. After all, in direct contrast to fire, which always seeks to ascend, water always flows downhill.

Most of our Eath is covered with water – so what of the seas and oceans? Even today they hold many mysteries. Countless species as yet unknown to marine biologists lurk in the depths, while discoveries are constantly being made of bizarre creatures inhabiting aquatic environments hitherto thought too hostile to sustain life. There are currents in the deep oceans that take 1000 years to turn full circle. And there are currents too, deep in the mind of man, that are prodigious in their power, and equally ponderous in their motion.

Few people now believe in mermaids, sea monsters, floating islands, or any of the other wild-sounding yarns old seafarers would happily spin for the delectation of the youngsters. Like the myths of past millennia these tales, although only a few centuries old, have largely lost their credibility, even though many people still seek and claim to find the vein of truth which runs through the old stories, and believe them to be valuable charts revealing deep mysteries of the human psyche. For many, the sea retains its ancient mystique and romance: it has become a symbol of the subconscious in whose depths fantastic creatures and sunken cities still figure large, and where refugees from abandoned legends can still hold court and dwell in a timeless haven.

It is worth noting that although water is the most common substance on the planet, most of it is saline. Less than one per cent of all the water in the world is the flowing, fresh water that we all depend upon for survival. So precious is this liquid that many mystics regard rivers and streams as the arteries of the Earth Goddess, their precious fluid being her very blood. This water/blood analogy is curiously mirrored in the Christian mysteries: first Jesus performs the miracle of turning water into wine at a wedding feast, and then he turns wine into his own blood at the last supper – a mystery that is commemorated daily in the Eucharist.

At its heart, this element is concerned with change, transformation, fluidity and the ability to adapt to new situations. And this quality characterizes people born under the influence of water in the star signs of Cancer, Scorpio, and Pisces.

A meditation in the spirit form of an Undine (a lithe water-sprite) could take you not only through lakes of crystal clarity, but also through the uncharted depths of the deep ocean. As the sun sets behind a watery horizon, watch how a shining path appears to stretch toward you across the gently rippling surface. Walk awhile along this magical path before diving with dolphin grace into the warm welcoming body of the water.

The crystal that best symbolizes this blue element is the sapphire. Being unusually cool to the touch, sapphires were reputed to quench fire and, by analogy, the fiery human passions – not only lust, but anger too. It is a Buddhist tradition that this gem can assist the human heart to act with selfless devotion.

The North, Midnight and the Element of Earth

Except in extreme, polar latitudes, the sun never shines from due north. Neither does it shine in the midnight hour. This direction and time are both associated with the absence of warmth, and a consequent lack of vitality. These are likewise characteristic of winter. And they are all particularly associated with death and repose. It is no accident that the corpse is poetically referred to as inert clay, which is returned to the earth at burial. Yet the soil is fertile and, in due course, brings forth an abundance of vegetation and life.

We cannot naturally soar to heaven's heights with the birds, swim to the depths of the sea with the fish, or enter an inferno. Our species has evolved to feel secure only on solid ground. Appropriately, the most down-to-earth of the twelve signs of the zodiac are those three that are particularly influenced by the earth element: Taurus, Virgo, and Capricorn.

Earth is the only element we can hold in our hands and literally get to grips with. There is tremendous exhilaration in mountain climbing, trekking across a desert or exploring caves. Anyone purposefully facing the sheer enormity and raw indifference of elemental Earth can experience a life-changing sense of awe. The emotion is strong enough literally to shake them to their bones, yet it gradually resolves itself into a feeling of intense stillness and peace.

Of course, the Earth is not really still or solid at all. Not only is it spinning on its axis and whirling round the sun, but the sun itself is rapidly orbiting the galactic hub, which has, like all the other galaxies, been violently flung through the immensity of space-time by the Big Bang. . .

If we cast our minds away from this movement through the infinity of space, we may turn to consider the "solidity" of the infinitesimal. When you look at it closely enough, matter is composed of molecules that contain vastly more empty space than actual atoms, which in turn are comprised of enormous gaps and a few minuscule subatomic particles, which probably don't exist as real matter anyway – just minute quanta of energy. After contemplating these extremes, it is comforting to return to our normal perception of the world, where rocks are solid and stay firm under our feet! Such is the meditation of elemental Earth however, and the traditional form for undertaking the journey is that of the gnome. Not the decorative garden variety, but the elemental being, whose body is harder than rock itself, and can tunnel through strata in the blink of an eye.

It is always worth remembering, when we start getting bogged down in the mundane trivia of day-to-day life, that we are literally children of the stars. Many of the chemical elements that form both the Earth and ourselves are incomprehensibly ancient. Some, like hydrogen, were created in the first few minutes of the Big Bang. Others, like iron, were forged in the nuclear furnace of an ancient star that blew itself to smithereens. These are the very same elemental particles that we now wear as flesh and blood, clothes and jewellery.

Many minerals, especially crystals, exercise a powerful attraction on us, and we have responded by making them a part of our everyday lives. People all over the world still use traditional tokens at rites of passage. The giving of a silver spoon for a birth, for example; the gift of a diamond for an engagement; the exchange of gold rings at a wedding; the wearing of a jet or onyx brooch at a funeral . . . Likewise, designer or costume jewellery, club badges, and competition medals are all symbols of personal status, and can be viewed as the direct descendants of the prehistoric shaman's talisman. Divining how these traditions arose is a complex but fascinating operation. It is rather like being a special kind of archaeologist who is painstakingly examining how an ancient temple was constructed – not out of stone but from the thoughts of its priests.

The crystal most commonly associated with the element of Earth is the emerald. One recurrent Medieval notion was that an emerald was dislodged from Lucifer's crown when he fell from heaven to hell. From this stone (known as the Lapis Exilis) was sculpted the Holy Grail, supposed repository of man's ultimate mystical liberation. The ancient Emerald Tablet of Hermes Trismegistus was thought to be an imperfect copy of an earlier document written by Thoth (the ancient Egyptian god of wisdom), that reputedly contained all the lore necessary for humanity's ultimate magical liberation. Mines in Columbia, long before the Spanish conquest, supplied Inca kings, temples and graves with emeralds that were held sacred as representing the green, fertile Earth. The goddess Umina was symbolized by an enormous crystal, and was worshipped with gifts of smaller stones, representing children. The Spanish conquistadors, of course, zealously destroyed this pagan holy family.

Incidentally, please bear in mind when trying any of the meditations outlined above that, when we get in touch with the planet we are connecting directly to a primal and hugely powerful force. It can be (if you'll pardon the word-play) an earth-shattering experience to make contact with the chaotic energy that is still moving the entire universe. Some people call this energy God, others call it the Big Bang. Perhaps they are the same . . . Investigating Earth Energies is one way to find out for yourself.

The Sun – Fountain of Life

The planets of the solar system, including the Earth, coalesced out of an accretion disc orbiting the sun around 5,000,000,000 years ago. Because the Earth's equator is not perfectly aligned with the plane of its orbit, we experience seasons during our year-long journey. These seasons are directly related to the movement of the sun on its annual voyage through our sky, and were very well known to the ancient astronomers. The seasons follow one another in an apparently endless cycle: spring, summer, autumn, winter, spring, summer . . . This natural fact of life had a dramatic impact on the thoughts and hopes of ancient man. When so many plants die in the autumn, decay in the winter, and put out new growth in the spring, why couldn't people – in some magical way – do the same?

It seemed perfectly natural to assume that they could. The doctrine of reincarnation was an attempt to rationalize this perennial hope. Of course, reincarnation also accounted for the similarities that were passed from one generation to the next, the similarities that we now know to be genetic. To the casual observer though, it must have seemed obvious that the spirits of the ancestors lived on and were reborn in their children and grandchildren.

The seasonal extremes of midsummer and midwinter were thought to be the two great turning points of the ancient year.

Although in desert countries the high summer sun could be vilified as fierce and destructive, in Britain and other temperate countries, its impact has usually been beneficial. The sun's warmth is particulary welcome during the cold winter months! Nevertheless, if summer carried on even just a little too long, the soil would begin to parch, streams would start to dry up, and drought could bring suffering and death to man and beast alike. Similarly, if the icy grip of winter was slow in lifting its oppressive hand, and the bounty of spring's welcome return was delayed too long, starvation would visit the land.

It is no coincidence that, in the Christian tradition as in others, the child who would bring perennial salvation was born at midwinter. Many students of comparative religion see in the Nativity a metaphor for the solstice birth of the new year, which grows through the lengthening hours of sunlight and, in maturity, will become the glorious champion which overthrows winter's cruel reign.

Some anthropologists also speculate over the origins of commonplace Christmas customs, seeing in some the survival of pagan influences. One such notion is the careful attention devoted to the hearth fire's yule log and, indeed, the traditional Christmas candle. These have been interpreted as magical supports which nurture the weakening sun as it sinks to its midwinter low. These homely fires also warm and succour the feeble new year's sun that rises the next morning, as vulnerable and adorable as an infant.

The Inca culture of South America was one of many that regarded the sun as the source of their livelihood, and the power behind the throne. Each year at the winter solstice, the god was ceremonially tethered to a pillar, the Intihuatana, at Macchu Picchu. This pillar, rather like the gnomon on a sundial, is part of a complex solar observatory and chronometer, and the rituals were designed to ensure that the god did not stray from his appointed path through the heavens.

Thousands of temples to the sun god (Inti) were erected throughout the Inca empire. Girls as young as eight were chosen from their communities to live a cloistered life as "Virgins of the Sun". Their solemn duty was to ensure that the sacred flame in the temple was never allowed to go out. They themselves were only freed from a lifetime of service if they were selected to be the bride of a high-ranking official. Infidelity during their years of service was punishable by death.

Sun gods have not always proved popular. When the pharaoh Amenhotep changed his name to Akhenaten in the fourteenth century BC, he signalled his absolute decree that Egypt would embrace monotheism. The only god, he declared, was Aten, the visible disk of the sun. Aten was glorified as the supreme creator and sole benefactor of the world, and the pharaoh was his chief priest and representative on Earth. Akhenaten went so far as to order the destruction of all the ancient temples to other deities, and he sought to confiscate their treasures for the greater glory of Aten. His inspired vision even extended to the building of a magnificent new capital of Egypt (on the site of present day el-Amarna).

Naturally enough, the established priesthood was discomforted, to say the least, by being made so rudely redundant. The vast majority of the population also resisted losing their favourite deities, especially those rather maternal goddesses who, they felt, bestowed special mercies on the lowly and afflicted.

When Akhenaten died, his son (whose name meant "Living Image of Aten") renounced his father's icono-clasm, restored the cult of the older god Amon, and changed his own name in favour of that elder god. The new name of that young pharaoh was Tutankhamen, perhaps the most famous of all Egyptian pharaohs.

The Moon – Our Guide Through the Darkness

Although often called the Earth's only natural satellite, astronomers treat the moon as a planet in its own right, making the Earth/moon relationship a double planet system.

Certainly the moon's gravitational alignments with

The solar eclipse of 29 July 1878, as seen in Colorado.

the sun, revealed in its phases, affect the height of the tides of the sea, and its rising and setting likewise determines the times of the tides themselves.

Perhaps because it is at its brightest during the dark of the night, the Moon has long been associated with dreams, fantasy and illusion. Moreover, the way that it changes, visibly altering from each day to the next as it waxes and wanes, has made it a byword for inconstancy. Its regulation of women's menstrual cycles (with the associated hormone-related fluctuation of moods) has linked it securely with the feminine mysteries. This is perhaps the origin of the dichotomy between male as solar, and female as lunar. This mistaken belief sometimes resulted in women being damned by solar priests. Women, they argued, were clearly governed by the nocturnal realm and, therefore, were creatures of the dark, the antithesis of light, and therefore unquestionably evil! The violent obliteration of the sun during a total solar eclipse was an additional compelling reason to fear the moon's power.

Certainly, the Moon has been linked with the mysteries of the night, such as dreams, and that greater sleep, death, since time immemorial. If the moment of sunset is likened to the moment of death (it is, after all, an extinction following which warmth gradually ebbs away), then the simultaneous rising of the full moon marks the entry of the soul into the afterlife. It is hardly surprising then, that many ancient mythologies talk of the realm of the dead being dark and relatively dismal.

The moon is also powerfully associated with sleep, and many psychics train themselves to hover between wakefulness and unconsciousness, to carefully explore the nightly descent into the otherworld of dreams.

Clearly, the coming of the night can either be welcomed as harbinger of rest from toil, or dreaded as the herald of nightmares.

Mankind evolved to operate at optimum capacity during the daylight hours, and so is relatively ill at ease and nervous in the dark, being more vulnerable to predators (either nocturnal wild beasts or other humans), and natural disasters. In addition, moonlit nights are traditionally the favoured haunt of supernatural beings, especially those of a malevolent nature.

The phases of the noon are particularly significant. There is a wealth of anecdotal evidence, for example, suggesting that acts of random violence and mental aberration are most common during the full noon. The very words *lunacy* and *lunatic* commemorate the ancient idea that the influence of the lunar cycle extends into the intimate reaches of our minds.

The thin crescent of the waxing moon is associated with youth and virginity, as well as innocence and inspiration. Diana, the Roman goddess of the moon was a virgin goddess. She was also a renowned hunter and archer, the thin crescent being the arc of her drawn bow.

If the full moon represented the full-blown maturity of womanhood, then the last quarter was the age of the crone. She was the ancient one, wise beyond telling, who speaks in riddles and acts with a vengeance! She was often feared because she was so powerful (and she was also incorruptible, unswayed either by inducement or threat), but in truth she was a staunch protector of the weak and vulnerable (although she would never tolerate a fool!). She was personified as Hecate, queen of witchcraft.

The moon has been lauded by innumerable generations of romantic poets and artists, and the sheer beauty of her shining white face has entranced many a sensitive soul. However, anyone unfortunate enough to be stranded by night in a comfortless wilderness might find the glare of a cold and distant moon almost mocking in its intensity!

The moon's message is always one of change, perpetually reminding us that the "absolute truths" of yesterday are, in the light of a new day, often seen to be illusions.

Sacred Landscape

When people started cultivating land the soil became of prime importance, although even before this human beings had already forged a close living relationship with the Earth.

Each of the different habitats of seashore, plains, riverside and mountain had its own distinctive varieties of plants and animals. Very often nomadic tribes would move from one terrain to the next, in a cycle dictated by the seasons. After autumn's harvest of woodland fruits, for example, winter might take them down to the shore, to reap the sea's bounty, while spring might tempt them back to the uplands where the fresh plants and flowers would make appetizing eating. Moreover, we all know that some environments are more comfortable for us than others. The sea air, for instance, is often rich in ozone, which can have a mildly tranquillizing effect. Sun-drenched waterfalls emit clouds of invisible ions, which also calm and relax the mind.

The human imagination might also play a part in our

interaction with the landscape. After all, who knows what manner of terrible creatures might be lurking below the surface of "bottomless" lakes? Stories of lake monsters were once abundant, although nowadays only a few examples are widely known. The Loch Ness monster is probably the most famous, but other bizarre aquatic animals have been sighted in lakes as far afield as Africa, Australia, Japan, Ireland, New Zealand, Russia, Sweden and the USA. Canada is particularly rich in these mysterious creatures, with examples such as the Ogopogo, which haunts Lake Okanagan in the west of the country. Then there is the Turtle Lake monster of Saskatchewan, the black beast of Lake Ponenegamook, and the Manipogo of Lakes Manitoba and Winnipegosis.

Although anecdotal evidence is not scarce, hard physical evidence has been harder to find, and the scientific community is yet to be convinced of the existence of these legendary creatures. But that does not mean that they are simply figments of the imagination, merely that they may be rare and understandably publicity-shy!

Another natural source of water, so essential to human well-being, is the well, around which many mysteries have been woven. Medical science certainly supports some of the claims for the healing powers of certain holy wells. Those rich in iron, for example, can help alleviate anaemia; while alkaline waters can neutralize stomach disorders caused by excess acid. However, many wells are reputed to have magical properties that far exceed any conventional explanation.

The wishing well is a prime example of a miraculous well, which is supposed either to be the home of a magical creature, or a gateway to the world of the gods themselves. Valuable votive offerings and even human sacrifices were lavished upon such wells by people from early cultures on both sides of the Atlantic, by British Celts for example, and by pre-Colombian peoples of Central and South America.

Caves too have often been the subjects of dark legends telling of the subterranean creatures that sometimes venture out and wreak havoc in the countryside. On the other hand, it seems likely that these mysterious entrances were also anciently regarded as a sort of entry into the very womb of the Earth Goddess herself. The famous caves of Lascaux (France) and Altamira (Spain) contain thousands of paintings and drawings of lifelike animals and people. It is tempting to imagine, more than fifteen thousand years ago, a series of sacred processions penetrating the perpetual darkness of the inner sanctum. Once inside, they would solemnly present their offerings and, with painstaking care, paint their representations. The whole proceedings would be inspired and fired by the ardent hope that the fertility goddess would become magically pregnant and produce a plentiful supply of the game animals they had depicted.

Mountains too have been viewed with awe and venerated as the dwelling-places of the gods. Mount Olympus is probably the most famous residence of an entire pantheon, but many other high places have been noted as the focus of mysterious powers.

Uluru (or Ayers Rock as it is incorrectly but more commonly known), is a huge sandstone monolith in the midst of the Australian desert. It is certainly a magnificent sight, drawing pilgrims and tourists by the thousand, and every crevice, contour and feature is full of meaning and mythic significance. Aboriginal legend tells that it was formed during the Tjukurpa or "Dreamtime" and forms the centre of a vast symbolic landscape, of which they remain the natural custodians.

Glastonbury Tor, England, is remarkably similar in that it rises in splendid isolation out of a broad plain, the Somerset Levels. The Tor, well known for its legends of King Arthur and the Holy Grail, is also reputed to lie at the heart of a vast and enigmatic figure traced on the ground. Known as the Glastonbury Zodiac, the figure encompasses all twelve astrological signs each of which has been identified in the local landscape. Their outlines are drawn both by natural features such as meandering streams, as well as manmade features such as modern roads. However, many scholars dispute the validity of this colossal drawing. Because, they argue, the components of the design differ enormously in age, the Zodiac cannot be the result of an intentional design, but is merely the product of pure chance.

If natural rock formations and solitary hills attract attention as Earth energy hotspots, imagine the forces unleashed by a volcano. Mount Fuji, in Japan, for instance, is more than a source of limitless inspiration for artists and poets, who see in its almost perfect symmetry a blueprint of absolute beauty. The volcano was named after Fuchi, the native fire goddess, and 2000 years ago in the midst of a period of eruption a shrine was built at the summit in an attempt to pacify the angered spirit. The peak in general and a certain path in particular (at a height of 1.5 miles (2.5 km)), has long been believed to be a mystical gateway between the realm of men and the realm of the gods. Legend has it that they dwell there still, invisible to the prying eyes of the near half a million pilgrims and tourists who struggle to the top every year.

It is not difficult to understand the poetic link between the earthshaking roar and massive spurts of fire unleashed by an active volcano, and dragons. These mythical creatures are said to nest inside vast hollow hills and cause the Earth to rumble when they twitch fitfully in their sleep. And, when they wake, then their great billowing wings darken the sky and their terrible and unquenchable thirst for destruction is wantonly vented on their long-suffering neighbours!

Such are the myths and mysteries that have accumulated round one of the Earth's most terrifying manifestations, the volcano. Earthquakes, too, have given rise to bizarre and inexplicable phenomena but, here, modern science may offer an explanation. The study of Earth Lights is a relatively new field of research that hopes to solve a whole collection of mysteries with a single explanation.

It is well known that quartz produces tiny amounts of electricity when it is rubbed or knocked (piezoelectricity). Because of the abundance of this mineral, not only in pure veins but also as the primary constituent of sandstone, it is suggested that many earthquakes trigger enormous amounts of piezoelectricity as the rocks of the Earth's crust are fractured and crushed. Researchers claim that vast clouds of ions are released in the run-up to the actual slippage and quake. These may be responsible for some of the many observations of bizarre animal behaviour in the hours and minutes before a major quake. Indeed, it is thought that people too can sense these changes in the electromagnetic environment, although we have become unused to reacting to this instinctive warning of imminent danger.

Another feature of this theory is that, under certain circumstances, these clouds of ionized gas could become faintly luminous. Again, we are reminded of the dragon motif. Moreover, it is claimed that this phenomenon could be the reason why many reports of UFO sightings seem to congregate near active geological fault lines, and have been noted to peak in the weeks and days before even minor earthquakes.

It is possible that ancient shamans and other tribal leaders were chosen because of their unusual sensitivity to these and other subtle signals from the restless Earth. Perhaps they could read the invisible landscape of electromagnetic and gravitational anomalies like a map. If so, then they could readily sense and avoid the over-active areas, and lead their people to safety, where the Earth's energies were calm, balanced and conducive to a happy and fruitful settlement.

A Glimpse of Faeryland

It may seem odd that faeries are included in this study of Earth energies but, having explored the sacred landscape, one thing has been surely notable by its absence – life. Our planet is unique, so far as science can tell, in that it supports life. We ignore this simple fact at our peril!

We have already uncovered dragons lurking in the hollows of volcanoes and peering impishly out of earthquake zones. We have plumbed the bottomless depths of lakes and climbed to the tops of the world's high places – to find each populated with gods and bizarre mythical creatures. What of the flowers, trees, insects, animals, and birds that inhabit the surface of our world?

Birds in particular have always exercised a powerful effect on the human imagination. The mysteries of migration, for example, are even now not fully understood, although science is revealing their secrets one by one. Some birds' eyes are sensitive to polarized light, which helps them to navigate even when the sun is obscured by cloud. Others have traces of magnetite, a naturally-occurring magnetic ore, in their beaks, which may help them to sense the slight variations in the Earth's magnetic signature. This may also be one of the mechanisms which enables them to pick up advance warning of impending earthquakes. Years ago though, people thought that migrating birds, such as swallows, actually hibernated in the muddy beds of streams and rivers (an echo of their habit of making their nests from mud), or flew away to spend a season on the moon!

It is our ability to empathize, to imagine what it must be like to be a bird or an animal, that gives our species a magical window on the world.

We can run with the deer, soar with the eagle, swim with the salmon, and explore in our imaginations aspects of the world that we could never otherwise experience. If we listen attentively, these creatures can even speak to us, spirit to spirit.

Above all other birds, it is the majestic eagle that has most captured our imagination. The height to which eagles can soar affords them a magnificent panoramic view that is analogous to the clear perspective of spiritual enlightenment. Throughout the world, the eagle represents wisdom and knowledge, and was usually the consort or totem animal of the king of the gods, such as Zeus or Jupiter.

The king of trees was the oak. This tree has long been symbolic of strength, endurance and courage, and various species have therefore been associated with the heads of patriarchal pantheons, including Allah, Dagda, Jupiter, Taranis, Thor, Yahweh and Zeus. There is also a recurring relationship with lightning, and the oak's ability to survive lightning strikes has greatly enhanced its reputation for perseverance and continuity. Oaks were venerated with votive offerings, rituals and dances by their worshippers – all in the hope that the trees might be induced to share their secret powers of longevity and strength, and to protect the community from adversity both physical and spiritual.

Oak trees have long been credited with the power to withstand magical attacks, and to remain unaffected by charms and incantations. Magicians, it was thought, would weave their snares of illusion in vain, and be unable to warp their victim's minds, if only an oak was nearby. It was to protect himself from the subversive magic of Christianity that Ethelbert, king of pagan Kent, listened from beneath the boughs of an oak tree while St Augustine preached the Gospel. Of course, Christianity despised the ancient ways and dutifully destroyed as many of the sacred sentinel trees, and indeed, entire groves of holy trees, as they could find.

To the pantheist though, there is nothing that does not have its own spirit, each taking its natural place in a seamless hierarchy of existence. In the same way that we can tell what our pets are feeling, and vice versa, many people believe it is possible to communicate with wild animals and even plants.

The Findhorn Foundation is famous around the globe for its intuitive approach to producing healthy plants in an overtly hostile environment. Deliberately choosing infertile land, the members of the Foundation have developed a working relationship with the soil and plants, which has produced remark- ably healthy specimens. At the heart of their technique is a quasi-mystical belief in plant spirits. Calling them devas (derived from a Hindu word meaning "beings of light"), instead of the traditional but now-debased term faeries, Foundation members communicate with the garden as they work. Every species of plant has its own unique deva, which collectively control the forces of nature. The Foundation even recognizes the existence of a Landscape Angel who takes care of the entire locality. This Angel teaches them through psychic impressions and spiritual messages how best to nurture the Findhorn Garden for the mutual benefit of people, plants and the entire ecosystem.

The idea is that by eating such plants, whose own energies have been cared for and strengthened, we fill ourselves with their vital essence and become more closely attuned to the spirit of Mother Nature herself. Of course, some plants would not be eaten, but allowed to grow to their full term, and their seeds carefully harvested for planting next spring.

Eating certain other plants was always a matter of strict taboo. Most notable among these are the psychotropic or hallucinogenic plants such as the peyote cactus and the fly agaric toadstool. When eaten, the plant spirit readily enters not only the stomach but the very mind of the consumer, and can have cata- strophic effects on the unwary! It is notable that such plants were never consumed for recreational use (in the common sense of the phrase), but as a way to access the chimerical landscape of magic – a realm where meeting faeries and a whole host of other mythical beings is a commonplace experience.

Sacred Sites

We live in the heart of a vibrant, living world. We could learn much by listening to a babbling brook that winds through a bluebell glade in springtime, but the wisdom of the rocks atop the craggy mountain peaks is beyond the power of words to express. These are the energies and mysteries of the Earth, but what of the nature of mankind? We too are born of the Earth, and our own story is also important.

Many women find an almost mystical sense of fulfil-ment in giving birth. It is almost as if, by bringing a new life into the world, they share in a timeless moment of triumph over our traditional arch-enemy, Death. And the grand mystery of death is still the subject of mankind's deepest consideration.

Churches are usually built so that the congregation faces the altar to the east. Most Christian burials are similarly aligned, and this is usually explained in terms of the dead being able to rise comfortably from their graves on the Day of Judgment, and to face with joyous expectation their first sunrise in heaven.

It is remarkable, however, that the same burial align-ments have been noted in many ancient cultures. Indeed, some megalithic tombs are aligned so that the light from the rising sun enters through a narrow window and illuminates the sepulchre. Significantly, at Newgrange (Ireland), the date of this special sunrise is the midwinter solstice, the date that the sun is born again as the new year. These capacious New Stone Age barrows were periodically cleansed and old bones taken out, leaving the chambers mostly empty. Is it possible that these tombs were repositories for the bones of the dead who had yet to be reborn into the community? Once reborn, of course, the spirits no longer needed to be housed and venerated in the womb-like burial mound, and their remains could be removed.

The celebrated alignment of Stonehenge with the midsummer sunrise, which has been made famous by the controversial dawn ceremonies of Druids and other New Age pagans, has recently been challenged. It is now thought likely that Stonehenge was at least as important during the time of the midwinter sunset – which is on precisely the same alignment but in the opposite direction. Even less certain is the reason why its Bronze Age architects felt compelled to use stones taken from the crags of west Wales. Encircled by the huge and familiar ring of sarsen stones, is an arrangement of Presscelly bluestones, which were transported some 155 miles (250 km) – as the crow flies! Exactly what powers or special properties made those particular stones so necessary for Stonehenge is just one of many enduring mysteries that fire the imagination to seek answers in places where conventional science dares not look.

Man's fascination with the heavens in general, and solar alignments in particular, is prodigious. The pyramids of both Egypt and Central America were painstakingly aligned to the cardinal points. If nothing else, these immense relics remind us of our instinctive urge to measure and understand nature.

It was an attempt, though, to understand the human mind and spirit that inspired the ancient tradition of maze-walking. Perhaps best remembered in the Greek legend of Theseus and the Minotaur (where the hero escapes from a terrifying labyrinth by laying a thin thread of string along his route), it seems likely that an element of risk or danger was an essential part of the original design.

It is thought that following a maze presents pilgrims with a test that not only measures their powers of self-control, but may even allow their spirit to undertake a parallel journey in its own realm. Perhaps this is the purpose of the weird processional paths known as the Nazca Lines in Peru. Many of these Lines trace the outlines of huge animals, and may have played a part in shamanic ceremonies designed to contact the totem creatures, ranging from spiders to monkeys, whales and birds. It is notable too, that some of these figures are aligned with the heavens. The beaks of certain birds, for example, point toward the place on the horizon where the sun would rise on Midsummer's Day.

In North America there are over 100,000 earth mounds. Although most are fairly small funeral mounds, some are large. Monk's Mound in St Louis covers an area larger than that of the Great Pyramid of Giza. A significant number too are shaped to represent animals. In Georgia, for example, the Hopewell people moved tons of boulders to build a stone bird with a wingspan of 40 yd (36.5 m). The largest so-called effigy mound in North America though, is the Serpent Mound in Ohio. This meandering mound measures over 440 yd (400 m) from tip to spiral-shaped tail, and has been described as a snake biting an egg. It is

The maze is a map showing the tortuous route into the spirit world.

thought that it might represent a solar eclipse, interpreting it as the sun being devoured. Other researchers dispute this prosaic claim and, among various other theories, it has been suggested that the pattern traces some powerful form of Earth energy that wells up at the "egg", and vibrates along the surface before spiralling back into the ground at the tail.

Psychic dowsers (heirs to the ancient tradition of water dowsers, but who mentally "tune in" to Earth energy instead of water), have often claimed to find phenomena similar to this formation in Britain and elsewhere.

Some authorities have even speculated that ley lines, marked by prehistoric mounds and other artifacts on the ground, are not the "old straight tracks" they were first thought to be. Instead, it is now proposed, the antiquities that are apparently spaced along the path of the ley actually mark the nodes where two (or more) undulating lines of Earth energy intersect. The caduceus, where two serpents twine around a staff, might supply the appropriate visual image. The caduceus was a magic wand borne by the Roman god Mercury, with which he could make people fall asleep, or even wake them from the dead. Who knows what powers could be tapped from the Earth, if this latest theory proves to be true?

Another relatively recent branch of ley lore is concerned with discovering not lines but geometric shapes, mapped out by ancient sites. One such, in the fertile lee of desolate Dartmoor's looming bulk, apparently represents a giant who is the subject of primeval legends still current in the locality.

Other figures drawn on the ground are easier to spot. The famous White Horse of Uffington, for example, was drawn simply by cutting away the turf to reveal the layer of white chalk rock underneath. The Horse has recently been investigated by the same team that dated the Turin Shroud and, using the new technique of optical dating, it has been found to be much older than previously thought. This magnificent beast has been galloping over the hillside for over 3000 years.

What of the highly publicized crop circles? Well, they are certainly not an exclusively modern phenomena. However, with the rare example of a mini whirlwind to flatten the corn, I'm afraid that human not extraterrestrial agencies lie behind the many and varied, and often highly imaginative designs that, if you'll excuse the pun, crop up every year. Of course, these people may be answering an unconscious call to mark and invest a particular site with special importance. Perhaps they are actually following in the footsteps of the ancient shamans who decided on the locations of the primeval sacred sites. Who knows?

One thing is for sure though, there is usually more to things than simply meets the eye, and if you can't keep a sense of humour and perspective, you could end up missing much more than just a joke!

Feng Shui – Oriental Geomancy

The words Feng Shui translate as Wind and Water, and the concept of flowing is at the heart of this ancient oriental system.

By observing the laws of nature, Chinese sages drew up a series of guidelines to help people live in harmony with their surroundings. In the closing decades of the twentieth century, these formulae have taken root in the Western world too, as they appeal as much to our common sense as to our love of the arcane and mysterious.

Originating, according to legend, more than 5000 years ago, Feng Shui is a means of controlling Chi (also spelled Qi or Ki), which was the name given to the life energy that permeates and vivifies the entire universe. If you have too much Chi, you will be overwhelmed by stress and conflict. If you have too little, you will sink into a morass of lethargy and despair.

Chi can be controlled and channelled by landscaping your garden, home and lifestyle. Bright, shiny or pointed things attract Chi and keep it moving, whereas dark, fluffy or rounded objects tend to repel Chi or block its path. With the correct combination of objects then, it is possible to draw Chi into your home, and help it to circulate throughout every aspect of your life. You might want it to revitalize your lounge, for example, or make your study a haven of peace and relaxation.

The routes taken by the Chi are sometimes called Dragon Lines, and these can flow for hundreds of miles. Some may rise from the ground at mountaintops, and meander down through the foothills until they gradually spiral and sink into a distant lake or marsh. The similarity with ley lines has not been lost on researchers, especially in the light of the modern idea that leys might represent not straight but wavy lines.

The ideal situation for a house, so far as Feng Shui geomancers are concerned, is to have a tall hill immediately to the rear (the northward side), with smaller hills either side, and with sweeping views to the front overlooking a little lake. Such a position could be likened to sitting in a comfortable armchair and soaking your feet in a bowl of warm water! The Chinese give expressive names to these four directions. The northern mountain they call the Black Tortoise, the south vista is the Red Phoenix, the eastern flank is the realm of the Azure Dragon, and the west is the abode of the White Tiger. If these are all harmonious then your house will be the focus of tremendous good fortune.

Few of us are so lucky, of course, so the geomancers (or sorcerers as they are sometimes known) have devised a wide range of practical suggestions for improving the flow of this Earth energy through your home. Evergreen trees and bushes strengthen the energy flow, although the front of the house should be kept reasonably open, so as not to impede the passage of incoming Chi. A small water feature before the front door can more than double the positive energy that enters your property.

Internally, mobiles help to swish Chi from one place to another. Clutter will tend to trap Chi and create a stagnant pool, bringing an unhealthy atmosphere to that part of the room. Sharp corners are not conducive to keeping Chi circulating smoothly; positioning tall plants or bright ornaments in such places can help to neutralize the problem.

We are particularly sensitive to the effects of Chi while we are asleep. Beds, therefore, should not directly face the bedroom door or disturbing dreams will be generated as the Chi continually sweeps over and through our bodies.

By focusing our attention on the way we build our homes, especially in city environments, Feng Shui has much to offer the West. Its sensitivity to the detrimental effects that tall buildings can create by dominating smaller ones, and the way they can oppress the people who live and work in them, demonstrates that there is much to recommend it.

Once the inevitable claims of miracle cures have died down, and Feng Shui is accepted as a practical and largely common sense approach to living in harmony with our environment, its principles could even help solve the perennial problems of urban sprawl and inner city degeneration. Learning to live in harmony with Earth energies certainly offers us the hope of a brighter prospect for future housing development.

Gaia – the Living Planet

Many members of the scientific community are recognizing that our study of the Earth is coming full circle. Primitive man thought of the world as a whole, a mother whose mate is the heavenly father. In direct contrast, historically, science has tended to compartmentalize the world, breaking it down into distinct departments. Labels such as geology, chemistry, biology and meteorology have drawn arbitrary boundaries between topics that are really all facets of one vast subject – our world. A new, holistic view is now attempting a dynamic synthesis of all our accumulated knowledge. And the results may be startling.

In 1979 maverick inventor and biochemist, James Lovelock, published a book that sparked a popular revolution in thinking about our planet. "Gaia: A New Look at Life" presented the hypothesis that the Earth actually behaves as if it were a single entity. Lovelock argued that all the different environments and species that inhabit our globe interact in much the way that the various organs in a healthy human body cooperate and sustain life. Many people welcomed his theory, named (at the suggestion of his friend and neighbour, the novelist William Golding) after the Greek Earth Goddess, Gaia. Even its dire warnings were hailed as plain common sense. Polluting the land, sea and sky would eventually trigger a strong reaction from the ecosystem, which will automatically strive to stabilize the damage and rid itself of the cause.

Although there have been efforts on a global level to reduce the increasing degradation of our environment, most people feel that more could and must be done. There is no doubt that much more will need to be done before Gaia will feel content that she has raised her children well!

It is not easy to imagine our world populated by people at peace with themselves, but it is well worth the attempt. Then imagine if everyone was sensitive to the forces that dowsers feel, and learned to sense the subtle clues that the ancient shamans and tribal leaders intuitively knew and followed. And what a difference it would make, if they could recognize the spirits dwelling in the animals, plants and even in the landscapes that they encountered.

What a wonderful thing it would be then, to meet another *person*...

PART THREE

Powers of Healing

••••••••••••••••••••••••••••••••••••

A Matter of Faith

Healing by unconventional means, call it faith healing, laying on of hands or magic, owes much of its current popularity in the Western world to Spiritualist healers who performed their brand of magic in the middle of the twentieth century. The greatest of such healers in Britain was a man called Harry Edwards, whose public demonstrations of healing drew audiences of thousands. Edwards always invited medical professionals along to his demonstrations to examine a sick person before and after the healing had taken place, but there was little that was theatrical about his healing. Harry's treatments involved a very simple laying on of hands and a short period of silence. He did not rub or otherwise manipulate his patients, yet many were able to throw away their crutches and walk off the stage. Others rejoiced when their sight or hearing was improved after the healing process.

So how did Harry induce healing by a simple touch? Many of his patients reported feeling a very warm glow when he administered the healing; more heat than would be expected from a simple touch by a warm hand. Where did this extra heat come from? Harry's

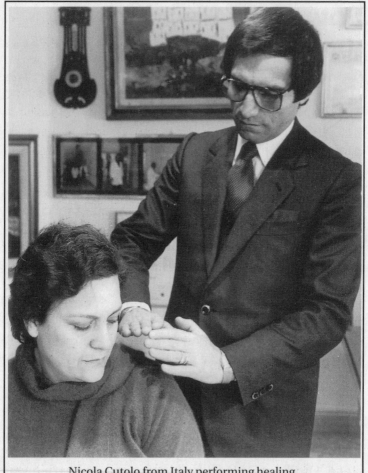

Nicola Cutolo from Italy performing healing.

own explanation was that he was transferring energy. Sounds simple really, except that this energy was being channelled through Harry from highly-skilled, but deceased physicians from the spirit world. All Harry had to do was to attune himself to the spirits, and *they* were the ones who did the healing.

One of the fastest growing forms of spiritual healing, based on the laying on of hands, is Reiki. *Reiki* is a Japanese word meaning "universal life-force-energy", and it is a system of channelling that energy to someone for the purpose of healing. The system originated in Japan. Its founder, Dr Mikao Usui, is said to have discovered the technique while on a spiritual journey on a sacred Japanese mountain, not so much by chance as by sheer force of will.

The story goes that Dr Usui went to the mountain to fast and meditate for twenty-one days, in the hope that he would receive revelations about how Christ healed the sick. During the final night he saw a ball of light on the horizon; the ball gradually came closer and closer. Naturally his first instinct was to run away, but he realized that this might just have been what he was waiting for, so he sat there while the light drew nearer and eventually hit him directly on the forehead. As the light struck him he was taken on a mystical journey and shown bubbles of all the colours of the rainbow – in which were hidden the symbols of Reiki. When he returned from the mountain, Dr Usui found that he had acquired an incredible power to heal. He returned to the monastery at which he was studying, and immediately upon arriving he healed the broken toe-nail of a monk, a tooth ailment, his own starvation, and the Abbot's sickness which had kept him bedridden for months. These have become known as the first four miracles of Reiki.

Dr Usui spent the next seven years healing the sick in the poorest areas of Tokyo, with dramatic results. During this period he trained another man in the art of Reiki, who in turn passed on the skills to Mrs Hawayo Takata, who became responsible for the introduction of Reiki to the West. Reiki applies an energy quality commonly known as "vibration", and is very simply performed. A practitioner places his or her hands upon the person to be healed with the intent for the healing to occur, and the energy then begins to flow. Practitioners believe that this energy form has its own intelligence and knows where it should go within the body in order for the healing to take place. Nonetheless, there is a prescribed set of hand positions traditionally taught that give good coverage over the recipient's entire body.

If the healing process is as simple as a laying on of hands, then it might be explained as some kind of transfer of energy from one person to another. Some people are naturally in tune with this energy and are more capable of passing it on to others. But this doesn't explain the many cases where healers can perform their magic without actually touching the patient. The phenomenon of distance healing is one that seems to defy explanation, yet which appears to have worked for thousands of people.

An early practitioner of distance healing was an aris-tocratic Roman Catholic priest called Prince Alexander Leopold Franz Emmerich von Hohenlohe-Waldenburg-Schillingfürst. Von Hohenlohe became famous for his ability to heal without ever meeting his patients, and on 10 March 1824 a plea for his skills was sent by the then mayor of Washington. The mayor's sister was lying paralysed and dying, and had been written off as incurable by the medical profession. A group of people gathered by her bedside at 3.30 in the morning in order to coincide with the time of a special mass which von Hohenlohe was conducting in Germany for the purpose of sending healing vibrations to her. The *Catholic Spectator* reported what actually happened: "At the moment of receiving the Blessed Sacrament (which, her tongue being quite parched and dead-like, she could hardly effect) she rises up in her bed, and lifting up her two arms, one of which she had not been able for a long time even to move, she exclaims – 'Lord Jesus, what have I done to obtain so great a favour? What shall I do to acknowledge so great a benefit?', asks for her clothes, dresses herself, sits up, throws herself down on her knees with the priest, the Rev. Stephen Dubuisson, who had given her holy communion, and who was prostrate on the ground, lost in a transport of admiration and gratitude, then rises, walks through the room . . ."

Reiki practitioners now also claim to be able to heal at a distance. To the world of the spirit there is no such thing as time or space; the world we see around us is only a small fragment of all that exists. Since there is no time and space to limit spirit, Reiki practitioners believe that they can operate without the normal limitations of space, and that they can bring healing to a patient regardless of distance. In conducting remote healings, the recipient must be objectified somehow, by using something (for example a teddy bear) to represent the body of the patient. The practitioner then practises the Reiki on the object, and the patient, who could be anywhere in the world, receives the healing powers bestowed upon it.

The National Federation of Spiritual Healers

explains that distance healing is achieved by healers who "attune with the Divine source to beam healing energies to the patient". To the average sceptical observer, this isn't very convincing and, as a definition, it would never appease the scientific community. Much of the evidence for distance healing is purely anecdotal, but there have been attempts by the scientists to investigate the phenomenon.

Dr Robert Miller of the Holmes Centre for Research in Holistic Healing in Los Angeles devised an experiment to test distance healing. The unique thing about this experiment was that the subjects did not know that they were taking part. Dr Miller gathered together a team of eight healers from different backgrounds and beliefs, and they were asked to treat a series of patients suffering from high blood pressure by distance healing. Miller also brought in a team of regular physicians who were asked to monitor whether the patients showed any alterations in blood pressure and heart rate over a long period of time. He did not tell the physicians what "treatment" the patients were receiving, nor did he tell them that many of the patients were part of a control group who were receiving no treatment whatsoever.

There were ninety-six patients in total, forty-eight of whom were to receive distance healing, with the remainder as the control group, receiving conventional treatment. The results were not conclusive, but did show a trend in the data. Four of the healers were exceptionally effective, producing ninety-two per cent improvement rates in their patients, compared with a seventy-five per cent improvement rate in the control group who received conventional treatment for high blood pressure. It seemed that the healers had indeed greatly helped their patients, more so even than modern medicine. Some might have put this down to mind over matter – a simple process of faith, whereby the patients believed that the healers' abilities would help them, and therefore it did. But the patients were never told that they were going to be healed by such a means.

It would appear that there are people who have an ability to heal. This could mean that they possess some kind of magical energy which they can somehow transmit to others, and this energy restores balance to the sufferer. Or it could mean that we are surrounded by a healing force which some individuals are able to channel, tap into and pass on to the sick. For many, this force is represented by a deity – for Christians, that deity is, of course, God. Many people firmly believe in the healing power of prayer and faith, that God will bestow upon them incredible restorative powers in response to their beliefs. One only has to look at the millions of people who have flocked to Lourdes on pilgrimages in search of miraculous healing.

Lourdes is seen by many Roman Catholics as a shrine impregnated with magical healing powers. Over six thousand people who have visited Lourdes claim to have received miracle cures for their ailments. This sounds like an incredible advertisement for Catholicism, yet the Roman Catholic church has been very reluctant over the years to endorse these miracles. Only sixty-five cures have been officially recognized by the Roman Catholic church as miracles in over 150 years – a rate of just one every two years on average. Anyone who claims to have been healed at Lourdes is carefully examined. Once they have passed through the examination process, they are passed on to a

Pilgrims visiting the grotto at Lourdes.

twenty-five-member international committee of specialists who carry out further, exhaustive examinations. Diagnoses are verified to determine their authenticity, and any treatment being received at the time of the visit to Lourdes is assessed to see if it could be the reason for the cure rather than divine intervention. Only those cases which appear to be a genuinely spontaneous remission from a serious disease have any chance of going on to the next stage, which is a medical tribunal in Paris. If they pass this stage, then an ecclesiastical tribunal declares the case to be an official miracle.

One of the sixty-five officially authenticated miracles concerned a twenty-two-year-old Italian called Vittorio Micheli, who was admitted to Verona military hospital in April 1962. Micheli had been diagnosed as suffering from a form of cancer which had eaten into the bone at the top of his left leg. For over a year he was immobilized, and his condition gradually deteriorated. He knew that medical techniques could only take away the pain, and he announced that he wished to visit Lourdes. By the time he was taken there, his hip had become grossly deformed, his leg was utterly lifeless, and his doctors could no longer feel a bone beneath the ever-growing tumour on Vittorio's leg. But amazingly, as soon as he was immersed in the water of Lourdes, he felt cured. He described the sensation as a feeling of electricity passing through his body.

When Vittorio returned to the hospital in Italy, he found that his pain was rapidly decreasing and that he was regaining his appetite. Within just one month, he was up and walking, even though X-rays showed no noticeable change in his hip. Eight months later, he underwent further X-rays, which showed what doctors described as "a remarkable reconstruction of the bony tissue of the pelvis". He was completely cured of the cancer, and had actually regenerated the destroyed tissues of his body.

The latest authenticated miracle cure to happen at Lourdes occurred in 1987, but was not officially declared a miracle by the Roman Catholic church until twelve years later in 1999, after vigorous investigation. Jean-Pierre Bely had developed multiple sclerosis in the 1980s, which caused his body to deteriorate to such an extent that he was unable to walk. On his visit to Lourdes, he felt a coldness, then intense heat all over his body, and "a marvellous, liberating force". The next evening he heard a voice in his head saying, "Get up and walk". He did, and to his surprise he managed to stumble around for a while. Since that time, he has made a one hundred per cent recovery.

Lourdes, it seems, is blessed with a magical healing power that has directly touched the lives of thousands of people, not just those who are among the sixty-five authenticated miracles. The real mystery, however, is the source of these healing properties: is it the water, the air, the prayers of the believers or the minds of the believers?

Religious groups would have us believe that the power of prayer and belief in deities is what charges the healing power of such sites as Lourdes. This belief has in turn led to a growth in the number of faith healers who claim to use the power of prayer to channel divine healing to the sick. Many such healers, in the form of tele-evangelists and healer-preachers, have accumulated vast wealth in the course of their "miraculous" healing. Fair enough, you might think, if they have provided a wonderful service of healing which has been of immense benefit, but the problem arises when certain people take advantage of people's faith. There are many charlatans currently operating who prey on the sick and take money from them while providing little benefit. Some descend to unimaginable depths to attract funds to their "spiritual campaigns", often using simple trickery to convince their congregations that they possess magical healing powers.

One of the worst examples of this was Peter Popoff, who ran a religious television empire in America and Canada. Popoff came under investigation by James Randi, a well-known debunker of psychic and supernatural frauds. Randi was convinced that Popoff was an elaborate fraudster, and attended one of his healing shows to prove it. Popoff was certainly a showman. He would run up and down the aisles of the audience, claiming that he had the divine gift of knowledge. He would then call out people's names, and tell them things about themselves that he could not have known, including what their ailments were. Then he would call them up on to the stage and perform a "healing", assuring them that they would be fully recovered in a matter of days.

Randi had spotted that Popoff's wife would interview members of the audience in the foyer before they were admitted into the theatre, and that she would transmit this vital information to her husband when the show was underway, using a radio. Popoff himself had a receiver in his ear, and would pretend that what he knew about his audience came to him through divine powers bestowed upon him by God. Before Randi exposed him as a fraud Popoff was making up to $1.25 million every month with his scam, a sign of how eager many people are to believe in faith healers.

But there *are* faith healers who appear to possess genuine healing abilities. Perhaps a simple rule should be followed if one is to put one's faith in someone who purports to be a healer: the bigger the show, the better the chance it is a confidence trick. Many genuine healers claim that they are nothing special, that the healing process is brought about simply by a faith in God and the power of prayer. Sceptics would argue that this could again be a case of mind over matter, a form of "placebo effect" (which is discussed later), and that prayer is simply one way of channelling the mind's power to influence the physical body. The simple truth is that nobody really knows how such amazing healing occurs, be it magic, faith or by the placebo effect. Demystifying the process could well dispel the essential ingredient of faith, thus destroying the healing power.

Acupuncture

When considering the use of alternative medicines, most of us in the Western world naturally turn to the East for guidance. Eastern medicine is responsible for Reiki, as we have already seen, and a whole host of other therapies that are not to be found in the offices of your local general practitioner. One of the most popular, and many would say, effective, remedies that has come from the East, is *chen-ts'u* (literally "needle stab"), more popularly known in the West as "acupuncture" (Latin for "needle stab!").

The system of acupuncture dates back thousands of years. Needles of flint, bone, bamboo and pottery made up the Stone Age acupuncturist's kit – archaeologists in China have found some dating between 4000 and 5000 years ago, which makes acupuncture the oldest form of organized healing known to man. The earliest written references to acupuncture appear in an ancient work completed approximately 4000 years ago, entitled the *Nei ching*, or the "Yellow Emperor's Classic of Internal Medicine". The work consists of thirty-four books which comprise a series of conversations between the Emperor Huangti and his minister Ch'i Pai about the causes and treatment of diseases. In the books, acupuncture was seen as just one part of a complete system of medicine that included massage, herbalism, diet, exercises, all bound up in a philosophy of healthy living.

Traditional Chinese medicine is still based on the *tao* – meaning "the path", or "the way of life". In Eastern philosophy, mind, body and soul form one unit, and Man is an integral part of the Universe as a whole, with its season of cycles and its ebb and flow of energies. A person who lives in harmony with the *tao*, according to the laws of nature, is a healthy person. Breaking natural laws leads to disharmony and imbalance, which in turn displays itself in the form of disease.

Health is expressed in the form of *qi* (also written as *shi* or *ch'i*), the life-force or vital energy. If *qi* is not flowing smoothly through the body, mental or emotional disturbance or sickness will be the inevitable result. *Qi* is manifested in the opposite and complementary forces of *yin* and *yang*. *Yin* represents that which is receptive, female, dark, hidden and watery, while *yang* represents that which is dynamic, masculine, light, open and hard. Good health requires a balance of both forces in one's body, activities and diet. An excess of either *yin* or *yang* causes ill-health, and the purpose of acupuncture is to restore health by restoring the balance of energies.

Qi is believed to circulate the body through a series of meridians – invisible channels flowing beneath the surface of the skin. There are twelve main paired meridians on each side of the body, each of which is linked with an organ – the heart, bladder, gall bladder, small intestine, kidneys, lungs, liver, colon, spleen and stomach. You may have noticed this makes only ten organs, with twelve meridians, but that is because the other two are linked to organs which are not recognized by Western physiologists – the *heart constrictor*, which controls circulation, and the *triple heater*, which keeps the body and the emotions warm.

On each meridian lie a varying number of points known as acupuncture points, which are seen as the entrances and exits for *qi*, the vital energy. The practice of acupuncture targets these points. Stimulating them with needles produces an effect in a corresponding part of the body through which the relevant meridian travels. Originally there were 365 points, based on the calendar year, but by the fourteenth century the number had increased to 657. New ones are continually being discovered, and there are now in excess of 2000 acupuncture points for the specialist to deal with.

The classical 365 points are indicated on charts, some of them centuries old, but modern practitioners refer to them by number, for example, "spleen number two". Their original names are much more poetic, with such terms as "the great eliminator" or "released stream". The point which in modern times is referred to as "heart number seven" on the heart meridian (classically known as "spirit gate") is found on the wrist, and can be used both for alleviating physical heart symptoms and for the relief of fear.

In the West, acupuncture is not yet accepted in mainstream medical practice. Many medical practitioners, who readily accept that it works as a treatment, continue to say that the concept of *qi* and the meridians is pure baloney. This is something of a contradiction – a bit like saying, "I accept that this car is capable of taking me from A to B, but I do not believe in the concept of the internal combustion engine." But those practitioners would argue that there has to be a better explanation, more in keeping with Western scientific thought. Despite there being no universal acceptance of the traditional basis for acupuncture, however, there are acupuncturists in the West, who, like their Eastern counterparts, base their treatments on the concept of balancing *yin* and *yang* and *qi* energy flowing freely through the body.

Methods of diagnosis vary considerably, but most reputable acupuncturists will take a medical history of the patient and, if possible, work in cooperation with the patient's conventional doctor. Where the conventional medical doctor will inspect a patient's tongue, look at their general complexion and check their pulse as a first method of inquiry, the acupuncturist uses a very different method of inquiry, called pulse diagnosis. Based on the Chinese discovery of twelve wrist pulses, six on each wrist, with each pulse relating to one of the twelve meridians, and therefore to a main organ, the acupuncturist is able to tell where an imbalance lies within the meridians according to whether a pulse is too weak or too strong. A major advantage of using pulse diagnosis is that, by detecting imbalances at an early stage, an acupuncturist can restore the body's energy balances before any negative symptoms actually occur. A word of warning, however. This opens the possibility for unscrupulous practitioners to keep patients under lengthy treatments for non-existent diseases, assuring them throughout the treatment that they are practising preventative medicine. Such people exist, and care has to be taken to find a genuine practitioner.

Once the pulse diagnosis has been made, the practitioner will decide which acupuncture points to treat, and how. The most common form of treatment is to insert needles a short way under the skin. This can cause a slight pain, but is less uncomfortable than most people at first imagine, and is worth the discomfort if it relieves a much greater pain. The needles the acupuncturist uses are very fine, between 1 and 1½ inches (2½ and 4 cm) long, and rarely cause bleeding when inserted. The acupuncturist will assess the patient's needs in order to determine how long the needles are to be left in the skin, and whether they should be rotated. Further energy can be added using "moxibustion", in which a pinch of a herb called moxa, or similar substance, is placed on the point, set alight, and removed when the heat is felt, before the skin burns.

The results of treatment vary dramatically. Sometimes a patient experiences instant relief of pain. On other occasions, the improvements are slower, over a period of weeks, or even months for severe cases. Patients often report a feeling of well-being, ranging from a mild tranquillity to a sudden rush of energy. Sometimes they actually feel worse for a period of time before improvements begin. In some cases they experience nothing whatsoever.

With such a wide range of results, sceptics often refer back to the placebo effect for an explanation. The reported benefits, they argue, could simply be a matter of faith. But although faith plays an important part in all forms of medicine, including conventional methods, sceptics cannot use this argument against the use of acupuncture in the treatment of animals, who obviously lack this faith in the ability of the acupuncturist. There are also a great many people who have lacked faith in the treatment but who have still received the benefits.

In Western thinking, no one fully understands why the insertion of a needle into the skin should have a positive effect. The traditional acupuncturist will claim that successful treatment is the result of a restoration of the body's energies, which in turn has a positive effect on bodily and emotional symptoms. Medical practitioners who believe that acupuncture can be used to effect treatment, but who dismiss the concept of *qi*, advocate that the prick of the needle stimulates nerves under the skin, which transmit electrical impulses to the spinal cord and to the brain, and the brain then activates healing to the diseased area. This explanation would go some way to solving the mystery of how sticking a needle in one part of the body can affect another.

Regardless of just *how* it works, acupuncture has been used successfully to treat a wide range of diseases. It can be of great benefit in almost any condition where there has not been an irreversible organic deterioration, and is particularly useful in conditions where conventional medicines are generally ineffective, such as allergies, migraines, rheumatism and arthritis. Acupuncture has been found to provide instant relief from neuralgia, and its pain-relieving effects are such that it has even been used as an anaesthetic in some surgical operations. If properly practised, it will cure or alleviate a vast number of conditions, without any damaging side effects whatsoever.

As with so many ancient arts, modern scientists are baffled by how it was discovered so many years ago. How, for example, did Stone Age acupuncturists know where the acupuncture points were located on the body? In fact, this is less of a mystery than might first appear. Many of the acupuncture points are well known to practitioners of the martial arts, both as knockout points and revival points, and could have been discovered accidentally during combat. But what of the many acupuncture points that are located far away from the area which they help to heal? How did the ancient Chinese work out, for example, that stimulating a point on the foot would have an effect on the liver? How indeed did they discover the system of the twelve meridians? Though some acupuncturists state that they can sense the state of a person's energies, no one has yet proved that the meridians actually exist. Is it possible that the ancient Chinese, who seemingly lived by a philosophy based on harmony with the Universe, were able to sense the healing possibilities of acupuncture in a way that modern scientists have lost through centuries of rationalism?

One of the greatest mysteries surrounding the treatment is why it took so long to reach the West, when it had been established in the East for millennia. But even in China, acupuncture has had a varied history. In 1822 it was decreed inferior to herbal medicine and banned from the imperial court of the Ching Dynasty, although it remained popular throughout the countryside. In the 1920s, when a plague struck Manchuria, Chiang Kai-shek banned the use of acupuncture as a treatment, in favour of Western medicine. Under the communist regime that followed, acupuncture was considered to be a form of treatment offered only by witch doctors, and the government sought to ban it. However, under Mao Tse-Tung's iron rule, acupuncture was actively encouraged, and several research institutes were set up to investigate its use. With so many troubles surrounding the use of acupuncture in its homeland, perhaps it is unsurprising that the treatment has been slow to catch on in the West.

Although there has been gradual acceptance in the West, even the more enthusiastic doctors continue to struggle over the question of *qi*, the vital energy on which acupuncture is based. There is an ongoing argument between conventional doctors who promote acupuncture and the traditional acupuncturists. Where the conventional doctor will dismiss the concept of *qi* as nonsense, the traditional acupuncturist will complain that such doctors are only treating the symptoms, thus giving short-term relief, rather than restoring complete health by treating the body energies.

In China this argument is not an issue, and the use of acupuncture is now more widespread than ever. The most dramatic way in which acupuncture is seen to work is in surgery. Over two million operations have now taken place in China in which the only form of anaesthesia consists of one or two needles rotated in, say, the patient's leg before and during the operation.

Patients undergoing this type of surgery are fully awake throughout the procedure, without any pain, and can even eat and drink. Between fifteen and twenty per cent of all operations in China are now performed using this technique, and the success rate (success being a patient who suffers no pain) is around seventy-five per cent.

The possibilities for this in the West are vast. When one considers the cost to the public of general anaesthetics, not solely the cost of the drugs, but also the machinery, then the fact that the burden of paying the bill could be lifted through the use of some strategically placed acupuncture needles is hard to ignore. And this economical advantage is clearly taking effect; France and other Western countries are now increasingly adopting the practice.

Another important application of acupuncture is in helping to cure addictions, from heroin to cigarettes. Treating the right points can help alleviate cravings and withdrawal symptoms, and induce calmness and reduce anxiety. This form of acupuncture has in fact become extremely popular in the West, and many studies of drug addicts (particularly in the US) treated by acupuncture have shown very good results.

I shall leave the final word on acupuncture to the British Medical Acupuncture Society. On 12 November 1998 they issued the following press release:

> *Who would have thought that burning Chinese herbs over an acupuncture point on a pregnant woman's toe could really effect a baby's movement and position inside the mother's womb? Well, we now know that it can. A randomized control trial published in the Journal of the American Medical*

Association . . . proves beyond reasonable doubt that burning the herb Artemesia vulgaris (moxa) over the little toe of a woman at thirty-three weeks of pregnancy with a breech presentation (i.e. the baby is the wrong way round in the womb) caused a significant increase in foetal movements. More importantly, after two weeks, over seventy-five per cent of those women treated with moxibustion had converted to a cephalic presentation (head-first – the right way round) compared to under half those women who did not receive acupuncture, a result of great statistical significance.

The most interesting part to sceptics will undoubtedly be the statement "a result of great statistical significance". What we appear to have achieved is a scientific test to prove the worth of acupuncture, with a control group present to confirm the results – and the numbers are in favour of the practice! But even with studies such as this, the cause for the phenomenon has remained elusive. Modern science does not like to have an effect without a cause. For acupuncture to be completely accepted in the West a conclusive scientific cause for its action must be found. At this stage in our knowledge, what can be said is that acupuncture achieves positive results – and the evidence for this is persuasive. It is hardly likely that a practice could survive for 5000 years among an intelligent and civilized society unless it worked.

Hypnosis

If the magic of healing can be ascribed to an individual's belief that they will be healed, then there is a very strong case to be made for the theory that the mind can directly affect the body in seemingly miraculous ways. Modern medicine is primarily concerned with the physical body and the effects that certain drugs and techniques have upon it. Various alternative therapies, however, are more concerned with accessing the power of the mind to affect the physical body, one such being hypnotism.

Although hypnotism has been practised throughout history, it only really came to prominence in Western societies through the work of Franz Mesmer (hence, "mesmerism") 200 years ago. Mesmer made two discoveries of great significance. First, he found that if a patient who was in a trance was told that he would feel no pain, he would indeed feel no pain. Mesmer showed that surgical operations could be performed without any discomfort to the patient, and this was before the discovery of anaesthetics. The medical profession at the time shunned Mesmer, thinking him to be a crank. (This always seems to happen when anyone develops a technique which goes against the scientific establishment's thinking.) Leading physicians were invited to watch him perform the amputation of a leg, and on seeing that the patient, who was awake throughout the operation, felt no pain, they insisted that he was merely pretending not to feel any pain. This would make him a rather accomplished actor by any accounts!

Mesmer's other discovery was that some of his hypnotized subjects acquired talents which they did not have when not under his spell. Some became adept at drawing, and a few appeared to gain clair-voyant capabilities, describing events that they could not possibly have witnessed.

The discovery of anaesthetics, coupled with an ever-sceptical medical community, meant that mesmerism or hypnotism was rarely used in healing practices, and it became marginalized over the years. In the modern world most people when asked their opinion of hypnotists think immediately of entertainment shows where a hypnotist makes members of the audience perform puerile acts for the amusement of the rest of the audience. But hypnosis can be used for far greater purposes than entertainment, including healing.

Nobody really understands fully how hypnosis achieves healing in an individual, but most theorists support the notion that a hypnotist shuts off certain parts of the brain, thereby enhancing other areas which usually lie dormant. These areas can then act to heal the body in significant ways, suggesting that we are all capable of incredible healing abilities, if only we knew how to access them within ourselves.

Joe Keeton is one of Britain's most experienced and respected hypnotists, and in his book, *The Power of the Mind*, he quotes numerous cases in which individuals have overcome serious health problems through hypnosis. One case involved a young woman whose heel bone had been shattered in a motorcycle accident. She underwent hypnotherapy, and the results were truly startling. Her recovery actually included new growth of the damaged bone. Her conventional doctor was stunned by what had happened, saying:

"the improvement which occurred in the condition of her heel was much greater than any of her medical advisers anticipated. I can offer no incontrovertible proof that the hypnosis did provide growth stimulus, but I am convinced in my own mind that it did affect the healing process."

Accessing the incredible powers of the mind is a very useful tool for healing. Dr Dabney Ewin of Tulane University, New Orleans, began to use hypnosis to treat burns victims in the 1970s. Some of his results have defied even the harshest criticism from sceptics. In one case, a patient's arm was badly damaged by an explosion of acetylene, which burns at 5432° F (3000° C). The patient was rushed to Dr Ewin's surgery and placed under hypnosis within an hour. Dr Ewin used hypnotic suggestion to persuade the patient that his arm felt cool and comfortable. He then dressed the wound and sent him back to work. The next day the patient came back to be checked over by Dr Ewin, who noted that the skin was still charred, but there was no swelling, infection or pain. Within twelve days, the arm was completely healed, something which would never have been anticipated had conventional medicine been the only treatment given.

This evidence was dismissed by sceptics as purely anecdotal, but the findings of two California doctors have them truly baffled. Dr Jerold Kaplan and Dr Lawrence Moore at the Alta Bates Hospital burns unit in Berkeley performed an experiment to test the healing power of hypnosis. They selected five patients who had been burned badly on both sides of their bodies. Using hypnosis, they suggested to the patients that one side of their bodies was in fact not burned at all. In four out of the five patients, the healing was significantly more advanced in the areas at which the hypnosis was directed than in the areas which received only conventional treatment.

Another case in England caused a stir when it was reported in the *British Medical Journal*, as it appeared to treat a condition largely thought of as incurable. A sixteen-year-old boy was suffering from a condition which left large wart-like excrescences all over his body. His skin was covered in a "rigid, horny casing", and he had been subjected to skin transplants for years. Within a month, however, the skin grafts themselves would always succumb to the condition. Dr Albert Mason, a senior registrar at the Queen Victoria Hospital in East Grinstead, was finally called in by sceptical colleagues to try hypnosis on the patient, always under strict laboratory conditions.

Mason first persuaded the boy that the warts were going to fall off his left arm. When the boy returned a week later, his arm was completely clear from the shoulder to the wrist, but there was no noticeable change to the rest of his body. Dr Mason took the patient to his colleagues, and told them that he had used only hypnosis to cure the arm. One of the surgeons present was utterly astounded, and ordered Dr Mason to go to the library to look up the condition, which he told him was a case of congenital ichthyosiform erythrodermia of Brocq. Mason duly did so, and discovered that the condition was untreatable, as it meant that the patient's skin had none of the essential oil-forming glands whose function is to make the outer layers flake off and renew themselves. The bacteria-ridden warts would simply continue to build up, whatever was done to them.

Undeterred by his finding that the medical profession had written the boy's condition off as incurable, Dr Mason continued with the hypnotherapy, and went on to achieve an impressive improvement on all areas of his body. The horrible scaling fell off the other arm, his hands, 90 per cent of his back and 70 per cent of his legs and buttocks. One year later, Mason called the boy in for a check-up, and was delighted to see that the condition had not returned.

The mind, therefore, can most definitely affect the body. Hypnosis is just one method of helping it to do so, but there are several others. Many believe that this is not a magical technique, but that hypnosis, and other methods, are simply activating the powers of the mind to fool the body into thinking that it will recover, which it duly does.

Herbalism

Herbalism is a form of medicine so ancient that its origins are lost in the mists of time. Compared with conventional medicine, herbalism has a completely different emphasis on the way in which it acts on the body – in most cases treatments are geared to supporting the powerful recuperative and defensive forces of the body against deteriorating influences, rather than attacking the disease directly.

Herbalism has traditionally been associated with witchcraft, and many practitioners of the therapy are Wiccans, or new age witches. The image of someone in a black pointed hat toiling away over a boiling cauldron instantly springs to mind, but this is most definitely not the case. Most modern witches are just

Herb	Ailment	Dosage	Administration
Aconite	Neuralgia Sciatica	Highly dilute	External application over unbroken skin
Agrimony	Colic Intestinal tract infections	1–4 grams of the dried herb three times per day day	Taken orally
Aloe Vera	Cuts, grazes, burns, rashes, bites, stings	120–300mg dried sap three times per day	External application on the affected area
Angelica	Colds and flu Asthma	1–2 grams of dried root three times per day	Prepare as a warming tonic
Aniseed	Bronchial infections Whooping cough	0.5–1 gram of dried fruits three times per day	Prepare as tonic
Asparagus	Urinary infections Kidney disorders	20–50ml of freshly prepared juice	Liquidized and taken as a drink
Burdock	Skin problems, such as acne	1–6 grams of dried root three times per day	Apply to affected area
Chamomile (wild)	Tension Insomnia Menstrual cramps	1–4 grams of dried flowers three times per day	Prepare as a warming tonic

Herb	Ailment	Dosage	Administration
Comfrey	Wounds Fractures Ulcers	1–4 grams of dried root three times per day	Apply to the affected area
Dill	Colic Flatulence	1–4 grams of dried fruits three time per day	As a tonic
Echinacea	Septic conditions	0.5–1 gram of the dried root three times per day	Depending on the condition, either as a tonic, mouthwash or douche
Feverfew	Migraine	1 fresh leaf 1–3 times daily	Best taken fresh
Lavender	Nervous irritation Exhaustion Depression	0.5–2 grams dried flowers three times per day	Oil used locally for headaches; tonic used otherwise
Marigold	Ulcers Eye infections	1–4 grams dried flowerheads three times per day	Used as eyebath for eye infections; applied locally to ulcers

normal people who simply have an interest in the healing properties of herbs and spells, a form of therapy that is conventionally ignored.

Treatments claim to be able to aid in curing a whole range of medical ailments. For example eliminative remedies encourage one or more of the body's eliminative functions. The purpose of such an agent is to increase the removal of toxic material from the body. Alteratives are herbs which alter the processes of metabolism so that the tissues can best deal with the functions of nutrition and elimination. Remedies most often thought of as alterative include burdock, nettles, echinacea and figwort. They are frequently applied to toxic conditions such as skin diseases, arthritis and auto immune diseases.

A list of common herbal treatments for everyday ailments is contained within the table below.

The table shows just a handful of the herbal remedies prescribed by practitoners of the art. It is not advised to try any of the remedies at home, as many of the herbs used can, in the wrong dose, or if applied in the incorrect manner, be poisonous. Practitioners spend a great many years learning which herbs to use for any particular ailment, and if you are thinking of trying herbalism as a means of healing, it is best to contact a registered herbalist.

The treatments offered do, however, use very gentle stimulations to provoke healing. When used in the right hands, herbalism has confounded the medical industry, and therefore its use is becoming more wide-spread. All manner of mysticisms have been attached to this alternative medicine, with claims that the herbs have in some way been blessed by practitioner, and that is what has endowed them with healing powers. This is generally regarded as nonsense by sceptics, but once again, if a patient has faith in the practitioner, and believes that they have healing powers, then the mind can be activated to produce wondrous effects upon the physical body.

Homeopathy

Homeopathy is an example of making sympathetic magic work to cure ailments. The motto of the homeopathic system is "*Similia similibus curantur*" ("Like cures like"). Homeopathy is a system of medicine that uses specially prepared, highly diluted substances in order to activate the body's own natural healing mechanisms. It uses a variety of substances taken from plants, animals, minerals, chemicals and conventional drugs, all in tiny amounts, using a special preparation process. This process involves diluting the substances by shaking, and the finished product is then tested on healthy individuals to determine its effects. These effects are then used as guidelines for administering the remedy to the sick patient. The shaking is vital to the cure, as it is believed that the vibrations of the diluted solution are still present and actively work on the patient.

Homeopathy differs from conventional medicine in that it seeks not to treat a single symptom, but to direct the healing process towards the whole range of symptoms a patient may have. It is also directed towards self-healing, and therefore can only proceed at the rate at which the human body can naturally change.

The system of homeopathy was the brainchild of Samuel Christian Hahnemann, who developed the procedure over a period of fifty years. The principles that he devised at the beginning of the nineteenth century are essentially the same as those being followed today. Hahnemann was translating a herbal book by British author William Cullen in 1790 when he had the brainwave that led to the creation of homeo-

pathic medicine. Cullen had explained that the reason
that the drug quinine was effective against malaria was
because it was bitter. Hahnemann saw this as
nonsense, for there were many other drugs which were
far more bitter than quinine and which had no noticeable effect against malaria. He therefore decided to
perform an experiment upon himself to demonstrate
the real reason why quinine was so effective against
malaria.

Over several days, he administered quinine to
himself twice daily, and noted down the effects. He
found that his feet and fingertips became cold and,
after a while, he started to feel drowsy. His heart began
to palpitate and his pulse to quicken; he felt an incredible anxiety and started to tremble uncontrollably. In
short, he experienced all the symptoms usually associated with a fever, but without actually having the
disease itself. He found that this occurred every time
he administered a dose of the quinine, but that it
disappeared after about two hours. Hahnemann
suggested that a drug acts therapeutically when it
produces symptoms in a person without a disease that
are similar to those produced in a person who has the
disease – the basis of homeopathic teaching. He began
to test other drugs in a similar way – administering
them to healthy subjects – and observing what
symptoms were produced.

Hahnemann used a holistic approach to his therapy;
he looked at all the symptoms of an ailment.
Conventional medicine, by contrast, uses a drug to
cure only one symptom. And all symptoms were given
equal importance, as Hahnemann believed that some
"force" controlled all human health and illness. This
force is considered by some to be the spirit, the soul or

the life energy. Homeopathy therefore became a system that focuses on the individual and how they react in whole to an illness, physically, mentally and emotionally. Where science was trying to pinpoint single diagnostic categories which are the same in all of us, homeopathy began to look at the whole situation of a single individual, a system known as "holism".

Hahnemann's next discovery was to prove the most curious. Having proven a remedy by his unusual methods on healthy people, he began to see if he could actually apply it to the sick. At first he administered his treatments in the usual doses, but he found that many of the drugs were semi-poisonous and produced harmful side effects on his patients. He therefore began to dilute the drugs, making the doses smaller and smaller. What he found was that, contrary to popular medical beliefs, the smaller the dose, the better and longer the cure. He found that homeopathy worked by inducing a mild but specific set of symptoms similar to those already experienced by a sick patient, and thus the patient's natural healing processes were speeded up, thereby curing the original complaint that much faster. His treatments, in other words, helped the sick to heal themselves.

The practice of homeopathy became very widespread for about half a century. It was found to be extremely effective during large-scale outbreaks of cholera which were rife during the latter half of the nineteenth century. Death rates during such epidemics using conventional medicine were as high as 60 per cent, but statistics showed that homeopathic methods reduced this figure to as low as 10 per cent. In spite of its successes, however, homeopathy had its opponents. Apothecaries (pharmacists of the time) hated homeopathy because the system involved doctors making up their own medicines from fresh herbs, and using only one remedy at a time. This was not good for their business, which involved mass production and long-term storage, and they sold directly to patients and doctors. If doctors were to make up their own remedies on a need-to basis, the apothecaries would go out of business. The second body of opposition was the doctors themselves. They relied on quick and dramatic treatments to cure illness which required specialist knowledge and training in order to make a living, and any treatment which patients could both make and administer to themselves was an obvious threat to their profession. Homeopathy began to decline after about fifty years of prominence, largely due to opposition from the doctors and apothecaries, but also because of an ever-expanding medical industry. As science advanced, the system of homeopathy seemed more and more archaic, and by the turn of the century, it was practically obsolete.

Interest in the field was revitalized in the 1960s, as even scientific thinking began to realize the importance of providing individualized health care. Homeopathy is a system that is based entirely on that principle, so it is not surprising that it made a comeback. Its popularity is particularly marked in the developing world, where conventional medicine is far too expensive to be widely available, and the idea that the body can help to heal itself is more generally acknowledged.

Homeopathic treatments are more popular today than ever before, though it is generally used as a complementary adjunct to conventional treatment rather than as a complete replacement. It is not a system that is applicable for all illnesses, but its use is expanding into areas where it had previously been thought of as being quite useless. In India, for example, practitioners are investigating its use in the treatment of malaria, dysentery, cancer and AIDS, but it is generally used for significantly more minor conditions. The ten most common ailments treated by homeopathy are:

1. Asthma
2. Depression
3. Otitis media
4. Allergic rhinitis
5. Headaches and migraines
6. Neurosis
7. Nonspecific allergies
8. Dermatits
9. Arthritis
10. Hypertension

The greatest attribute of homeopathy is that it can be practised at home. There are a good many trained practitioners who would be better able to cure chronic health problems or enhance overall health, but for simple things such as cuts and grazes and minor illness, anyone can help themselves to heal themselves using basic homeopathic techniques and with a minimum of knowledge. Homeopathy is generally a safe and gentle healing system that any family can use to help relieve the everyday minor medical problems that occur. Basic homeopathy kits can be bought over the counter in many pharmacies. In the table below is a list of common homeopathic treatments and the symptoms that they can cure, whether those symptoms be states of mind (*Mood*) or physical ailments (*Illness*).

Remedy	General	Mood symptoms	Illness
Monkshood (Aconitum napellus)	Restlessness Tingling, coldnesss, numbing	Fear and anxiety Restlessness	Emotional trauma Colds Croup Earache Eye injuries Fever
Horse chestnut (Aeschulus hippocastanum)	Slowness of body functions Blood stagnation in the veins	Irritable and depressed	Haemorrhoids Varicose veins
Fools' parsley (Aethusia cynapium)	Childhood illnesses, diarrhoea, colic, teething	Restless crying Uneasiness	Childhood diarrhoea Colic Teething
Antimony sulphide (Antimonium crudum)	Exhaustion Milky coating on the tongue	Irritability Sulkiness	Chicken pox Gas, heartburn and indigestion
Honey bee (Apis mellifica)	Swelling Itching Exhaustion	Listlessness Poor concentration	Heat-stroke Insect bites Skin rashes
Trioxide of arsenic (Arsenicum montana)	Weakness Burning pains Acrid discharges	Nervousness Anxiety Fear of death	Gastro-enteritis Influenza Pinkeye Vaginal infection
Deadly nightshade (Belladonna)	Red, hot throbbing High fever	Delirium Nightmares Violent rages	Boils Fever Headache ☞

Remedy	General	Mood symptoms	Illness
	Burning pain		Menstrual cramps Styes Toothache
Barberry (Berberis vulgaris)	Wandering, burning pains	Listlessness	Urinary tract infections
Spanish fly (Cantharis)	Violent inflammations	Anxiety Frenzies Raw, burning pains	Burns Painful urination
Unroasted coffee (Coffea cruda)	Overexcitement Hypersensitivity Nervous palpitations	Excitability Overactivity of the mind	Insomnia Toothache
Meadow saffron (Colchicum)	Weakness Tearing pains Cold sweats	Depression Mental confusion	Morning sickness
Boneset (Eupatorium perfoliatum)	Fever with shaking Pain and soreness of the bones	Sadness	Influenza
Marsh tea (Ledum)	Puncture wounds Swollen extremities Joint pains		Cuts and bruises Insect bites and stings Sprains

Remedy	General	Mood symptoms	Illness
Phosphate of magnesia (Magnesium phosphorica)	Sharp, shooting pains Spasms and muscle cramps	Pain Inability to think clearly	Abdominal pain Colic Menstrual cramps
Poison-nut (Nux vomica)	Hypersensitivity to pain, light, noise Cravings for alcohol, drugs etc	Irritability	Common cold Constipation Gas, heartburn, indigestion Hangovers Haemorrhoids Menstrual cramps
Rue bitterwort (Ruta graveolens)	Strained muscles Weakness Burning, stinging pains	Quarrelsome Anxiety Restlessness	Acute back spasms and sciatica Ganglion cysts Sprains Tennis elbow
Tobacco (Tabacum)	Nausea Irregular pulse Collapse	Despondency Forgetfulness Insomnia	Motion sickness
Tree of life (Thuja occidentalis)	Copious sweating Green, foul discharges	Irritability	Warts

If in doubt about using homeopathic medicine, it is always best to seek the advice of a registered practitioner, but there are many instances when even that will not help. If a treatment is either having no effect, or even having an adverse effect, it is very important not to continue with the homeopathy, and to seek an alternative therapy as soon as possible. If a disease is serious and destructive, or if there are good conventional methods available, then it is best to avoid homeopathic treatments in order to prevent harm by progression of the illness.

There are, however, incredible stories of the healing powers of homeopathic treatments. In one case, a seventeen-year-old girl who had been severely ill since the age of fourteen seemed very unlikely to improve, as she was completely unresponsive to conventional medicine. She had recurring stomach ulcers and had become a manic-depressive. She would go for days where she was completely hyperactive and would not eat or sleep, apparently completely out of her mind. This would then be followed by a period of extreme depression, almost constant sleep and bingeing. She started to mutilate herself with razor blades, and had been under the care of psychiatrists and counsellors for several years. She did not seem to react to the usual antidepressants such as lithium, and had even attempted suicide by overdosing on them.

She also suffered from acne, morning headaches and cravings for salt, all of which were dismissed as unimportant by the medical profession, but when she finally went to see a homeopath, he took these conditions very seriously as part of the holistic approach to curing her. She was given a dose of *Natrum muriaticum* (table-salt) by the homeopath, when she was in the middle of a violent ulcer attack. Within two weeks, she had stopped self-mutilating and her ulcer pain went away. Her violent mood swings abated and her headaches stopped. She continued to use the homeopathic treatment in smaller doses for two years, taking an application whenever she felt stomach pain. She is no longer a manic depressive. Where conventional medicine had completely failed her, a simple dose of highly diluted salt had come to her rescue.

Colour and Sound Therapy

It is a widely held concept that we are all spiritual beings and highly susceptible to both positive and negative energies. These energies can cause imbalances that make us depressed or even physically ill, but those same energies can also uplift us, make us well and keep our lives in emotional and mental balance. Everything in the universe responds to light and tone, and the theory behind colour and sound therapy is that every human being responds to that being's own particular keynote and colour vibration. Therefore, learning an individual's tone and colour can aid in applying the proper energies for that person.

The magic of colour and music therapy is an ancient one, known to the sages of old. Centuries ago, it was used for healing in ancient Greece and Egypt, India and China. This therapy works because we, as spiritual beings, are highly susceptible to positive and negative energy forces, although we are more often than not unaware of this. For example, simply looking at a bright red colour evokes a particular response, while being in a blue room evokes another entirely different emotion. One colour may be effective for stimulating the brain cells, another to bring peace and quietness to the mind. When used in combination with accompanying and complementary music, the effect will be greatly enhanced.

Music is the most subtle of the art forms, but many would say that it probably has the greatest influence on our psychic centres and our nervous system. Everything in the universe vibrates to certain frequencies, and we are influenced by them according to our own nerve responses. It follows, therefore, that illnesses too have their own vibrations, and if we can find musical tones with a sympathetic vibration, then we could combat that ailment.

Music and colour therapies are based on healing energy centres within our bodies called *chakras*, in much the same way as yogic teaching. Each chakra is responsible for the welfare of parts of the physical body and the spirit, and different colours and music affect different chakras in various ways. There are seven of these chakras, and what they relate to, and which colours and music types seem to magically affect them, are listed in the table overleaf.

Colour and music therapists believe that, in recognizing that colour rays and musical tones have a direct, vibratory correspondence with each other, we can utilize these energies for our benefit. It is natural that there will be different responses to colours and music, even though there are some generalities that can be applied to each one of these energies. For example, the colour red is a very powerful colour, maybe too powerful for some. People who respond in a positive way to red would probably be characterized by their high energy and independence, but for others it may have a negative effect, providing too much energy where it is not needed.

Red relates to the first, or root chakra, and to the note of C. It represents our life energy, the blood. It offers intense stimulation and brings about increased circulation in the body, but should be used with care, as the stimulation offered could be too great for some people. Since red is such a physical colour, it can be used to stimulate those with low blood pressure, anaemia, arthritis and poor circulation, or any problem related to congestion of one form or another. Using the colour red to heal would be maximized using powerful music in the note of C, such as the Sousa Marches, or *Mars* from the Planet Suite by Gustav Holst.

Orange is a warm, invigorating colour, and can be used to revitalize. On the physical level, it can often help in cases of anaemia, arthritis, diabetes and any form of congestion. On the mental level, it is useful to lift people out of depression, and can bring self-confidence to those with low self-esteem. If faced with a stressful situation, it helps to be enveloped in this colour, perhaps by wearing an orange jumper, and the good sensations can be enhanced by playing music in the key of D, such as *Jupiter* from the Planets Suite, or *Capriccio Espagnole* by Rimski-Korsakov.

Yellow is the colour most associated with the emotions, but it is also used to aid mental activity. It can stimulate the nervous system, enhance emotive feeling and activate the mental faculties. Yellow should bring a happy outlook on life, and is also very useful for intense mental activity, so would be a good colour to wear during an examination. The musical correlation to yellow is E in the middle octave, and a good piece of music to play to accentuate the powers of the colour would be *Piano Concerto No. 26* by Mozart.

Green is considered to be the great balancer, and therefore is the safest colour to use in any situation. The best way to experience the power of the colour is to go outside and lie on the grass. Green can

Colours	Musical Tones	Chakras	Glands	Body affected	Characteristics	Healing applied for
Red	C	Root (base of spine)	Ovaries Testicles	Physical	Physical strength and independence	Anaemia; Apathy; Bad circulation
Orange	D	Sacral	Spleen Liver	Ethereal	Courage	Nerves; Fear; Low blood pressure
Yellow	E	Navel	Pancreal	Astral	Thought Emotions	Stomach problems; Depression
Green	F	Heart	Thymus	Lower mental	Balance Tranquillity Healing powers	Heart; Circulation; Ulcers
Blue	G	Throat	Thyroid	Higher mental	Coolness Calmness Peace	High blood pressure; Fevers; Dermatitis; Cancer
Indigo	A	Third Eye	Pituitary	Spiritual	Intuition Memory Dedication	Nervous disorders; Some mental disorders
Violet	B	Crown	Pineal	Divine Monad	Awareness of one's divinity	Lack of motivation; Some mental disorders

restore energy and tired nerves, and also aid in the curing of boils and ulcers. Chlorophyll, the very essence of the colour green, is now being used in conventional medicine to balance heart rhythms. The ideal musical accompaniment, in the key of F, would be *Neptune* from the Planets Suite or *Melody in F* by Rubenstein.

Blue represents spiritual awareness, coolness, calmness and inner peace. It is also a reflective colour, helping people to enhance their memories. A very clean colour, blue can be used to cure various skin eruptions. High blood pressure is often stabilized through the use of blue, as it seems to calm the system, and it can be beneficial against some cancerous growths as it is considered a retardant. Music in the key of G is ideal to enhance the spiritual growth attained through the use of the colour, and pieces such as *Air on a G String* by Bach or *Ave Maria* by Schubert would be the ideal music to play.

Indigo is associated with the pituitary gland, believed by many to be the "Third Eye", responsible for our intuitive senses. This colour is used as an aid in finding the spiritual self, but can also be used to help in conditions affecting the eyes, ears and sinuses, such as cataracts, earaches and coughing. The note associated with indigo is A, and accompanying music should be something along the lines of *Venus* from the Planets Suite or *Traumerei* by Schumann.

Finally, violet is the colour of the highest spiritual vibration. It is an excellent colour to use in meditation, but it can also be used to help heal physically. Violet can help to alleviate epilepsy, cramps and kidney infections. The musical note relating to violet is B, and the best examples of this are in the Gregorian Chants, or something along the lines of *Piano Concerto in B Minor* by Tchaikovsky.

So, those are the colours and the music, but how are their beneficial elements accessed? With music therapy, it is relatively straightforward – simply turn on the right music. But what of colour therapy? Some of the physical aids that can be used are coloured light-bulbs or clothing, or simply visualizing the colour enveloping you.

But are the healing powers of colours and music really magic and beneficial? This has caused considerable debate. On the one side, there are the colour and music therapists, who, naturally, would argue strongly that yes, they are indeed powerful tools for healing. On the other side are sceptics, who would argue that the whole field of colour and music therapy is utter nonsense, and that any benefit derived comes purely from the belief in the mind of the patient that something good will come of it, a kind of placebo effect (see below). It is not an area that is easy to quantify, but if the sceptics are right, and patients are receiving benefit from the therapy purely on the basis of their beliefs, then what is the harm in that anyway?

The Placebo Effect

Faith healers, herbalists, colour and sound therapists and homeopaths alike have all, over the years, claimed magical abilities which aid them in their healing. "Magic" is a word which sceptics and scientists naturally scoff at, and they would seek to provide alternative, rational explanations for the healing process which others believe merit such a mystical definition.

The mind is still a mystery to all of us. We don't know how it works, or even where it is, though most theories locate it somewhere deep within the brain. We do know, however, that its capabilities are vast. We know that hypnotism can induce the mind to heal the body, but what of cases where the mind works without such influence to aid in the healing process?

In his book, *Health and Healing*, Dr Andrew Weil described a true case of mind over matter. All conventional medical treatments had failed to cure a man in his fifties who had suffered for years from warts covering most of his body. Finally, his doctor told him that there was a new, powerful but potentially dangerous treatment available that might help, involving strong X-rays fired at the body. The patient agreed to undertake the treatment, despite the possible risks described by the doctor, and he undressed and stood in a darkened room next to the machine. The machine hummed impressively for a few minutes, and then the doctor entered the room to announce that the treatment was over. The next day, all the warts on the man's body had melted away, and he returned to his doctor to thank him. It was only then that the doctor informed him that the machine had in fact not emitted a single X-ray. The doctor was simply trying to create a belief in the patient's mind that he would be cured. It proved to be sufficient that the patient *believed* that he was receiving a new, special treatment, for his mind to produce a healing miracle. This process is known as the "placebo effect".

A very famous case of the placebo effect concerned a cancer patient called Mr Wright. Wright was dying from cancer of the lymph nodes which had produced tumours the size of oranges in his neck, under his arms and in his groin, chest and abdomen. He had been written off by his doctors as "in a terminal state", and was untreatable save for sedatives and pain killers to make his situation more bearable. Wright then heard of a new wonder drug called Krebiozen, and although he was too sick to warrant its use, eventually his doctors gave in to his pleas and administered a dose. This dose made him so sick that they thought he was on the point of death, but three days later, he was found walking around the hospital ward chattering happily to anyone who would listen.

When the doctors examined him, they found that "the tumour masses had melted away like snowballs on a hot stove, and in only these few days, they were half their original size". Within ten days, he was discharged from hospital; his cancer had virtually vanished. But the story did not end there. Shortly afterwards, Mr Wright read newspaper reports which declared that the new wonder drug Krebiozen had not lived up to expectations, and that only very few patients had improved after taking it. After just two months of relatively good health, Wright found himself back in hospital, the tumours were back, and he was in danger of death at any time.

His doctor was well aware that Wright's initial recovery was largely due to the belief in his mind of the power of the new drug, and he decided to capitalize on that. He reassured Mr Wright that a shipment of "super-refined, double-strength" Krebiozen was on its way. He wrote that "by delaying a couple of days before the 'shipment' arrived, his anticipation of salvation had reached a tremendous pitch. When I announced that the new series of injections was about to begin, he was almost ecstatic and his faith was very strong." After this series of injections, Wright's recovery was even more dramatic than it had been the first time round. His tumours receded and he soon found himself the very picture of health, ready to return to a normal life. What he did not know was that this second series of injections did not contain a super dose of Krebiozen; all that was in the hypodermic needle was sterile water. The power of Wright's mind had been so strong that he had healed himself in the belief that he was receiving a miracle cure.

Again, Wright's life had been saved by the placebo effect and the power of his own mind. Unfortunately, this very power proved to be his undoing. Not long after his recovery, the American Medical Association made a formal announcement that "nationwide tests show Krebiozen to be a worthless drug for the treatment of cancer". Wright heard this announcement, and within days he was re-admitted into hospital. Just a short while later he was dead.

The placebo effect is a phenomenon that has baffled scientists ever since it was first discovered in the 1950s, quite by accident. When tests are conducted to determine the effects of a new drug, a control group is always used. The control group is given something that looks exactly like the new drug, but is in fact a plain sugar pill. In a good number of such trials, the control group exhibits exactly the same beneficial results as those who take the real drug, and this has become known as the placebo effect. Many believe that the placebo effect is scientific proof that the mind, when under a suggestive influence, can directly affect the body, in particular, the healing process.

The placebo effect is not simply limited to the development of new pharmaceutical drugs. Placebo surgery has produced some astounding results. During the 1950s, a new surgery was developed to help angina sufferers. The operation was surrounded by controversy, as the medical community debated its worth as a technique, and there were conflicting reports about the degree of pain relief experienced by patients. The Institute of Noetic Studies published *The Heart of Healing* to show the results of an amazing new "surgical" operation which had been performed to test the new angina technique. Their report showed some truly startling results:

> *Several surgeons decided to test the angina operation by performing placebo surgeries in which they cut open their patients and then closed them back up again without tying off the artery. These patients experienced everything the medical system could offer – the attention of their doctors, the drama of preparing for surgery, the surgical incision, nurturance during recovery, and the expectation that the new and widely hailed treatment would improve their condition – except the treatment itself. The doctors found that the phoney surgeries proved no less beneficial to patients than the real thing. In one study, more patients who had undergone the sham operation reported relief. Placebo surgery reduced the patients' use of nitro-glycerine, the most common pain reliever for angina. It also increased patients' capacity for exercise and the amount they could work."*

The *World Journal of Surgery* made a report in 1983 into the effectiveness of chemotherapy for the treatment of cancer. The technique has some disturbing side-effects, such as nausea, diarrhoea and hair loss. The report also showed that people who had undergone placebo chemotherapy – believing that they were receiving chemotherapy, but in fact receiving nothing – not only experienced the positive effects, namely the reduction in their cancer, but also the negative. Nearly one third of the placebo patients lost their hair as a result.

It would appear, therefore, that just believing that something will make you better seems to be enough for many people's bodies to start the healing process. This could be an explanation for the successes of faith healers, hypnotists and all manner of other healers. Some believe that the healing process is activated through a closer connection to God, others to the application of mystical herbs, yet others to magical vibrations or the hypnotist's suggestive powers. Perhaps these people are all wrong, and the magic of healing is actually located within our own minds – we just have to believe in ourselves.

One person who did just that, using a technique that may seem to some quite bizarre, was fifty-six-year-old Doris Phillips. In 1982, she was informed by her doctor that her throat cancer had spread to her lungs. Over a period of twenty years, Doris had undergone two major operations and thirty radiation treatments to keep her cancer at bay, but it always returned. Her doctor suggested that she try chemotherapy, which he explained might temporarily shrink the tumours, but would not cure them. Mrs Phillips had had enough by this time, and she decided instead to put her affairs in order, and prepare for her death. She was terribly depressed and turned to a counsellor for help, who presented her with a book entitled *Getting Well Again* by Carl Simonton. Reading this book proved to be a major turning point in Doris's life.

The book advocated visualization techniques which could be used in meditation to create a "healing force". Several times a day, Doris would sit in the corner of her bedroom, and imagine her body fighting the cancer. She saw it as a game. The healthy immune cells she saw as gobbling up the cancerous cells like a Pacman video game. She even obtained an X-ray of her chest so that she could visualize exactly where her army of Pacmen should attack. After several months practising this technique, Doris again visited her doctor to see the results of her latest X-rays. The doctor was stunned to report that her cancer had been eradicated, and he asked her hundreds of questions to determine what she had been taking to cure herself. A decade later, Doris was alive, well and still free from cancer. The cure had been within herself all along – she just had to believe it for it to happen.

The Future of Healing

Conventional medical science has made incredible advances over the last century. Diseases once thought of as incurable have been virtually eradicated; transplant operations are becoming commonplace. But throughout the world, hospitals and doctors' surgeries are stretched to the limit. Healthcare costs an enormous amount of money, and this cost rises with every new discovery. In America, the healthcare system costs $2.5 billion every day, accounting for 12 per cent of the country's gross domestic product.

Faced with ever increasing healthcare costs, many people have turned to complementary medicine. In the United Kingdom, according to a 1997 survey, half a million people regularly visit its 20,000 registered spiritual healers. Many doctors even have "seen the light", and are referring patients to alternative practitioners. Above all, there is a growing realization that we play a significant part in our own healing process.

The use of complementary medical techniques are on the increase, but it would be foolish to suppose that they would ever provide a replacement for conventional medicine. Most people think that they deserve the term "complementary", because they should run alongside conventional medicine rather than provide an alternative. Investigation into healing techniques is continually evolving. For those with a scientific frame of mind, there are many questions for which the doctors must find answers. For the majority of healers and those who have received the magic of their cures, it is the end result that matters, not how it was achieved.

PART FOUR

Witches and Witchcraft
• •

Witchcraft – the Old Religion

> *"Double double toil and trouble;*
> *Fire burn and cauldron bubble ..."*
>
> (Macbeth, Act IV, scene I, 10–11)

Generally speaking, when we think of witches, one of two images comes to mind.

The first is the wizened old crone, her hooked nose almost meeting her long, curved chin, her tiny eyes twinkling malevolently as she cackles over noxious potions bubbling and frothing in the cauldron in front of her. This is the Halloween witch with the tall, pointed hat, who terrifies her neighbours with her "Evil Eye". This hag is a figure of fear when present, and of derisive bravado when not in the vicinity. The other image is far more attractive – and perversely, often far more dangerous ... The lithe, seductive young woman, her sleek black hair unbound and shining in the candlelight, sensual red mouth inviting, sparkling eyes bewitching as she uses her considerable powers to get exactly what she wants ... The truth, of course, is both far less lurid, and far more intriguing, than either vision.

So what is witchcraft? What, exactly, *is* a witch? At its simplest, a witch is someone – not necessarily female – who practises Wicca, the Craft of the Wise. Also sometimes called the Old Way or the Old Religion, at its most fundamental level Wicca encompasses the wisdom to live in harmony with the rhythms of nature, with the needs of the planet and the creatures upon it, with our own inner patterns, rhythms and desires. It teaches ways to act upon those innate abilities to enrich and empower ourselves, those around us, and our world. Those who practice the Wise Craft practice the three "R"s – Responsibility (for oneself and one's own actions), Respect (for oneself and others) and Reverence (for the planet, and for the life force that invests all things.) Everyone, male or female, has the potential to be a witch.

One thing Wicca is most emphatically *not*, is Satanism or devil worship. The notion of devil worship, of the Devil himself, as perceived by most people today, is basically a Christian concept, although its origins go back much further – at least as far as the Egyptian deity Set, brother, rival and arch-enemy of Osiris (the "Good One"). To a very large extent, Wicca was deliberately accused of being party to devil worship in order to "prove" that it was evil and should be stamped out. After all, a lifepath that needed no expensive buildings, no priestly hierarchy, no donations or taxes to a power-hungry Church, and which, worst of all, regarded women as absolute equals to men, would be anathema to patriarchal monotheism – wouldn't it?

Intolerance is at the root of such dualistic thinking: a thing is either right, or wrong, and if it's wrong, it must be destroyed. Wicca is not a dualistic lifepath: all things are equal in importance and significance in the scheme of things (in the words of Leon Rosselson, "All life is sacred, all life is one, from the rocks on the mountains, to the children unborn."). Wicca takes the good things of the earth and uses them to build and to heal; it promotes tolerance and compassion; and it advocates harmony, creativity and love.

The Power of Creation

Almost from the dawn of the human species – in the late Paleolithic when *homo sapiens* superceded *homo neanderthalensis* – there has been a reverence for the mysterious ability of the female to bring forth life. The bearing of children, bringing a new life into the world, is a thoroughly magical thing – even these days, when the mechanics of genetics and generation are fairly well understood. Back then, it was nothing short of miraculous. And it invested the female with awesome power. Without her ability to bear the next generation, there could be no continuance – the race would die out. It really requires no great leap of the imagination to make the association between the fertility and creative powers of the female animal, and the fertility and powers of creation of the earth itself. The planet, of course, is larger and all-encompassing, but the comparison is clear: the earth also brings forth life, magically, in the form of the innumerable plants that feed the animals – and the people – which roam across its surface. It's not surprising that the earth began to be revered as a deity, and considered as a nurturing parent – in short, it became the Mother Goddess.

Of course, mothers don't just nurture their young. They also protect and teach – and discipline (or punish) when the child does wrong. The Mother

Goddess behaved in the same manner: usually she was protective, caring for her children, but sometimes she could be angry, and chastise her children. And she also did something else that no woman could do, at least as far as the human race was aware: she gently took the dead back into her embrace. And in the following year, flowers blossomed from the grave. . .

So the Mother Goddess became the Great Goddess, the giver of life, but also the one who took life away: "the womb and the tomb", the One who embodies all of human existence. She manifested and personified physical matter, space and time; she was the spark that filled the newborn with life and the fire that kept life going; she was the body of all things, whether animal, plant, rock, air or water; and she was the renewer of all things in an endless cycle of birth, life, death and rebirth.

She has had many names and many forms throughout the ages, reflecting her different aspects and manifestations – Maat, Nut and Isis in Egypt, Inanna and Ereshkigal in Sumeria, Ishtar and Tiamat in Babylon, Astarte in Canaan, Bride in Albion, Gaea in the classical world, Kujum-Chantu and Kali in India, Una in Australia, Kuma (amongst others) in South America – but she was always revered and, in the main, cherished.

The Moon has been the outward symbol of the Great Goddess since time immemorial. The changing face of Earth's sister planet, from thin crescent to full to dark moon, is almost inextricably bound up with the birth-death-rebirth cycle that is so much a part of the worship of the Great Goddess. The Moon's intimate affinity with the female capacity for reproduction, itself closely linked with female menstruation, empha-

The Moon, the celestial symbol of the Goddess.

sized the association. The changing Moon also symbolized the phases of female life – maidenhood, maturity and the capacity to bear children, and old age, when the reproductive capacity ceased and left time for the woman's innate and intuitive wisdom to come to the fore, to make her the ideal teacher of the next generation and *confidante* of younger women. It may be that the Christian Church's perception of God as tripartite – Father, Son and Holy Spirit – was originally an attempt to emulate the mysterious nature of the Triple Goddess.

The Moon, of course, isn't just a night-time phenomenon – she can often be seen during the day – but she is at her brightest and most beautiful at night, and this led to the association of the night and the mysterious dark as being very much the preserve of the female (it wasn't until much later that masculist propaganda substituted "sinister" for "mysterious").

The Great Goddess was the eternal mother and the source of life, but it was recognized, even in early times, that nature is divided into opposites: heat and cold, dry and wet, male and female, light and dark. (This sort of dualism isn't the entire story, of course, because it disregards the subtle gradations in between absolute opposites – but as a rough and ready way of organizing the experience of life, it has served for hundreds of thousands of years.) So the Goddess "gave birth" to a son, the Horned God, the Lord of the Animals, hunting, plants and crops, and the Wild Wood, who also became her consort. The Horned God has been a feature of ancient religions for a very long time. He has gone by different names (indeed, he isn't always portrayed as being horned, although he often has some animal characteristic to indicate his aspect as the God of the wild things in nature), and has had different powers throughout the ages, but his primary function is to symbolize male fertility. He is very often associated with the Sun, and the cycle of Wiccan festivals follows his year-long story from birth to death.

The Wiccan Year
Reflecting the perception of life as a cycle of birth-death-rebirth, Wiccans see the year as a wheel, rolling through time, and the eight major fire festivals, or Sabbats, of the year form the spokes. The festivals in turn tell the story of the Great Goddess and her son and consort, the Horned God, the Lord of the Greenwood.

Yule, the winter solstice (around 21 December; it can vary by a day or two each year) marks the birth of the Goddess's son, symbolized by the Sun itself. The winter solstice is, of course, the longest night and correspondingly shortest day of the year: from this point onwards the nights grow shorter and the days longer until the summer solstice. Candles and fires are lit, to reassure the infant God that he is welcome and not alone, and to encourage him to gain strength. Homes are decorated in red, green, white and gold: red for vitality and the sun, green for fertility and the natural world, white for purity and spirituality, and gold to honour the God, and in hopes of the wealth (health, a good harvest, happiness) to come in the following year.

Imbolc (1 February) is the Feast of the White Lady. The young God increases in power, warming his sleeping Mother and consort-to-be; her invigorating power stirs beneath the covering of snow and frost, encouraging the first signs of life in the seeds that have lain dormant all winter. The festival is celebrated with purification rites, white candles, and solemn devotion.

Eostre, the spring equinox (when the Sun enters the Sign of Aries; around 21 March), celebrates the great abundance of the springtime, and is a significant fertility festival. The Goddess wakes from sleep and, helped by the burgeoning warmth of the God, showers the earth with fecundity. Green things are growing fast, flowers are springing forth: it's a time to plan and commence new enterprises, make new resolutions, and plant the seeds which will nourish the folk in later months. Eggs are the most potent symbols for this festival – the egg represents limitless potential – and are decorated and exchanged. It's extremely lucky to catch sight of a hare, Eostre's sacred animal, at this time.

Beltain, better known as May Day, marks the start of the Bright Year and is one of the most important festivals of the year. Beltain celebrates the union of the Goddess and the now fully-grown God, and the conceiving of new life. Wiccans celebrate the festival with a feast, flowers, Maypole dances (the Maypole is a very unsubtle, positive fertility symbol!) and, frequently, the conception of their own children . . . Children born as a result of the Beltain celebrations were known by the delightful name of "Merrybegots"!

Midsummer, the summer solstice (around 21 June), is the longest day and shortest night of the year. It celebrates Love, the love between the God and the Goddess, and between Wiccans everywhere. Midsummer is the ideal time for handfastings (Wiccan "marriages"). The festival is celebrated with flowers, especially roses, and sometimes feathers. It is nevertheless tinged with a certain sadness because the bright days of summer are drawing to a close, and the Dark Year is on its way.

Lughnasadh – "loo nah sah" or "loo-sar" – on August 1st marks the Harvest of the First Fruits. The God is weakening as the year grows old, although the Goddess can already feel the child of their love in her womb, even as the fruits ripen on tree and bush and the grain turns golden in the fields. The feast is celebrated with sun-shaped loaves of bread, honey and mead.

Harvest, the autumn equinox (around 22 September), sees the God preparing to die and return to the Earth Mother, to nourish the soil from which will spring next year's harvest. The Goddess's deep sadness at her coming loss is tempered by the expectation of their child, and she brings all things to harvest in memory of their love. Harvest is a time for giving thanks for the good things of the earth, and for feasting.

Samhain – "sah-wen", "sah-veen" or "soe-en" – is the Wiccan New Year. Better known to most people as Halloween (31 October), the festival commemorates the death of the God, looking both backwards to the year that is ending, and forward to the new life to come at Yule, when the God is reborn. Samhain marks the start of the Dark Year, and is celebrated with bonfires, candles and a feast, especially of pork and apples. Before midnight on 31 October, take a broom and sweep thoroughly through the house, finally brushing any dust out of the back door (assuming you have one, of course), asking all misfortune and bad luck to leave with the sweepings. Perform a little piece of money magic: after midnight, have someone throw a silver coin through the front door, and ensure it lies where it falls for the entire year (place it under the rug or carpet if necessary). It will make sure there is always enough money in the house to meet your needs.

Ancient symbol of the Earth Mother with wheat and bread.

The correlation of the ancient festivals with Christian holy days – Yule with Christmas, for example, and Eostre with Easter – isn't accidental. The Sabbats were, and still are, profoundly important to Wiccans, and the Church authorities, recognizing this, adopted and adapted the existing feasts into the new faith as a way of making it more palatable to those who followed the Old Ways.

As well as the eight Sabbats, Wiccans also honour the esbats, the festivals of the Full Moon; there are usually thirteen of these each year. The ritual of "Drawing Down the Moon", which honours the Goddess, is usually performed at the esbat: the high priestess draws the power of the full moon down into herself, thus becoming an embodiment of the Great Goddess in her ever-changing Lunar aspect. Filled with psychic force, she will often experience visions which enable her to give wise advice to the others at the ritual.

Esbats are also opportunities for the members of the coven to exchange news and views, discuss any problems they may be having and ways of resolving them, and perform any special rites for healing. The ceremony concludes with a light meal, where, as is normal in Wiccan celebrations, a small amount of the food and drink available is solemnly poured onto the earth as a thanksgiving to the Earth Mother for her goodness and nurture.

The Burning Times
In the fourteenth century, after millennia of relatively peaceful practice of their faith, worshippers of the Great Goddess, now called witches, became the object of fear, contempt, and the most terrible hatred. No one was safe: friend turned against friend, neighbour

against neighbour; as the hysteria grew, even children came to testify against their parents. For 300 years thousands of innocent people were tortured, maimed and murdered as witches and devil-worshippers. How did it happen?

As with most social and cultural change, it was a combination of a number of factors. There is a school of thought that suggests it probably started far back in time, when men began to find the idea of an all-powerful Great Goddess a source of frustration and intense jealousy. Slowly, aggressive male deities took over from the beneficent, bountiful Earth Mother, she who both gave life and took it in her role as the regulator of the natural way of things. The Great Goddess was relegated to a secondary rôle, and was joined by representations and images of the darker, more destructive side of her nature which gradually supplanted her nurturing side. Tiamat, once revered as the mother of all the Babylonian deities, suddenly became a menace to the world. Lilith, supposedly Adam's first wife, became a killer of children. (It's interesting to note the traditional reason for her spurning of her assigned husband: a vibrant, independent figure, she refused to lie under Adam, insisting instead that she should be on top! The legend itself provides an insight into the thought processes that led to the subjugation of the female half of the human race.) The Goddess in her Lunar aspect as the Crone, the wise, revered, and venerable giver of knowledge, was transformed into Hecate, the evil queen of the dead, the underworld and witches.

Women, as representatives of the Great Goddess, met with equally unpleasant treatment. From being revered as the bearers of life, in tune with the natural rhythms of the world and wise in its ways, they were gradually regarded as being untrustworthy, helplessly prey to those very rhythms for which they were once venerated, cruel and capricious. Of course, it wouldn't do to allow such creatures to have any real control over their own fates. To start with it was a gradual process. It speeded up significantly when the patriarchal religions took hold, and women were reduced to nothing more than baby machines and chattels, owned by the men to whom they were, effectively, sold (by other men, their fathers or brothers). But the worship of the Great Goddess continued, quietly, inconspicuously, in secret. After all, for a lot of women, it was all they had to sustain them. The situation varied from country to country, and from year to year. In more tolerant climates, the worship of the Goddess was sanctioned, if not welcomed. Women were accorded honour as healers and teachers, and their function as mothers and nurturers of the family was both appreciated and respected. In the main, however, their fate was to be considered little better than slaves.

The new Christian religion, in the form of the Roman Catholic Church, was primarily responsible for perverting the image of the worship of the Great Goddess from a nature-loving, nurturing lifepath into something so evil its practitioners must be tortured and brutally murdered. This isn't the place to examine quite how a faith, whose creator advocated love and forgiveness, changed into an intolerant, vengeful, greedy and power-mad institution – that subject deserves a book to itself. Suffice to say the Great Goddess was metamorphosed into the sinister queen of witches, and the Horned God suffered an even worse fate. He became the Devil, the seducer of the innocent and origin of all evil on earth.

In part, this was an attempt by the Church to denigrate and suppress the ancient deities, and to some extent the endeavour was understandable. The Church was, to a large degree, the only stable institution in a changeable, often-chaotic world, and its monasteries and convents were oases of learning and repositories of knowledge. It charged itself with the sacred duty of converting the world to its own faith, and worked diligently to accomplish that aim. (That being said, if the monarch of a country was converted to Christianity, it was assumed that the entire population was also converted although, of course, to the vast majority of the people the king was a distant figure whose personal situation had no bearing whatsoever upon their lives.) The ancient festivals and the seasons they celebrated were too profoundly embedded in the people's consciousness to be easily dismissed, so the Church incorporated them into its own festivals. An uneasy truce existed for several centuries between the Church and the followers of the Old Ways, while the Church grew richer and more powerful.

It was probably the case of the Cathar "heretics" that sparked off the real problems for the ordinary individual. The Cathars believed that the entire world was evil, Satan its ruler, and all worldly institutions, riches, works of art, indeed anything that gave any pleasure, were designed by the Devil to deliver human souls to hell. Since the Church was a worldly institution, wealthy and rich in works of art, it too must be a device of the Devil. Such thinking, needless to say, did not endear the Cathars to the Church, and at the beginning of the thirteenth century the Inquisition, the official instrument of the Catholic Church's law enforcement, was created. It was to continue its work of wiping out heretics, i.e. anyone who did not conform to the Church's teachings, for 500 years.

Initially, only religious heretics attracted the attention of the Inquisition, but by the middle of the fourteenth century witches began to be drawn in. The infamous book *Malleus Maleficarum, The Hammer of the Witches,* by Kramer and Sprenger, a pair of German inquisitors, was used as both pretext and guide for the discovery and destruction of witches – who were, of course, mostly women, for women were "lustful, vain, false, vindictive, mean-minded and weak-willed". Moreover, as the book points out: "So heinous are the crimes of witches that they even exceed the sins and the fall of the bad Angels; and if this is true as to their guilt, how should it not also be true of their punishments in hell?" As the belief spread that witches were involved in the Devil's work, suspicion fell on anyone who seemed at all strange or adept in any unusual skill. Individuals were encouraged to denounce their fellows, and it's fairly certain that amongst those few who sincerely believed their victims were guilty of evil works, there were also a large number who accused people of whom they were jealous, or to whom they were indebted in some way, or with whom they had quarrelled, or simply to avert suspicion from themselves.

The Witch Trials were terrible things. A confession was necessary before an execution could take place, and to wring confessions from those who at first refused to comply, the science of torture was refined to a hideous degree. Instruments of torture included such devices as bone-crushing vices (often spiked on the inside) that could be applied to any part of the body and reduced the bones to splinters; a chair (again, often spiked) with a

The witch trial at Salem of George Jacobs, who was hanged in 1692 on the evidence of a child.

metal seat that could be heated by a fire below it; and the rack, which dislocated the joints of the body. Methods of torture included such horrors as *strappado*, where the arms were tied behind the back, the victim raised by a rope attached to a pulley, then dropped nearly to the floor – a procedure that resulted in the arms being pulled from their sockets – whipping, flaying, cutting out the tongue (generally reserved for blasphemers), hacking off limbs (mostly reserved for those accused of dese-crating the Host, the wafer that assumed the body of Christ during Mass), and the water torture (water and a length of soft fabric, often knotted, were forced down the accused's throat and into her stomach, resulting in the sensation of choking. After a while the material was wrenched out, tearing the victim's innards). An untold number of accused women were also raped. The results of torture were pretty much a foregone conclusion: either the victim confessed, or she died in the process. And if she survived the torture, she was consigned to the stake and burned. Those who confessed and begged divine forgiveness were often garroted before being burned; those who confessed and did not were burned alive. The witch-hunts of the Inquisition became known to Wiccans as The Burning Times.

No one knows exactly how many people died during those times, it could be thousands, tens of thousands, hundreds of thousands depending on which record is read. The fact remains, however, that an unforgivable number of people were murdered in the name of the Christian Church, a terrible indictment of male power gone mad. Most will always be nameless; in England we know the names of just a few. It's a sad litany of names of individuals, mostly women, mostly innocent of anything more than a knowledge of herbalism and a small gift of healing, who inspired jealousy and mistrust in their neighbours, women like Anne Bodenham, Joan Prentice, Joan Flower and her daughters, and Agnes Brown. There were a few individuals, it's true, who for reasons of mental instability or a wish to appear more important than they were, boasted of their abilities, but in the main the Burning Times saw the needless and cruel deaths of those whose only crime was a little knowledge and the wish to worship in the way they felt was right.

Nevertheless, the worship of the Great Goddess continued, disguised and "underground". Her image was transposed into that of Mary, Mother of Christ, and she was, and still is, adored in that form, especially by women. But it wasn't until the English witchcraft laws were repealed – in 1951! – that Wiccans and other followers of the Old Ways dared to make their allegiance publicly known.

The Good, the Bad and the Downright Evil . . .
The history of witchcraft resounds with famous, or infamous, names: nearly everyone has heard of some of them, even if most people are unaware of the stories behind them: Gilles de Rais, Johann Faust, Urbain Grandier, Isobel Gowdie, Matthew Hopkins, Cotton Mather and the witches of Salem, Aleister Crowley.

Some, of course, were innocent individuals, persecuted through no fault of their own, the victims of the malice of others. Some mistakenly thought they were doing good. Others used the temper of the times to gain power over their fellows. And some deliberately and consciously worked to be as evil as they could, allowing free rein to their basest and most depraved urges.

One of the earlier accounts of the kind of persecution a charge of witchcraft could raise concerns Lady Alice Kyteler, a rich and influential woman who lived in Kilkenny, Ireland, around the beginning of the four-teenth century. Not at all popular with her neighbours, and altogether too powerful for her own good, Lady Alice and her household were accused of all manner of evil deeds, from refusing to enter a church and partake of the Eucharist, to making potions and charms to incite love, hatred or bring about death. These potions were said to include ingredients such as the hair and brains of unbaptized children, worms and the intestines of a cockerel, boiled together in the skull of a beheaded robber. Lady Alice was also reputed to have a lesser devil, Robin Artisson, as her servant, and to use flying ointment on a beam of wood to transport herself to any part of the world she wished. After a protracted ecclesiastical battle, Lady Alice was forced to flee to England, where she lived for the rest of her life. Her supporters weren't so lucky, suffering excommunica-tion and imprisonment and one, Petronilla de Meath, was the first woman in Ireland to be burned as a witch.

Gilles de Rais was born around 1420 into one of the richest and noblest families in Brittany, France. From the time he inherited his father's fortune, at the age of twenty, he lived a life of absolute luxury, denying himself nothing. But such complete dissipation even-tually led to boredom, and the nobleman found himself giving in to darker cravings. Children began to disappear from the countryside surrounding his castle, and it was rumoured that he had them kidnapped and brought to him, subjecting them to the most awful physical and sexual abuse before killing them slowly, believing that by so doing he honored the devil.

Gradually, his extravagant lifestyle ate into his inheritance and de Rais was forced to consider ways of recouping his fortunes. Not being in a position to do any kind of work – having never needed to – he decided the only thing he could do was to become an alchemist and *make* the gold he needed to replenish his squandered wealth. His attempts to recruit alchemists from all over Europe resulted in his fortunes being degraded further, as unscrupulous fakes arrived to take advantage of his hospitality. Finally one of the alchemists, an Italian called Prelati, offered occult help in the search. Gilles de Rais gave his own blood to draw up a contract with the devil, and offered the heart, eyes and blood of a young child as a token of his sincerity. The attempt failed, and rumours of the nobleman's activities became so strong the Church finally intervened. Gilles de Rais was tried, confessed, convicted and burned along with his accomplice Prelati. As befitted his aristocratic status, de Rais was strangled before being thrown into the flames, although Prelati was burned alive.

Johann Faust was probably little more than an early sixteenth-century astrologer and soothsayer, but his name has passed into the popular imagination as the magician who sold his soul to the devil for earthly powers. He was allowed twenty-four years of wealth, influence, everything he desired in fact but at the end of that time he was torn to pieces and condemned to hell for all eternity. He was by no means the first to have entered into such a pact. There is a tale, dating from the sixth century, about Theophilus, a priest of an important church in Asia Minor who, frustrated in his desire to be made a bishop, made a covenant with the devil to achieve that end. (In his case, however, years of prayer and remorse resulted in his forgiveness when the Virgin Mary interceded on his behalf and the contract was destroyed.)

Alison ("Mother") Demdike, best-known of the witches of Pendle Forest (on the Yorkshire borders in England) was most likely initiated into the cult of witchcraft in her youth; at any rate, at the time she and the rest of her coven were hanged, around 1612, she had been practising witchcraft for over half of her eighty years of life. The Pendle witches were believed to keep their familiar spirits as pets – Mother Demdike had a black dog called Tibbs, which was a disguised demon who did her bidding. They were accused of bewitching their neighbours' animals, and causing death through burning wax images in the likeness of the person they wished to harm.

Urbain Grandier, a proud and ambitious young Catholic priest from Loudon, in Anjou, France, seemed to have made a habit of annoying his superiors, not to mention other influential people. He is known to have fathered at least one illegitimate child (with the wife of a powerful local official), his financial dealings left a lot to be desired, and his legal quarrels with his fellow priests, in which he was usually the victor, made him enemies amongst his peers. Finally, Mignon, a priest whom Grandier had defeated in a house-property case, began to work on his downfall.

Mignon became the confessor to the nuns of the Ursuline convent, established in a house in Loudon. The Ursulines were a very poor Order, and paid their way by educating the daughters of wealthy families. It came to Mignon's attention that both the nuns and their charges were dreaming of Grandier (not altogether surprising, since he was tall, handsome, and fascinating to women). Mignon saw this as an ideal opportunity, and set out to convince the women that devilry was afoot, that Grandier was sending devils to seduce them as they slept (the timely offer of a "gift" to enrich the impoverished convent also helped convince the Mother Superior that agreeing to the plan might not be such a bad idea. The culmination was that in August 1634, Grandier was convicted of sorcery and trafficking with the devil. The evidence was provided by the devil Astaroth (who had, supposedly, possessed the Mother Superior), and eleven other powerful and malignant devils. On 18 August, Grandier was burned alive at the stake, guilty not of witchcraft, just of being overly self-confident and a little too human.

Isobel Gowdie, the famous Scottish witch, was almost unique in confessing to her "crimes" voluntarily, no torture was used. Amongst other acts, she claimed that she and the coven of which she was a member caused thistles to grow in place of crops in their neighbours' fields; bewitched to death every son of a local landowner; raised storms; were able to kill people at a distance using "elf-arrows" (ancient flint arrowheads still found in Britain); and shape-change themselves into hares. Isobel also went into great detail about the rites and rituals undertaken by the coven. The records of her fate have been lost, but it is most likely that she was hanged, or burned, as was the custom at the time.

Matthew Hopkins, the notorious and sadistic "Witchfinder-General", plied his trade up and down the English countryside in the middle of the seventeenth century. He would let it be known he was about to start operations in a particular area, then charged twenty shillings to each town to which he was invited. Those accused of witchcraft, almost without exception women, were assembled before him and subjected to a series of ordeals, designed, quite simply, to force them to confess.

First they were compelled to walk up and down a room, with no food or rest, for twenty-four hours. If that didn't work, the next step was to thoroughly and minutely inspect the accused's body for a "devil's mark" – anything from a prominent birthmark to an extra nipple – from which the witch was supposed to feed her familiars, or "imps", with her own blood. The devil's mark was reputed to be insensitive to pain, and was often jabbed with a bodkin to test whether it was genuine or not. These bodkins were not infrequently made with a retractable blade, so of course the accused would feel no pain, and could therefore be confirmed as a witch. The final step, if all else failed, was to "swim" the suspect. Her thumbs were tied to her toes and she was thrown into the local pond or river. If she floated (which happened quite often, since air trapped in the voluminous skirts worn at the time could easily keep the body afloat) she was guilty; if she sank, she was innocent, although she usually drowned anyway, since even if the woman could swim, tied as she was, she would be unable to save herself. Hopkins's career lasted only a little more than a year, from March 1645 to late spring 1646, before he was forced into retirement, but in that time he was responsible for the hanging of several hundred "witches".

Even in the twentieth century there have been memorable characters. Perhaps the most familiar is Aleister Crowley, the self-styled "wickedest man in the world" (for more information see *The Magical Arts)* but also worthy of note are Helen Duncan and Anton LaVey.

Helen Duncan was a spirit medium, active during World War II. Although not actually claiming to be a witch, she was the last woman to be tried in England under the Witchcraft Act of 1735 (section 4 – "the conjuration of spirits"). Ordinarily, any legal action taken against mediums was under the Vagrancy Act, but Mrs. Duncan had the misfortune to attract the attention of the military authorities when her spirit guide, Albert, spoke out about the destruction of two ships – within minutes of the torpedoing of HMS *Hood* and HMS *Barham* – and well before the news was officially released. Despite the source, this was viewed as a serious security breach, lending itself both to propaganda for the other side and as a cause for fear and despondency for those connected with the war effort. Mrs. Duncan was tried, effectively ridiculed, and jailed for nine months, the severity of her sentence far outweighing her unwitting "crime". It may have been that the announcement of the destruction of ships in time of war represented a fairly safe bet – after all, such events are far from rare – but there is always the chance that Helen Duncan was in fact psychic and privy to secret information. In any case, the authorities felt they couldn't afford the risk.

Anton LaVey was a colourful character. Again, not actually a witch, he deserves a mention here purely because of the common association of witchcraft and satanism. Founder of the Church of Satan, LaVey believed that man's true nature is that of a lustful, carnal beast, existing in a universe permeated and motivated by a dark force: that which is usually called Satan. LaVey died just before Samhain in 1997, but the

Church he founded still exists in Beverly Hills, California.

Salem
Although there was the occasional, isolated witch trial in America throughout the time of the European witch hunts (the first hanging of a witch took place in Connecticut in 1647, and there were others in Providence, Rhode Island in 1662), in the main the terrible hysteria passed the New World by, with one exception. Early in 1692 a strange kind of madness settled over the Massachusetts town of Salem.

The events had actually started in 1688, when the children of the Goodwin family began to act strangely after being "cursed" by the family's washerwomen, an Irish woman called Glover. On examination, by Cotton Mather (a respected and educated clergyman, and leading supporter of the witch trials), the first child went into convulsions when the Bible was read aloud to her, but was found to enjoy the words of "bad books" (i.e. any reading material not approved by the clergy). She also imagined that she rode to a Sabbat on a horse, performing the actions to accompany her story. The problems ceased when Glover was arrested, tried and executed.

Witchcraft mania resurfaced a few years later, in 1692. Elizabeth, the nine-year-old daughter of a minister of one of the churches in Salem, the Reverend Samuel Parris, and her eleven-year-old cousin, Abigail Williams, began to suffer convulsions, during which they swore and shouted blasphemies – horrifying in the extreme to the strict, rigidly-Puritan community. The town doctor, Griggs, found no physical cause for their outlandish and frightening behaviour, and it was suspected that the children had fallen under the Devil's spell.

In those days, and especially where the more fanatically narrow-minded Christian sects were particularly powerful, anything that couldn't be explained by the simplistic medical skills of the time must be the responsibility of Satan. The Devil was as real to them as the God they revered, and feared, so much. And it was known that Satan had many ways to influence and possess humans, especially women, who were weak and at the mercy of their emotions. The fact that Parris's West Indian slave woman, Tituba, regularly regaled an enthralled group of young girls, including Elizabeth, Abigail and their friends, with tales of witchcraft and magic, had nothing to do with the facts of the case, as far as the adults were concerned. At that time there was no understanding of the importance of allowing children's imagination an outlet, nor of the risks inherent on the sort of severe emotional and mental repression imposed on all sect members by the Puritans. The children, denied the sort of boisterous play now known to be vital for a healthy mental state and, it must be suspected, eager to attract the sort of attention ordinarily denied them, found it easy to do things that would normally result in harsh punishment. The Devil took the blame. Unfortunately, it didn't stop there. Other youngsters, eager for some attention of their own, were quick to copy. Convinced that the girls were acting under the influence of witchcraft, the town leaders questioned them; under pressure to answer, the children began to name names . . .

Sarah Good and Sarah Osborne – both of them unpopular women – were the first to be accused of witchcraft, along with Tituba. The slave enthusiastically confessed to witchcraft and all manner of devilish works, but the two Puritan women, understandably, righteously and indignantly denied all such charges. Tituba's testimony convinced the town elders that the Devil was at work in their community, however, and all three women were jailed to await trial.

It must have seemed like a dream come true to the girls: brought up in a religion that demanded strict obedience, first to their biological fathers, then to a severe and oppressive God, not even allowed the limited leeway granted to their brothers, suddenly they found the adults, the community leaders no less, paying them all the attention they could ever want, listening to their words and acting on them promptly. It's not surprising that they continued with the game. More people were accused of witchcraft; men and women, wealthy and respectable as well as poor and humble, were questioned and jailed. The wave of hysteria spread to other nearby settlements. And more children began to exhibit signs of demonic influence . . .

In May 1692 Sir William Phips, the governor of Massachusetts, set up a special court of *oyer and terminer* ("to hear and determine"), and the accused were brought to trial. Interestingly, unlike the witch trials in Europe, confession of witchcraft and dealing with the Devil was almost guaranteed to result in forgiveness and release (presumably permitting the church to bring the "strayed lamb back into the fold" as the New Testament would have it), and it's more than likely that many victims confessed in order to save their lives. Many others, however, staunch in their faith and their own righteous innocence, refused to confess to such an evil thing, even under torture. Theirs was pretty much a lost cause from the start however, for in the "jury" were the children who had accused them in the first place.

The girls' hysterical reactions such as moaning, screaming and convulsing as each victim denied their culpability, were effectively all the proof the court needed to convince them of the guilt of the accused. The children would scream that they were being pinched when the accused wrung their hands, or being bitten as the victim bit their own lips in fear. One child swore that a phantom of one of the accused had appeared and harried her. In the case of Martha Cory, the children insisted that she had appeared to them and tried to force them to sign a book; they also claimed that they could see a sinister black figure whispering in her ear at her trial, telling her what to say in response to the questioning.

It seems likely, too, that the judges themselves weren't above suggesting the names of unpopular individuals to the children, who then "confirmed" the adults' suspicions. And by this time, of course, the game had grown out of control: overwhelmed by the power they had gained, the girls couldn't – or wouldn't – shame themselves by confessing, thereby effectively admitting that they had been deluded, and lying, all along. On such flimsy, hysterical evidence, six men and thirteen women were convicted of witchcraft and hanged. Two more died in jail, and Martha Cory's husband, Giles, was crushed to death for refusing to reply to his accusers.

By the autumn, the community had become horrified by the goings-on and, supported by a band of ministers headed by Increase Mather (father of Cotton Mather), the acceptance of "spectral evidence" (as evinced by the children) was banned. Finally the governor dissolved the court and forbade any more arrests. The rest of the accused were set free, and life returned to normal. The "afflicted" children, not surprisingly, suddenly found themselves freed of any demonic influence and no longer troubled by witchcraft...

The Witch's Craft

Herblore and Healing

The use of herbs and other natural articles for healing is a traditional element of witchcraft. Indeed, those Wiccans who have made herbalism a lifetime's study often call themselves hedge-witches, in a delightfully modest tribute to the fact that the tools of their skill can be found in the most obvious and common places. The essential constituents of all kinds of plants, including herbs, flowers, trees and shrubs were, until the advent of synthetic, laboratory-manufactured drugs in the nineteenth century, the source of practically all medicines. These days, a large number of people are returning to the use of natural, herb-based medicinal preparations; in the main, they do not have the nasty side-effects often experienced with modern synthetic drugs. Such simple preparations as an infusion of willow bark – the original source of aspirin – for PMS and menstrual cramps, or raspberry leaf tea to ease labour pains, or a mint tisane to alleviate the misery of stomach cramps, indigestion or irritable bowel syndrome, are indispensable ingredients in the Wiccan first aid chest, as is honey. Best known as a food, honey is antibacterial, antiseptic, a wonderful salve for cuts, burns and blisters, and it promotes the growth of new skin. Obviously it's not wise to experiment with herbal medicine without knowing at least a little about the subject.

213

Many herbs can be dangerous if too much is used; foxglove, for example, the source of the digitalin used in heart disease, can be fatal at too high a dosage.

To the traditional witch, many plants had particular powers because of their shape or colour. For example, the mandrake (a poisonous plant related to the nightshade family) used to be used for the narcotic and anaesthetic properties of its juice. However, when uprooted, the whole plant often resembles a human figure (there is a medieval legend that the mandrake screams in agony when uprooted, and that anyone hearing the cry is doomed to die in anguish: at one time deaf people were employed to gather the root!) or, sometimes, male genitalia. The root is used in love and sex magic (placing one under the pillow is supposed to inspire lovers to prodigious bouts of lovemaking), and also has the reputation of increasing psychic abilities when worn around the neck in a small pouch.

Mistletoe is another very special plant. The white seeds were believed to be the semen of the sun, and carrying the berries or sleeping with them by the bed was reputed to help women conceive. Ergot, a poisonous black fungus that grows on rye, had the opposite effect: it induced labour, and when used correctly caused abortion. During the Burning Times, vervain was reputedly used as a painkiller to help those accused of witchcraft withstand the pain of torture. Rowan branches, dill, mallow and betony were said to protect the household against evil spirits and the ill-wishing of witches, either in bunches above the door or growing in the garden.

The infamous "flying ointment" used by witches to create the sensation of flying was a lotion comprised of a number of narcotic herbs mixed with fat and applied to areas of the body where the skin was particularly thin and sensitive, with the most usual area being the genitalia. The recipes for flying ointment included such deadly herbs as aconite (wolfsbane or monkshood), deadly nightshade, hemlock, henbane, white water lily, hellebore, damiana and thorn-apple.

Charms

A charm, in this context, is a physical object that can be dedicated or empowered to render a specific influence: a good example is a charm to bring good luck (even non-Wiccans have heard of the "lucky" four-leaf clover!). Others are charms to increase fertility, enhance love, to keep loved ones safe, or to raise money. The ritual that dedicates the object can be as simple as holding it in the hands and "willing" it to perform the desired task.

Wiccan charms are usually natural objects, happened upon without a conscious quest, and often simply and profoundly a "gift" from the Goddess. Holey stones (stones with natural holes right through them) are symbolic of the Great Goddess herself, and are considered very precious: stones are effectively the bones of the Earth Mother, which implies that crystals (found rather than bought) and stones with meaningful shapes or patterns can also be potent charms. A cast horseshoe, iron nails, feathers, seeds, driftwood, shells, animal claws or teeth, in fact anything found by an individual, with a particular meaning for that person, can become a charm.

Weather Magic

The ability to control the weather, and thus have more control over the fertility of the crops in the fields, has been a dream of farmers and agricultural workers for millennia, and it's a power that has been ascribed to witches at various times in history. Witches who claimed to be able to control the weather were traditionally called *tempestiarii*, "storm makers".

One of the most memorable cases, and one which had a significant effect on the way in which witches were viewed by the general public, occurred in the autumn of 1590, when King James (VI of Scotland, later James I of England) was on his way from Denmark to Scotland with his new bride. A coven of witches in North Berwick had assembled to raise a storm in order to sink the king's ship.

The Berwick witches' alleged method of raising the storm was rather grisly. A tortured cat was "christened", had the hands, feet and genitals of a dismembered corpse attached to the appropriate parts of its body, and was flung into the sea. Of course, under torture most people will admit to just about anything if it will stop the pain. Certainly a true Wiccan would have had nothing to do with such a cruel practice.

The real reason behind the attempt is unclear. Certainly Elizabeth I was unwilling to have James produce an heir, who would have been in line for the throne of England, and it may have been that Dr John Dee, her friend and tame magician, may have had a hand in the matter. Whatever the hidden motives, the attempt failed and the king survived.

A short while later in Edinburgh, one Gilly Duncan – a young servant girl renowned for her healing abilities and, most unfairly, therefore suspected of witchcraft – was tortured to discover the source of her powers. Not unsurprisingly she confessed to witchcraft, and implicated nearly seventy respectable Edinburgh citizens.

King James himself was present at the trials of the accused, and used the proceedings as the basis for his *Three Books on Demonology*. In 1603, when he became monarch of England on the death of Queen Elizabeth, he took steps to tighten up the lenient witchcraft laws of the country, which in turn led to life becoming ever more uncertain and dangerous for those who followed the Old Ways.

Whether it is actually possible for individuals to effect any kind of control over the weather is a matter for personal speculation and decision, but there are certainly rituals designed to do just that. Less unpleasant ways of controlling of the weather include such things as burning a handful of bracken in an outdoor fire to conjure rain, and the use of broom, which is reputed to raise or calm winds.

Familiars

Traditionally, witches had familiar spirits. During the Burning Times, these were said to be servant demons, given to the witch by the Devil to do her bidding and assist in her evil working. In fact, little familiars, often pets these days, are much-loved companions whose presence helps to strengthen the Wiccan's link to the natural world in which the Great Goddess reigns. Animals are also precious reminders of the vigour and power of the Horned God, whose creatures they are. Particularly sensitive individuals may find themselves able to communicate with their pets – it's a kind of telepathy, and it can work both ways if the animal involved is sufficiently attuned to its person. Being welcomed into an animal's mind, and sharing a little time with it, is an amazing experience. Catmint was often used to strengthen the psychic bond between a

The common family pet can become a psychic companion.

witch and the familiar spirit, especially in the case of cats. Other traditional familiar animals were toads, bats, lizards, owls, ferrets, and even foxes.

Rituals

"Merry meet –
Merry part –
And merry meet again!"

Human beings have a deep-seated need for rituals, for the marking of important times in their lives with some kind of meaningful activity or special festival. Birthday celebrations, anniversaries, even funeral wakes – every significant occasion demands its own commemoration. Wicca is no exception.

All rituals take place within a circle, either a literal circle drawn or built upon the ground, or a magical circle constructed from psychic energy. The circle doesn't need to be a permanent feature, although obviously such structures as stone circles or wood henges are pretty much enduring characteristics of the landscape! Aside from these, however, the circle is constructed afresh each time it is needed, and even the permanent circles should be cleansed and prepared before each use. The circle symbolizes the earth, the Earth Mother from whom we all spring, and also acts as a psychic anchor, protecting those within against negativity and any hostile energies emanating from either the mundane or the invisible worlds.

First the ground is swept with a broom or besom, the person wielding the broom focusing on sweeping negative thoughts away, then the outer edge of the circle is constructed. There are almost as many ways of doing this as there are covens: some draw the circle in chalk, or paint it on the floor, some use salt, or water, or small stones, yet others envisage the area being enclosed in a dome of silvery-blue light. Most covens then invoke the four "directions", a way of acknowledging the elements that make up all physical matter. North is earth, the physical senses, the body; east is air, the mental processes and the ability to think; south is fire, energy, willpower and determination; and west is water, the unconscious, feeling and intuition. The centre of the circle represents spirit and the individual in harmony, both with themselves and with everything around them. The actions and words used in casting the circle, as this activity is known, can be as elaborate or as simple as desired, and there is no right or wrong way for the ritual to be performed.

A group of Wiccans is known as a coven (the word simply comes from the Latin *convenire*, – to come together. Convent comes from the same root.) A coven can be any number of people: the "traditional" thirteen originally commemorated the thirteen full moons of the year, although with the advent of Christianity the number came to be seen as both sinister and unlucky. Wicca is a very democratic lifepath and all are equal in the sight of the Goddess. Nevertheless, there will always be those who have practised their faith for longer than newer adherents, and have more knowledge and wisdom, and such individuals usually take on the roles of teacher and instructor to the coven; in addition, they often find themselves taking the parts of the High Priest or Priestess in rituals.

Wiccaning, sometimes called "saining", is the

Wiccan equivalent of Christening; it is not practised by every Wiccan group, but is nevertheless a charming way for a newborn to be welcomed into the circle. The baby is presented to the group or coven within the circle, and a crescent traced on its forehead in water. The Goddess is given the child's name, and asked to guard and guide it on its journey through life. Next, a candle is passed over the child (out of harm's reach, obviously), with the request that the love of the Goddess will always warm the child. Finally, the scented smoke from a bunch of smouldering herbs is wafted over the child, with a request that the breath of the Goddess bless the child always. This simple rite is usually concluded with a quiet feast.

Initiation marks the entrance of an individual into the Wiccan lifepath, confirms their desire to embrace their new lifestyle and spirituality, and welcomes them into the coven. It's the culmination of several years' study of Wiccan history, divination, herblore and ritual, during which the initiate makes his or her own ritual tools, and sometimes Tarot pack, runes or other divinatory implements.

Traditionally, initiations were performed in a cave, as being symbolic of the womb of the Earth Mother, with the new Wiccan exiting the cave at the end as a symbol of their birth into their new life. The initiate is ritually bathed to symbolize the purity of their intent, then led naked, blindfolded and with hands bound, to the place of initiation; their helplessness at this stage is symbolic of the trust they must place in both their Wiccan fellows and the life they are about to enter. They are challenged, and must give their new name and purpose before being allowed to enter the circle. Once accepted, they are released from their bonds and blindfold, and presented to the coven and to the Goddess. The ritual concludes with a feast.

Handfasting is the Wiccan equivalent of marriage. The ceremony celebrates the love between the couple and their desire to be bonded to each other. Unlike Christian wedlock, however – which, with its overtones of "'til death do us part" is designed to literally "lock" the pair together, making no allowances for change – the union can be broken if both wish it in a corresponding ceremony known as handparting.

For some time before the ceremony, the couple spend time together braiding three cords into a simple rope. These must be made of a special material, or of leather, something that is symbolic to them both. As they work on the fabric, they should talk about their hopes and wishes for the years to come, and reaffirm their feelings for each other. At the chosen time, perhaps the summer solstice, or at full moon, the couple are welcomed into the circle and blessed in the name of the Goddess and the God by the High Priest and Priestess, who then tie the couple's hands together gently with the cord they have braided, symbolizing the binding together and interweaving of their lives. The pair may exchange vows if they feel so inclined, and there may be singing or dancing to celebrate the happy event. The ritual concludes, as do most Wiccan rites, with a feast.

Death Rites
Generally speaking, Wiccans believe in reincarnation, a conviction that influences their entire perception of death. For one thing, if you believe – *know* – that you are going to be reborn onto the planet, it makes good sense to do what you can to ensure it's a clean and

comfortable place to come home to. Enlightened self-interest of this sort tends to ensure that most Wiccans are deeply concerned with environmental matters.

In Wicca there is no heaven or hell. There are, however, the Summerlands, the otherworldly place where the soul goes after the death of the body to await its rebirth. The Summerlands are most often described as a place of eternal summer – hence the name – but otherwise similar to Earth, if brighter, better and without the ills and problems that beset the earthly life. It's a happy place, where the soul can rest and recuperate in comfort after the exigencies of physical life.

It follows that death is not something to be feared, certainly not for the person facing the great adventure. But what of those left behind? Even *knowing* that the soul of the dying individual will be reborn into another life in the near future, a certain sadness is inevitable for those who mourn. Wicca tries to ease the farewell to the departed: a Wiccan funeral is quite unlike the solemn occasion seemingly demanded by the Christian church. It has very often been scripted by the one for whom it is held, during their lifetime, and usually includes favourite songs or musical works, poems, literary pieces or self-penned prayers. The songs are generally cheerful, celebrating the life of the departed rather than mourning their death, and there is always a feast of some sort at the end, with speeches, toasts and stories. And in the close-knit, nurturing Wiccan community, there is an abundance of love and care for those left behind, to ease the first days of the separation.

The Tools of the Craft

Although it is certainly not necessary to own or use tools in order to practise Wicca, there are a number of implements that are generally employed in rituals, usually to symbolize or direct elemental energies.

The Cauldron and the Chalice

These two artifacts are considered symbolic of the feminine principle. The cauldron represents the body of the Great Goddess, the Earth herself as the Mother. Traditionally, the cauldron has three legs: the triangle or pyramid is symbolic of controlled power, and when coupled with the cauldron itself, represents both the power of the Earth Mother and the Wiccan's desire to use that power in a controlled (i.e. wise) way.

The chalice has its origin in the grisly custom of drinking from the cleaned skull of an enemy killed in battle. This was, in the beginning, a way of honouring the dead, of sharing in his bravery and valour and ensuring that his memory did not simply vanish along with his rotting corpse. Over the years the skulls were decorated and plated with metal, until eventually the metal chalice superseded the actual skull because it lasts longer, is less fragile, and is easier to obtain, keep and clean. The chalice is also, because of its shape and the fact that it can hold life-giving liquids (water, milk, wine or blood), symbolic of the womb. This, along with its gory origin, echoes the natural cycle of the world, the birth-death-rebirth that is so important to Wicca.

The cauldron is used ritually in several different ways. Filled with water, it can be employed as a scrying mirror: gazing into the flat, reflective surface of the water has the same effect as gazing into a crystal sphere. At the Sabbats it may be used as a vessel to hold a small fire to commemorate the festival. It may also be utilized to warm wine in preparation for such Dark Year feasts as Samhain and Yule. In elemental terms, the chalice represents the element of Water.

The Sword and the Knife

Because of their shape, and because they are both primarily designed for destruction, these are considered to be symbolic of the masculine principle. Each is something of a latecomer into the Wiccan lifepath since in a primarily Goddess-orientated religion the destructive masculine element plays only a small part. However, a knife of some sort was necessary, for example to cut herbs, and for the occasional sacrifice, so slowly the two weapons became an accepted part of the regalia. These days the knife (also known as an *athame*) is more likely to have a dull edge, and be used for directing masculine energies during rituals. Swords and knives are representative of the element of Air.

The Staff and the Wand

The staff is the most ancient Wiccan tool: its use stretches far back into the human race's earliest history. Originally, the staff was symbolic of the shaman, wiseman or wisewoman whose psychic and magical powers guarded and guided the tribe or clan. Both should be constructed by the Wiccan him/herself, of native woods: a female staff or wand is often made from elder (for power and protection) or rowan (strongly protective and useful to develop divinatory abilities), while a male Wiccan may use oak (sacred to Cernunnos) or ash (symbolic of the sacrifice of Odin.) Hazel, the tree that grants wisdom, is suitable for either men or women, and could be considered the best of all. The wand is effectively a smaller staff, but serves the same purpose – to absorb power from the earth and to project power for magical or ritual purposes (it is the origin of the illusionist's "magic wand"). Both the staff and the wand are often carved, or tipped with some natural object that can help with focusing and directing natural energies, such as a quartz crystal, pine cone, or animal tooth or claw. Less overtly masculine than the sword or knife, the staff and wand, because of their shape, are still considered masculine, but the much gentler, sympathetic, thoughtful aspect of the male. The staff and wand represent the element of Fire.

The Stone, Pentacle or Dish
Stones, pentacles or dishes symbolize the physical elements from which we are all made, as well as the physical body of the Earth Mother. The original altars were simply flattish-topped stones, open to the air and sunlight and with their roots deep in the Earth: today, the stone symbolizes those simpler times as well as reminding us that no matter how sophisticated the human race has become, it is still subject to the laws of nature. The pentacle, the familiar, five-pointed star, represents the human body when placed so that a single point is uppermost, or the Horned God when the single point is at the bottom. The stone symbolizes the element of Earth. Sometimes a coin or disc is used instead.

The Broom or Besom

The broom symbolizes hearth, home and cleanliness. It often has an ash wood shaft, broom sprigs for the bristles, and willow bindings. The broom is used to sweep the space where rituals are performed, and also to clean bad luck from the house at Samhain.

The Robe

Most Wiccans possess a robe, often one they have made themselves. It is usually undecorated, often black (to symbolize emptiness and thus the willingness to be filled with knowledge) or white (representative of death and rebirth and the unseen world) and worn only for rituals. For special occasions like Sabbats male Wiccans might wear red robes and female Wiccans green robes. (Some Wiccans prefer to work skyclad, i.e. naked, but given the vagaries of the weather and the legal system, this isn't always wise, or, indeed, possible!) The robe is usually tied with a cord, which represents both the umbilical cord and humanity's intimate link with the Earth Mother.

Jewellery

The subject of ritual jewellery can be something of a contentious issue – too many people give in to the temptation to wear far too much! Strictly speaking, jewellery is completely unnecessary. Nevertheless, sometimes a small talismanic or identification piece can be a comfort. A necklace of seashells, amber or jet is generally considered appropriate for a female Wiccan, and a small talismanic image or representation of a personal deity, on a leather cord or metal chain, apt for a male.

The Laws of Witchcraft – and what happens if you break them . . .

Despite what some ill-informed people might think, witchcraft as it is generally understood is subject to constraints. There are just two basic laws, but in them is concentrated all that is necessary to live in harmony with all things.

The Wiccan Rede
This is the Wiccan moral code. It simply states: "An it harm none, do what thou will". Far from being permission to do anything the individual fancies, this is actually a strong guide to correct living. It falls into two parts:

"An it harm none"; as long as it does no harm or damage of any kind to anyone or anything, *including yourself.* A simple-sounding instruction with global repercussions!

"Do what thou will"; you may do anything that your heart desires. "Will", in this context, can mean any or all of "want", "intend", "desire" or "have the willpower to accomplish". Note, also, that "thou" is singular. This instruction is designed for each and every individual who wishes to follow the Wiccan lifepath (although it would be an appropriate code for most non-Wiccans, too), and should be interpreted in the light of what each individual needs, wants or believes in. In other words, don't try to persuade other people into doing anything against their will.

The Law of Three
The karmic Threefold Law states that any good you do

will be returned to you threefold and likewise, any evil you do will come back to you three times worse! It therefore makes sense to do good. . .

While not a law, it is an accepted tenet of the Wiccan lifepath to respect other religions and their practitioners: all faiths are, ultimately, attempts to achieve union with the source of creation. It's a pity that other faiths do not return the compliment.

Today

Wicca is, above all else, a religion intimately connected with the natural world: the cycle of the seasons, the ebb and flow of the tides, the phases of the moon, growth, maturity, decay and death – and rebirth. Those who follow the Wiccan way aim for harmony, within themselves, with others, and with the world. This is not to say, of course, that they are simply reactive; Wicca is a very proactive, positive lifepath.

The world is, in the main, more tolerant these days. In some countries, especially America, Wicca is a recognized religion, afforded all the legal rights and privileges of any other faith – in theory, at least . . .

Of course, this does not mean that practitioners are necessarily safe from the sort of treatment meted out to their predecessors. Jealousy or misplaced fanatical zeal can inspire people to all sorts of unreasonable, irrational behaviour. These days, however, the crimes of which they accuse the objects of their hatred aren't those connected with trafficking with demons. They are more likely to fling accusations of sexual misde-meanours – especially of that most horrible crime, child abuse – at their victims instead. (True Wiccans find the very idea of abusing a child anathema, seeing children as the future, to be cherished, nurtured and loved. The idea of forcing a child to conform to another's mental sickness or lust for power is the province of the Satanist, not the Wiccan.) There are organized fundamentalist Christian groups who actively pray for all kinds of evil to be visited on those who do not conform to their own views. And there is the subtle harassment of Wiccans in the workplace, fortunately something that appears to be growing rarer.

There are many superficially-different forms of the Wise Craft around today, each giving reverence to that aspect of the Great Goddess, and the Horned God, which holds most significance for them; these aspects are called by the names of the traditional and historical deity that best embodied them. There are also solitary workers, Wiccans who, for reasons of isolation or personal preference, do not belong to a coven, but follow the lifepath alone (although even these individuals are conscious of being part of the warm, loving Wiccan community that embraces the entire planet.)

Reverence for the Great Goddess dates back at least 25,000 years (as evidenced by the Paleolithic "Venus" figurines), and it is probably safe to say that it will continue while there is a planet on which to live. And recently the human race's perception of their home-world is changing, seeing it more as an interlocking series of biosystems, each dependent on the others for health and even survival. People are finally realizing that while they depend on the earth for their very exis-tence, *She* doesn't need them, and in fact, she might very well be better off if the human race were wiped out!

Tolerance, a willingness to listen, reverence for creation, and all-embracing love is the Wiccan creed. We need more of it . . .

"Blesséd Be."

PART FIVE

The Magical Arts

●●●●●●●●●●●●●●●●●●●●●●●●●●●●●●●●●●●●●●

Introduction

We all know magic has something to do with conjuring rabbits out of hats, but neither psychologists, sociologists, anthropologists, nor even the ceremonial magicians themselves have managed to conjure up a single decent definition of what magic actually *is*. Dictionaries tell us that magic is all about influencing the course of events by the use of spiritual (as opposed to physical) forces. By inquiring into the word "spiritual" we can also learn to distinguish between black magic, which invokes evil spirits; white magic, which invokes angelic spirits; and natural magic, which primarily invokes the magician's own spirit. So what's the problem, what's wrong with that definition? Well, it does have one slight drawback: it is completely unacceptable to some of the world's major organized religions. Why? Because their own reliance on good relations between their flock and the angelic hosts implies that their priests are actually practising magicians!

The priests of some major religions actually endorse magic (Hinduism, for example, has a long tradition of using magical incantations), and their experiences and studies have greatly enriched and illumined the magical arts. Other religions however, an obvious example being Christianity, vigorously denounce all branches of magic and occultism. The combined dominance of the various Christian sects in the Western world obliterated most of the indigenous pagan magical systems that had flourished for millennia before the spread of the Gospel. In passing, we might note that some students of magic have argued that Christianity's historical persecution of other religions was tantamount to black magic. Its reliance on mind-control through spiritual threats (the everlasting fires of Hell, for instance), and vigorous suppression of ideas not expressly sanctioned by the hierarchy, are classic elements of the abusive treatment meted out by magicians who follow the path of spiritual darkness.

It is somewhat ironic that, at the dawning of the so-called New Age, people are so fascinated by ancient mysteries. For many, many seekers after spiritual truth, the allure of rediscovering half-lost secrets is almost as appealing as the thrill of actually discovering their own latent magical powers! There is no doubt that these beguiling temptations are fuelling a powerful, popular resurgence of interest in the occult arts in general and magic in particular.

Occult, incidentally, simply means hidden. To study it therefore, is to study that which is hidden. There are two main reasons why a subject is hidden: either it has been deliberately obscured (conspiracy theorists love this angle), or it has just never been found in the first place (this thought too inspires many spiritual adventurers). A third perspective, however, is that some truths about our world are so far beyond ordinary terms of reference that mere words cannot express them adequately. Unfortunately, this explanation is often quoted by charlatans as an excuse for not explaining their seemingly miraculous tricks, but it is also used by perfectly honest mystics who have had experiences that words are incapable of defining. Such people who have tried to find ways to relate their experiences have found it as difficult as trying to describe yellow to someone born blind! Many have turned to the arts, especially poetry, to describe their impressions, (but inevitably with only partial success). Perhaps this is why the magical arts are called arts – because so much relies on the point of view of the person experiencing them.

The problem of describing and interpreting magical truths has always emboldened detractors, who see even well-meant, if doomed attempts as a smoke-screen of deliberate confusion. Perhaps they are so embarrassed by their own lack of perception that they cannot admit even to the possibility of a natural veil, which only initiates guided by a higher power can penetrate.

Many spiritual teachers have found that the mysteries of life can, perhaps, be explored most concisely through parable. Although I make no claim to follow in such elevated footsteps, I think an example drawn from everyday life could aptly illustrate the subjectivity and power of certain experiences. I would like to preface this by observing that many superstitions are actually mini magical rites in the way they attempt to avoid misfortune by apparently irrational behaviour. For instance it is traditionally "bad luck" to walk under a ladder . . .

On their way to work, a couple of friends walk under

just such a ladder after a builder has been working overhead. One walks through without mishap, the other gets spattered with a rogue drip of paint (here, of course, we find the familiar grain of truth in the saying). The person who escaped unscathed might teasingly laugh at the other's obvious misfortune, and lightheartedly blame the superstition. The victim though, might not see the funny side so clearly, and may harbour a sneaking doubt that perhaps there is a more serious side to the situation – even apart from how exactly to get the paint off! Those gloomy suspicions may be reinforced when, while cleaning herself up in the ladies' room at work, the girl's unsympathetic boss enters to find her fussing and flustered . . .

The familiar domino effect has started to take over. How often do we find that, when one thing goes wrong, it seems to start a chain reaction? A whole succession of irritating nuisances can seem to accumulate and gather momentum – like an avalanche started by just one single snowflake too many! This simple observation is a key to understanding several branches of the magical arts.

For one thing, it demonstrates the power of suggestion: when one thing goes wrong, it puts the victim into a particular frame of mind. Psychology is replete with evidence that supports the idea that our mindset – the way we think and feel – affects almost every aspect of our lives. It's obvious and simple, but profoundly true: if we feel depressed or victimized then we're certainly not going to go to work brimming with self-confidence and willing and able to seize every new opportunity!

Some branches of magic (voodoo is a notorious example) use a sophisticated technique of suggestion as a weapon to exact revenge on a foe too strong or too far away to attack using purely physical means. Practitioners would stress that there is more to their magic than merely suggestion. But that very insistence on hidden forces further strengthens the suggestion itself, and suggestion alone can be a very powerful tool.

Other branches, for example talismanic magic, use physical objects to remind us of certain thoughts and emotions. If we are depressed, then handling certain crystals or even a scrap of paper with a certain emblem or design drawn upon it, can help us to balance our mood, overcome it, and escape its negative effects.

The domino effect can also offer a plausible scientific reason as to how magic can actually work. The idea that a single snowflake can wipe out an alpine village is, on the face of it, ludicrous. But, by tipping the balance on the avalanche that was waiting to happen, it can make the crucial difference. One tiny factor can produce an effect enormously out of proportion to its own size.

In magic, size definitely does not matter! Significance is the key: one significant factor can make or break anything. The sceptic might argue that placing a particular Tarot card on an altar couldn't change anything in the "real" world. But he would be forgetting the power of the snowflake. It is just possible that the card can set a particular train of events in motion, a snowballing cycle of cause and effect, that can achieve a prodigious and momentous result: the successful consummation of the magician's intention.

The scientific foundation for this sort of behaviour is known as Chaos Theory, and has been actively researched since its inception in the 1970s. Its relation to weather systems is often summed up in the observation that a butterfly beating its wings in Asia can cause a hurricane in America! Of course, people were well aware of this phenomenon long before modern scientists appropriated it. There is a well-known proverb, dating in part from at least the sixteenth century, that expresses the principle very well:

> For want of a nail the shoe is lost,
> For want of a shoe the horse is lost,
> For want of a horse the rider is lost,
> For want of a rider the message is lost,
> For want of a message the battle is lost,
> For the want of a battle the kingdom is lost.
> All for the want of a horseshoe nail!

There is also, unfortunately, a down side to this emphasis on every critical detail. Many ancient sources insist that if a magician makes a single error in performing a ritual, even to the slightest mispronunciation of one of the convoluted Barbarous Names of Power, then the outcome could not be guaranteed.

Many magicians would promptly abandon a rite, even if it had taken weeks of preparation, should the smallest imperfection occur. Why? Because they knew that the outcome could be very different from the one they intended. The result could, in fact, be catastrophic. This is one very good reason why there are such stern traditional warnings against people dabbling in magic. People who play with fire can get burnt – and I'm not talking about the Inquisition either!

This insistence on doing everything by the book puts the onus squarely on the magician rather than the rite. Cynics argue that this is rather like the small print in a contract: the notorious "let-out" clause. Fortunately, in most branches of the magical arts, the intention or will of the magician is far stronger and more significant than any one element of the ritual that is the embodiment and manifestation of that will.

Magic is a big subject, with many different divisions. There is certainly a world of difference between the shaman who works to avert the evil eye from his patient, the avaricious devil-worshipper who wants to dance naked on the grave of his arch business rival, and the idealistic student who attempts to transcend his ego while his friends go to a party. But they are all engaged in the pursuit and performance of the magical arts.

No wonder magic is so difficult to define!

Primal Magic

It is only natural that a baby, used to the muted sensations and the persistent rhythmic sounds of its mother's body, is bewildered by the startling clarity and intensity of its first experiences in the outside world. This impression is especially strong if the birth has been a traumatic one.

If the infant is fortunate it will swiftly overcome its shock, and discover that its every need is taken care of. Hunger, thirst and loneliness are all promptly relieved at the first signs of discomfort; and warmth, cleanliness and peace are also provided for as soon as they are missed. This is just as well. The human infant, unlike many other mammals, is unable to fend for itself in any way whatsoever. And it is not just completely helpless for a few vulnerable hours, but for months and, indeed, years.

With just a few cries for help, the baby can bring almost instant satisfaction for its every want – as if by magic. "Mother" truly is the name for God on the lips and in the hearts of small children. This is undoubtedly a potent source of our tendency to believe in magic and miracles. Little wonder then, that the earliest societies tended to start their religious activity with the cult of an all-embracing Earth Mother.

As long as 25,000 years ago, people started carving "Venus" figurines. Carefully sculpted from ivory, bone and stone, these works of art represent the idealized mother goddess, and are probably the oldest religious artifacts known. The statuettes are known as Venuses in honour of the Roman goddess of love, due to their overtly sexual features and obvious fertility. In fact, these figures are grossly misshapen by modern standards of fashion. Their hips, breasts, and buttocks are all greatly enlarged in order to emphasize their fecundity and fitness for child rearing. There is correspondingly little effort made to portray any facial features, or even arms or legs (which underscores the idea that these were not meant to depict particular women in the community, but a communal image of fertility).

People at that time were nomadic hunters, living in small bands and roaming the countryside in continual pursuit of plentiful herds of animals. Food was abundant and there was a real sense of security, born of living in perpetual harmony with their environment, that lasted not just a few months or years but was sustained throughout dozens of generations. Some authorities have observed that this period was probably the closest that mankind has ever come to enjoying a real Golden Age. Apparently the Earth

Mother did indeed warrant the idolization she received from her worshippers!

Magic, in such a society, is thought to have revolved around two interrelated problems. Firstly it is vital for the tribe to keep in step with the herds upon which its survival depends. Ceremonies that celebrate the changing seasons and mark the various points along the annual migration route, would also seek to magically ensure that river-crossings were not made hazardous by flooding, that the rains came in good time to prevent drought, that the herd of game animals kept healthy, and so on. This could all be effected by keeping the community on good terms with the spirits of the rivers, clouds, animals and vegetation. The other duty of magic was to ensure good relationships between the individual members of the tribe. Jealousy, envy, lust, pride, greed, all these vices that still plague our society today, have been part of human nature since time immemorial. All these require careful handling if they are not to develop into antisocial behaviour. Then, as now, these urges need powerful forces to hold them at bay. Unchecked, they can tear the living heart out of any community!

Here again, the authority of the Earth Mother, the divine mother of the tribe, is paramount. Apart from the persuasive good sense of cooperation over unbridled competition, the spiritual wellbeing of the malefactor would also be considered. Many shamanic rites are performed with the express intention of driving out evil spirits, spirits that are responsible for causing dis-ease and even disease. Bad dreams, bad thoughts, bad feelings and bad habits are all subject to purifying rituals.

Furthermore, the survival of the human spirit after

bodily death, and the spirit's eventual reincarnation, are primal beliefs. They are powerfully rooted in the obvious "proof" that personal characteristics recur time and again down the generations (we now recognize these features as our genetic inheritance). Since the Earth Mother is the goddess, the one who has the authority to give each and every individual continual rebirth, she wields ultimate power. She could, for example, withdraw the privilege of rebirth from anyone who repeatedly gives her offence instead of respect. Few miscreants would be willing to risk such complete extinction, and would be bound to submit to the judgment of the tribal elders or wise woman!

Venuses have been unearthed in a wide pattern of distribution, ranging from France to eastern Siberia. Archaeologists presume that they would have been brought into ritual or magical use during conception and childbirth but, as I have suggested above, it is likely that their significance extended into other rites of passage, including that other extreme and equally mysterious realm of death and rebirth.

Incidentally, some people find it notable that the religion described above is monotheistic. They wonder why the worship of a holy matriarch changed to that of a divine Father, and whether the same forces will, one day, bring a new figurehead into the ascendant. However, we should remember that the absence of ancient relics used in the worship of a Sky Father does not prove that he did not exist. Perhaps he may have been worshipped with idols that could not survive the passage through the millennia, or maybe without idols at all.

Of course, as we grow we learn that we must do more

than simply ask our mother for food and so on, we learn gradually how to take care of ourselves. Everything we need is somewhere out there in the world, as if waiting for us to take what we want. We just need to learn how to get it. We need, to put it simply, to strike up a working relationship with the Mother Goddess. If the asking for what we want is likened to a prayer or magical incantation, then the taking – or purposeful activity designed to get what we want – is equivalent to a magical ritual.

All parents-to-be promise themselves that they'll not make the same mistakes as their own parents. More pertinently, many promise themselves that they'll never use bribery or threats as inducements to get good behaviour. But how many, in the face of one obstinate mood too many, stick to those good intentions? It's so easy to say "If you eat your dinner, then I'll get you a pudding." Or "If you don't do your homework, then I'll not take you bowling at the weekend." Making deals is part and parcel of life. Negotiation, arbitration, compromise, it's actually important to develop and hone these skills while you're still young – you'd be lost without them in later life!

Trade and barter, wheeling and dealing, give and take, casting bread upon the waters, using a sprat to catch a mackerel. . . The euphemisms are endless, and crop up in every walk of life. Anyone who has ever written a BASIC program will be familiar with the logic of IF . . . THEN . . . statements. Our computers, it seems, run along the same lines as our parents, and so does our relationship with the Earth Mother. To get the Earth Mother to do what you want, you just need to do something to make her happy with you! Give her a present or, if you think she's punishing you for doing something wrong, take the hint and try to learn from your mistake. Then, to say sorry and make up, go out of your way to do her a favour. Such as? Well, why not give her something that you would like if someone gave it to you. Worth a try. Before you know it, you're offering up a sacrifice, just as your ancient forebears did thousands of years ago!

Talismanic Magic

Open the pouch of any shaman, witchdoctor or primitive magician (male or female), and you'll find a collection of bizarre artifacts. Most likely the contents will include items from a long list of traditional charms such as bones, teeth, feathers, crystals, twigs and leaves. Some people still carry a four-leafed clover for luck, and birthstones and other special crystals have made a very popular return to everyday use, whether worn as jewellery or simply carried in pocket or purse.

Although the particular items a shaman carries in his pouch naturally vary from culture to culture, the value and uses of this magical toolkit will be remarkably consistent. This is because people's basic needs are pretty similar the whole world over: physical healing, emotional support, spiritual security, social cohesion and protection from misfortune.

Depending on whether a seasonal festival was being held, or a sick child ministered to, there would usually be various ceremonial activities to accompany and enhance the use of the charms. These could vary from day-long communal dances on the one hand, to an evening's hypnotic chanting on the other. Whether the shaman used the bones to summon the ancestors to bless the harvest, or the feathers to sprinkle sacred water over a fevered child, all the elements of the ritual had a special meaning and power.

The means of summoning and directing this magical power was the subject of the shaman's lengthy and arduous apprenticeship. As a rule though, the magic relied on contacting and controlling the spirits of either the tribal ancestors or the natural world. In these groups of spirits, as among mortal folk, there would be some individual bearing grudges and bent on doing harm, although most would have benevolent or, at worst, neutral intentions. It was the shaman's job to learn how to defeat the evil spirits either by personal strength, or by finding magical allies. The charms that he would carry so carefully in his pouch, were gifts from supportive spirits. They were tokens or pledges of help.

Most of us have some personal experience of this, maybe not as a profoundly spiritual matter, but still significant. At the height of a holiday or other special trip, who hasn't chanced upon an item that somehow embodies the spirit of that time? Such a souvenir is the direct successor to the ancient charm. As soon as you glance at it, all the magic of the moment when you found it returns and fills you with its own personal energy. Often, incidentally, we are also filled with longing to return to that special time, and this is actually a powerful message that should not be ignored lightly!

To take a rather more prosaic point of view, we might conceive of the charm pouch as a sort of pocket address book. In it you can quickly find those essential telephone numbers – of your closest friends, parents, brothers and sisters, the local hospital, police station, fire station, taxi service, politician, plumber, anyone, in fact, who you could call on for immediate and professional help and advice. And, just as your contact phone numbers are personal to you, so the shaman's charms were often considered personal and worthless to anyone else.

Very occasionally though, the spirits made pledges that were not just to help a particular shaman, but to protect an entire community or tribe. In such cases the charm or totem became the property of the tribal chief, and passed from generation to generation. Totems belonging to a rival clan were sometimes sought in tribal wars, as capturing them would deprive the enemy of access to magical help and spiritual intervention. Most of us have had the misfortune to find out how absolutely lost we feel when we misplace our own personal organizers or address books – the damage to tribal morale when their most holy relic was stolen is difficult to over-estimate!

Although the pursuit and discovery of shamanic charms is a topic that strays into the provenance of shamanic vision-quests and even witchcraft, the ideas we have looked at are important for understanding how modern magic has developed. They have provided a continual and powerful undercurrent of interest in practical, everyday matters. Some magicians, though, have struggled to escape from these pursuits, hoping instead to find an ethereal, transcendental and ultimately mystical culmination to their occult careers.

Probably the single biggest development has been the transition from using purely natural objects as simple charms, to the deliberate and often painstaking construction of complex magical devices: talismans. Usually decorated with arcane symbols, and sometimes made of composite materials, these hand-crafted objects have a second significant difference from shamanic charms. Talismans are not viewed as passports that allow the spirits to come and influence the physical world, but are actually regarded as reposi-tories of magical power, rather like batteries. And, like some batteries, you can even recharge them when you feel their effectiveness is wearing a bit low.

We could leave the subject of charms by noting that the shaman had actually to find his four-leafed clover (or whatever magical plant he needed) himself, he had to personally pluck an eagle's feather, or extract the tiger's tooth by his own main force. The plant, feather or tooth was once physically connected to the plant, bird or animal whose spirit he needed. Importantly, this spiritual connection was not broken when he physically took the piece he required. When he produced the tooth to frighten away an evil spirit, the tiger is actually summoned to be there with him, ready and willing to fight in the spirit world.

This is known as "contagious magic". Wherever the charm is, there is a direct and instantaneous connec-tion to the spirit of whatever it was taken from. This is the same idea as is employed to such well-known and deadly effect in the voodoo doll. A contagious virus can begin with a ticklish sore throat, progress into a fully blown head cold (complete with inflamed sinuses and earache), and then even develop into a hacking chesty cough. The virus can spread very quickly from one infected part of the body to another. The same is true of contagious magic. Nail-clippings, body hair, or even personal items or clothing belonging to the victim, are incorporated in the voodoo doll. In this way, the voodoo witchdoctor can endeavour to ensure that whatever vengeful torment happens to the doll is transferred directly to the rest of the body of the victim.

The simple act of looking at a photograph of a loved one and wishing them well, could – strictly speaking – be construed as a benign act of contagious magic, using the photo as the link. This view of photography was at the heart of some rural folks' superstitious avoidance of the camera in its early days – they literally didn't want to risk putting their spirits in jeopardy.

As a rule, the modern magician would employ not contagious but homeopathic magic. The difference between the two forms is that in homeopathy the link does not need to be direct (actual hair, feathers, etc.) but only similar. Instead of a person's blood, for example, the magician could use red pigment; instead of a real tiger's tooth, the magician could simply paint its picture; instead of an ancestor's bones, only their name need be spoken. This single evolutionary step opened up a whole new game-plan for the would-be magician.

Imagine you are a warrior who wants to be as fierce as a tiger in battle. Perhaps, for one reason or another, you can't afford the time or trouble to confront the beast personally in order to come away with a tooth as a trophy and charm. What do you do? You buy a finger ring whose stone is carved in the shape of a snarling tiger's head. The stone would be, appropriately, tiger's eye, and the metal of the ring itself might be iron to honour Mars, god of war and warriors. By combining as many elements as you can, that all say "tiger + fierce", you get a composite talisman that is arguably just as effective as a real tiger's tooth (and far more environmentally sound!)

And anyone can do it. Although traditional charms like unicorn's horn and eye-of-newt still have plenty of exclusivity and cachet, the modern talisman is perfect for mass marketing and mass production.

However, for the serious magician, the best advice has got to be DIY. And for that you need a teacher or, less expensively, a rule book: a Grimoire.

Learning to Spell

"In the beginning was the Word, and the Word was with God, and the Word was God." These are the opening words of the most mystical of the Gospels, that of St John.

"The word creates all things: everything we love and hate – everything that is." So declares an ancient Egyptian text, continuing: "Nothing exists before it is spoken in a clear voice."

"And God said, Let there be light: and there was light." The story of the creation of the world, as given in the first chapter of Genesis, is a sequence of spoken commands.

"When on high, heaven had not been named, firm ground below had not been called by name. . ." These are the first words of the Sumerian Creation Epic, composed nearly 4000 years ago. It goes on to explain: "Uncalled by name, their destinies were as yet unde-termined. . ."

These quotations represent four major and influen-tial ancient sources, all clearly sharing a religious conviction of the creative, magical power of words (and the list could be continued at very great length).

Let us now consider an everyday example. You say to a friend, "I'm going shopping after lunch." You don't imagine you're making a big deal of anything but, in a way, your statement carries a lot of weight. You have spoken, and what you have said will (almost certainly) happen. You have stated your intention, and "given your word" that you will undertake the action. By speaking the truth, what you say predicts what will come to pass.

Now imagine that you are a king or queen and you say, "I'm going to build a canal from coast to coast." You needn't move another muscle, but it will be built – because you have spoken, and your word is law.

Magicians though, set their sights on an even higher power, and seek to wield the eternal forces of creation themselves. If they could only discover the words that set the universe in motion, they could rule the world. Even if they could just learn those magical syllables that control such relatively minor forces as the weather, floods, disease then they could take control of these devastating natural disasters, and avert the incalculable suffering they cause.

The prize was power almost beyond imagining, and, from earliest times, has inspired countless aspirants.

Pythagoras (born in Greece, in 580 BC) believed that all nature could be understood in terms of numbers, and every number (according to ideas that still inform the popular system of numerology) represents a unique creative power. He founded a school or brotherhood, to teach people to live in harmony with these natural forces (they were, for instance, strictly vegetarian). Pythagoreans also believed that each of the letters of the Greek alphabet had a numerical equivalent: A (alpha) = 1, B (beta) = 2, and so on. This process was called gematria. By adding the numbers of the letters together, any word could be reduced to a number, and its power understood.

A similar approach was applied to the Hebrew alphabet. After all, the Bible was revered as the "Word of God", so the Creator Himself could have deliberately left invaluable information encoded in its text. The students of the Qabalah ("Tradition") sought long and hard to uncover and understand those hidden or occult mysteries. Indeed, many are still searching. Besides numerous interesting correlations between words, Qabalists long ago found there were many other surprising discoveries awaiting analysis. For example Exodus chapter 14, verses 19 to 21, were found to have precisely seventy-two letters each. Scholars copied the letters of the first verse along a row, then they wrote the second verse underneath the first but in reverse order, then the third verse was written (in the proper sequence) underneath the other two. In this arrangement they saw seventy-two short columns of letters. Reading from top to bottom, they discovered seventy-two three-letter words that can be combined to form a single, comprehensive, name for God – the Shemhamforash. By adding either Al or Ih (both sacred syllables) they also derived the names of the seventy-two angels of Jacob's ladder.

The Gnostics, who employed Pythagorean numerology, agreed that seventy-two is one of the most holy of all numbers. But perhaps the best known example of turning Greek words into numbers is that of the Gnostic name (or formula) Abraxas. This was borne by the supreme deity of the Basilidian sect which adopted Qabalistic methods. By converting letters into numbers, and adding them, Abraxas amounts to 365, a clear reference to the days of the year. Hence Abraxas is regarded as a revelation (or revealer) of the mysteries of the solar cycle. Appropriately, he had 365 powers or virtues that were subordinate to his command. Abraxas, incidentally, is often depicted as a cock-headed human with two serpents instead of legs, carrying a circular shield and brandishing a whip.

Such angelic and holy names were some of the many snippets of secret lore that were garnered into medieval grimoires. Literally "grammars", these books taught the rules of how to spell and speak the names of power, and how to combine them into sentences (composed as much of ritual action as incantation) that could put truly stupendous forces under the magician's control.

Most grimoires pandered to the base appetites, and concerned themselves not with the spiritual elevation of the magician but only with the exercise of power over the earth (a notable exception being the largely benevolent Sacred Magic of Abra-Melin). Appropriately these grimoires concerned themselves not with the heavenly host of angels, but with the fallen angels who could be conjured up from their Hell. In this infernal hierarchy, a mirror image of heaven, even the seventy-two angels had their demonic counterparts. The Lesser Key of Solomon lists these seventy-two evil spirits, and provides detailed rites for calling them forth. Amon, for example, is one of the milder evil spirits: he stirs up feuds and foretells the future, appearing in the shape of a wolf with a tail like a snake, and breathing fire.

Sitri, a prince with a leopard's head and the wings of a griffin, inflames men and women to carnal passion, and can even induce them to parade themselves stark naked for the delectation of the magician (and, one might imagine, a paying audience!). Vepar, a merman, causes such putrefying sores that worms glut and breed there rapaciously. The victim suffers intensely yet takes three days to die. Andras, who has a raven's head, rides a black wolf and brandishes a sword, is a bit of tricky customer. He arouses such enmity and sows such discord, that the magician is advised to take precautions lest his assistants succumb to the demon's influence and slay him outright!

Surprisingly, perhaps, a good number of the other members of this infernal hierarchy of seventy-two fallen angels offer little of a sensational nature, merely teaching the magician the occult properties of herbs, gems and even geometry and languages.

Incidentally, the Greek and Hebrew alphabets are not identical, which gives students of gematria something of a difficulty. Although a few sounds have the same numerical meanings, most do not. So how can a sound in one holy language have a different magical meaning from the same sound in another holy language? Sadly, it seems gematria offers little hope of providing a universal translator.

Nevertheless, the ancient and mystical "Om" – the famous Hindu mantra or holy utterance, which signifies everything that is, was and will be – is thought to contain valuable phonetic clues. Intriguingly, it has been analyzed as representing the open throated "O" of unrestricted force rushing into being, which gradually but inexorably loses energy and condenses into the fixed, closed, state of material existence: "m". It is tempting to interpret this as an ancient prophecy of the "Big Bang – Big Freeze" scenario that contemporary astrophysicists are currently endorsing as the probable origin and inevitable end of life, the universe, and everything we know of.

Certain sounds actually do seem to carry a clear emotional value. The difference between a soft, soothing, sibilant sound like "Sssss", and the curt, gutteral grunt "Gr" is positively palpable! And anyone who has studied poetry will be well aware that professional writers choose their words carefully to carry their readers along on a gentle tide of euphony. Orators too use subtle but very effective patterns of speech to manipulate the emotions and minds of their audience. There is a special magic in the way these people use words. It is the same power exploited by ancient bards to hold their audiences captivated with stories of heroes and myth.

Words can reduce us to tears, or rouse us to wage wars.

But even that is only half the story.

Adepts or Impostors?

Words are powerful tools, but that is all they are. In the right hands they can heal nations, in the wrong hands they can bring civilization to ruin. Holy books, those containing the direct word of God, teach how mankind may return to the right path.

Despite a few charismatic but anarchic characters (notably Aleister Crowley, as we shall see a little later), and a crop of colourful charlatans, most magicians have been devoutly religious. Many sincere and saintly men and women have devoted intense scrutiny to the ancient holy texts throughout the millennia. At heart they seek personal salvation and liberation from sin and error. Some studied in the hope of learning the angelic password that opens the gates of heaven, others simply sought to commune with the angels themselves. Any magical powers picked up along the way were not always seen as an end in themselves but merely tools to do good deeds such as healing the sick. A few had grander ideas. Why not seek to establish the reign of heaven on earth?

One influential group of people inspired by the vision of building the heavenly city on terra firma were, of course, the Freemasons. A survival of a medieval guild of craftsmen, these "free masons" could see a clear parallel between their earthly livelihoods and their spiritual calling. After all, many of their commissions were to build churches and cathedrals that took generations to complete, and the establishment of Christ's kingdom on earth was also a labour that demanded devotion over the span of many lifetimes. Masonic tradition remembers that their brotherhood constructed the great temples of Jewish antiquity. As architects of sacred designs in stone, wood and precious metals, could they not also be considered as the architects of society in flesh and blood? "Social engineering" is the modern phrase that springs immediately to mind.

Although some apologists might decry the very idea that the Masons are a magical order or brotherhood, they have long been suspected of heretical ideas. As if awakening to the notion that their stern insistence on absolute secrecy renders them deeply suspect in the eyes of non-initiates, some modern Masons are trying to lift the veil (or, more precisely, one small corner of it) to show there's nothing sinister hidden there. Nevertheless, the Freemasons still exercise a powerful if covert grip on many vital organs of society. It is often claimed that in Britain, for example, almost the entire legal system is not only riddled with Masonic intrigues and hidden agendas, but is rife with incestuous self-interest.

There is no doubt that during its long and chequered history, Masonry has embraced magic and magicians alike. In the eighteenth century, for example Count Cagliostro toured Masonic Lodges performing elaborate magical rites designed to contact the spirits of long dead sages, such as Moses. Cagliostro, who claimed to possess the elixir of life (which could cure all diseases), announced himself to be the Grand Copt, the head of Egyptian Freemasonry, and founded several lodges where the rites were practised. In just one of these rites fully three dozen ladies were simultaneously initiated into the mysteries.

The rite began at midnight and, following a speech proclaiming the virtues of female emancipation, the ladies were accosted by scores of amorous men. Having resisted chastely the vigorous attentions of these debauched suitors (who even chased them into the moonlit gardens), the women were allowed to regroup inside the temple. Here, at the climax of the rite, the roof appeared to open and a huge golden orb slowly descended. Perched upon it was a naked man, with a star on his brow and clutching a serpent. This apparition, none other than Cagliostro himself, immediately commanded that his startled and still breathless audience of would-be initiates disrobe. He explained that for the ladies to hear and receive the truth they must themselves be as naked and open as the truth. After they had complied with his wishes, the magician instructed them that the purpose of the magical arts is to do good to humanity. Furthermore, he assured them that along with spiritual peace and understanding, the aim of Egyptian Freemasonry was to enjoy material pleasure. Indeed, when the rite was concluded, all the participants congregated in the ballroom to further celebrate the ladies' initiation into emancipation.

Whether Cagliostro is reckoned an avant-garde adept of the highest degree, or a rank charlatan, depends on your point of view. After a long and colourful career, the Inquisition found him guilty of being a Freemason, a heretic and a sorcerer. Although sentenced to death, his sentence was commuted to life imprisonment. The question of whether he died in jail or managed to escape, is still hotly debated in some magical circles. . .

The death of an even more infamous magician, Faust, is less uncertain. The life of this sixteenth century German magician has passed into legend, and has been told, revised and extravagantly embellished by innumerable writers, including of course, the redoubtable Goethe.

The young Johann Faust, it seems, was not a wealthy man, but he was a talented scholar and became a doctor both of medicine and divinity. His appetite for knowledge, though, extended far beyond the confines of the conventional curriculum. One night he left the comfort of his lodging and make his way into the heart of a dark forest until he reached a desolate spot where four roads met. Here, at the crossroads of his life, Faust conjured the Devil.

Protected only by his magic circle and a scattering of occult paraphernalia, he bargained with Satan himself. The Devil obligingly offered to provide unlimited assistance to his new disciple, for the span of twenty-four years, after which time Faust must surrender his body and soul to his diabolical mentor. The pact was duly signed in the magician's own blood, and a demon, Mephistopheles, was assigned to attend to his every whim. Mephistopheles took the delighted magician on a tour of the entire world, accomplishing all the travelling in the twinkling of an eye. The voyage did not consist of this world alone, but encompassed both heaven and hell into the bargain! His exploration of the spiritual realms was not confined to mere sightseeing, but included sexual adventures with more than a handful of succubi, female demons whose lasciviousness excelled that of any mortal woman.

Faust could, it seems, also conjure the ghost of anyone he cared to meet, and gained a considerable reputation for his powers of necromancy. For example, the emperor Charles V was more than satisfied when, at his royal request, Faust conjured the spirit of Alexander the Great. Faust was now, of course, wealthy beyond his wildest dreams and was rather overcome by it all. Many of his actions began to show less and less good judgment, and betray instead an increasingly strong sense of caprice...

On one occasion he made an enormous pair of stag's antlers appear on the head of a bewildered knight. The knight secretly vowed revenge and, with half a dozen fully armed accomplices, lay in wait for the magician as he travelled along a lonely road. When the lethal ambush was sprung however, Faust instantly conjured an entire regiment of cavalry to defend himself, and promptly routed his attackers.

On another occasion he used his powers to transport himself and a few drinking companions into a bishop's private wine cellar. Whilst enjoying the novelty (and the fine wines!) they were discovered by the butler. Before the servant could raise the alarm, however, a hasty spell struck him temporarily dumb and unable to move. After the party was over, the butler was found where Faust had left him, perched in the topmost boughs of a lofty tree!

Faust's fondness for banqueting was prodigious, and he loved to impress his guests by conjuring superb spreads replete with every conceivable delicacy, out of thin air. He could also magic entire palaces to appear, complete with towers and even ornamental lakes. As a finale, all these spectacular feats would vanish in an impressive flare of golden fire.

Although Faust's thirst for excitement and merriment certainly began to lapse into decadence, his impending doom cut his spree prematurely short. One stormy night, at a particularly lavish banquet, he confessed to his astonished party the truth of the diabolical deal he had struck. The price of his supernatural powers, he said at the climax to this bizarre travesty of the last supper, was now due for payment.

In the small hours of the night, after everyone had retired to bed, the sounds of a desperate struggle – from Faust's own chambers – awakened the household. His body was found, some distance from the house, horribly mutilated and eloquent of the presumed state of his immortal soul.

Mystics and Angels

Of course, not every magician has been obsessed with wealth and the extravagances of opulence and sexual licence. Many students of the magical arts have devoted themselves to the patient study of holy books in the hope of divining the Creator's will – not with the aim of exploiting the words of power for selfish purposes, but to better the lot of their fellows. Even in the Middle Ages, which is renowned for its appalling rituals of animal sacrifice in the name of magic, some magicians practised their arts in the name of the Christian God. One exceptionally tolerant fifteenth-century grimoire not only invited women to take the lead role in its rituals, but openly welcomed anyone of any faith whatsoever, as long as that faith acknowledged one supreme deity.

This book, the Sacred Magic of Abra-Melin the Mage, describes an exhausting ritual which starts at the Spring Equinox, and lasts for six whole months. During this time the magician systematically subdues his (or her) base appetites, purifies the desire for spiritual attainment and contemplates – in increasing humility – the majesty of their one god (whether Christian, Jewish, pantheist, etc. etc.) At the climax of this operation the successful magician is rewarded with a visit by his very own Guardian Angel, who appears in great beauty and with words of ineffable wisdom to enlighten, comfort and guide him. Following this encounter, the magician is introduced to the infernal counterpart of the angels, the realm of demons. Having won the support of his Guardian Angel, the magician is empowered to treat the diabolical hosts as underlings, and to command them to perform

The angel or holy messenger is a significant feature of many of the
world's religions.

whatever he wishes. By forcing them to do good works, despite their natural unwillingness, the magician may be sure that they are actually working toward their own salvation – in spite of themselves. The book specifies scores of particular magical acts that the demons can be relied upon to perform. These include many good deeds such as curing leprosy, uncovering theft and healing the bewitched. However, the Sacred Magic also gives instructions for the rather more dubious acts of destroying towns, sowing discord among ecclesiastics, and transforming men into asses!

The idea of having your own personal Guardian Angel, the holy mediator between you and the omniscient Immortal, has a lot of appeal. Being blessed with a face-to-face meeting, and having the opportunity of learning the truth and power of divine lore, is surely an opportunity not to be missed. This mystery lies at the heart of many modern magical systems. It is often termed attaining the Knowledge and Conversation of the Holy Guardian Angel. This sacred ambition is central to the aspirations of many contemporary magicians, even those who choose to work alone rather than in a formal society or circle.

The closing decades of the nineteenth century and early years of the twentieth, saw the rise of numerous magical orders and interest groups, including the Theosophical Society and the modern Rosicrucians. Another influential organization, the Hermetic Order of the Golden Dawn, chose its very name to commemorate the precise moment of spiritual illumination. Although couched in poetic terms of a glorious new day dawning, the impact of meeting your Angel is actually devastating. There is no turning back from this encounter with spiritual realms beyond the reach of the physical sciences. Everything the novice knew, or thought he knew, is suddenly transcended by a higher wisdom. The process is as visceral as resurrection from the tomb, or a rebirth. In fact, the Golden Dawn prepared their candidates well for the ordeal that faced them. Years of painstaking study and ritual were dedicated to the achievement of this single goal. Although it was, strictly-speaking, unnecessary (as the Angel would become the magician's personal guide), even the events following the meeting with the Angel were described. Indeed, the Order did not cast their new initiates adrift in the world, but continued to offer their members the support of ancient occult lore.

The magical ritual that the Golden Dawn performed to bring their worthy candidates into the light of a new era in their spiritual evolution, was particularly elaborate. Central to the ceremony was an awesome crypt, designed to emulate the vault in which a mystical hero, Christian Rosenkreutz (legendary founder of the order of the Red Rose and the Golden Cross), was interred in the fifteenth century.

Each of the seven sides of this chamber was painted with one colour of the rainbow, and every panel (including ceiling and floor) was filled with alchemical and magical symbols and pictures – all arranged in their most forceful combination. The language of symbolism spoke eloquently of the dual mystery of death and life, and the candidate, well versed in reading these arcane scripts, was confronted with the full meaning of the tomb. The rising of new awareness in the candidate's soul, echoed in all the detail and power of the resplendent temple, ensured a moment of great, even transcendental beauty that encompassed the extremes of personal humility and shared magnificence. This ritual echoed closely the Christian teachings of death and rebirth: a religious transformation that replaced the old with the new, as completely as when dawn's piercing light breaks into the sepulchre of spiritual darkness.

It is worth noting that although there are modern groups calling themselves the Golden Dawn, and which perform rituals modelled on those practised by the Order, the original Order itself has actually disbanded.

The Antichrist?

Aleister Crowley (1875–1947), is probably the single most influential magician of the modern era, yet he was denounced by the British press as "the wickedest man in the world."

Crowley claimed to reveal his true identity when he adopted the magical motto To Mega Therion – the Great Wild Beast! By gematria, converting the Greek letters of Crowley's motto into numbers, we arrive at 666, one of the most controversial and yet most widely known of all magical ciphers. In the Revelation of St John the Divine (chapter 13), we find the famous passage: "Here is wisdom: let him who has understanding count the number of the beast, which is the number of a man, and his number is 666." Bible scholars equate this number with the antichrist who tests the mettle of the faithful as they wait for Jesus's return to Earth. But why did Crowley choose to identify himself with the biblical beast of the apocalypse? Partly, simply to spite his mother. She subjected him to a particularly strict Christian upbringing (the family were members of the Plymouth Brethren, a secretive fundamentalist sect which, for example, abhorred Christmas and banned toys), and continually upbraided him for any childish misdemeanour. One of her scolds, particularly used for any blasphemous behaviour, was to call him a "Beast". Little did she know how his inquiring mind would eventually come to take her at her word! As he grew up Crowley rebelled against the confines of this very disciplined religion. Eventually, he embarked on a purposeful quest to discover and liberate the personal passion that was damned by its narrow creed.

Although the Plymouth Brethren were (and still are) an extreme example of doctrinal rigidity, Crowley profoundly resented the way that all branches of orthodox Christianity erect almost insuperable barriers between people and divinity. He particularly distrusted the established priesthood which, he felt, actually stands in the way, preventing the congregation from experiencing the immanence of the divine for themselves.

This iconoclastic attitude was tempered by a great deal of study and religious tolerance however. In a characteristically blunt statement, Crowley himself said, "I did not hate God or Christ, but merely the God and Christ of the people I hated." In particular, Crowley sought to release sex from the shroud of sin that Christianity had draped over the naked truth of human nature. His detractors say that he merely sought to return to the excesses of primitive orgiastic paganism. There is no doubt that sexual ecstasy (Dionysian, Tantric and so on) featured prominently in his way of life, but there was more to Crowley than that.

There were the drugs as well . . .

In 1910 Crowley staged a series of seven of his own plays (collectively entitled the *Rites of Eleusis*) at Westminster, London. These were designed to kindle a spark of divine fervour and enflame actors and audience alike with a glimpse of the sacred fire that purifies the soul. Certainly the plays involved the audience in a level of participation that formed a landmark in the history of theatre. The audience was invited to drink from a sacred "cup of libation," a particularly powerful potion believed to contain alcohol, mescaline and opium! Crowley himself nursed a drug habit throughout most of his life but his powerful physique and strength of will prevented the chronic debilitation and degeneration associated with many addicts. Practising the magical arts demanded discipline – especially in view of a revelation he received in Cairo, in 1904. Written at the dictation of his Guardian Angel, Aiwass, the Book of the Law became his own personal holy book, and marked the beginning of a new spiritual age – the Aeon of Horus; Crowley himself was the Prophet of the New Aeon.

Inspired by his vision of humanity, freed from the confines of exploitative religions, and armed with the authority of his Book, Crowley soon attracted disciples. He set up his own magical order, the Argenteum Astrum ("Silver Star"), in 1909 and even founded an Abbey (whose eventual dissolution was instigated by the Italian dictator, Mussolini).

In the sixteenth year of the new Aeon (1920), the Abbey of Thelema ("Will") was established on the island of Sicily. Psychedelic paintings soon adorned the interior walls of what was simply a farmhouse. The pictures in the so-called Chamber of Nightmares, for example, sought to represent all the terrifying images that could bedevil the imaginations of the unwary. Crowley's idea was to immunize the novice so as to avoid the full horror of the "bad trip." In these bizarre surroundings, the Thelemites practised a routine of daily observations, as would the residents of any conventional abbey. Instead of the solemn matins and vespers of Christian devotion, however, Crowley and the others would leave the abbey walls at dawn, noon, dusk and midnight to celebrate and salute the sun, the shining symbol of inner strength and liberality that they aspired toward.

Every morning they donned ceremonial robes and engaged in a group ritual around a hexagonal altar bedecked with candles, a copy of the Book of the Law, a bell, sword, cup and other instruments of the magician's craft. They even practised their own version of Grace, recited before meals, and dedicating themselves to accomplishing the Great Work of spiritual enlightenment. On special occasions they performed a dramatic ritual of Crowley's own design, a Gnostic Mass.

The Thelemic creed and commandment is "Do what thou wilt shall be the whole of the law". And the means of demonstrating devotion is enshrined in the phrase "Love is the law, love under will". The abbey was certainly the scene of an orgy of sexual self-expression and liberal experimentation with drugs, and these were combined with intense magical activity ranging from yogic meditation to the conjuration of spirits and even gods. In experiencing all forms of ecstasy the Thelemites aspired toward union with the divine.

The Book of the Law observes that "Every man and every woman is a star". And in this single sentence lies the heart of Crowley's philosophy. He believed that we should no longer regard the sun from the point of view of most primal religions (which, he would argue, includes Christianity), as something that dies at sunset and is reborn at dawn. Instead, he taught that each and every person should gaze from the perspective of the sun itself, constantly shining beyond the duality of earthly night and day, darkness and light, evil and good. The sun, as any ritual magician will know, is represented by the number 666.

As head of the abbey, Crowley – the Great Wild Beast – inevitably dominated proceedings, but he always urged his disciples to think and act for themselves. He did not wish for our species to continue to be blinded by superstition, nor enslaved by the seductions of corrupt political or religious leaders. Indeed, his insistence on banishing all traces of blind devotion to faith provided a memorable Thelemic motto and battle cry: "The method of science – the aim of religion". By subjecting his methods to the objective test of repeatability, Crowley sought to place magic on a scientifically credible platform. Nevertheless, he did not merely wish to get magic accredited with the scientific community: he regarded science as having much to learn from magic!

The magic of yesterday is often recreated in the science of tomorrow. It is worth reminding ourselves that our species has already all but mastered the technology of space flight, and solved the riddle of genetic engineering, and is in the course of unravelling the mysteries of the ageing process. We are on the brink of immortality, and of being able to create life in our own image. By the standards of our forebears, we are becoming a race of gods! Nevertheless, unless we take care to act with prudence, we face the traditional punishment meted out to the selfish gods of ancient myth. Only, this time, it won't be merely a continent – like the legendary Atlantis – that is destroyed: it could be our entire planet.

Like countless generations of magicians before him, Crowley firmly believed in the existence of "beings of intelligence and power of a far higher quality than anything we can conceive of as human". Consequently, he knew that the only logical course for mankind is to discover as much as possible about these beings: the immortal, universal custodians of the magical arts.

Can we really afford to ignore this directive?

To return to the problem that concerned us at the beginning of this section – how to define the magical arts – we should perhaps consider Crowley's own definition of magic (which he spells with a suffix k): "Magick is the Science and Art of causing Change to occur in conformity with will". And, as Tony Phillips, Thelemic magician, aptly comments: "One could say then, that Magick is simply the art of living."

PART SIX

Dreams and Dreaming

●●●●●●●●●●●●●●●●●●●●●●●●●●●●●●●●●●

The Mysterious World of Dreams

> *"... to sleep, perchance to dream ..."*
> (Hamlet, Act III, scene 1, l65)

For as long as the human species has been self-aware, it has been fascinated, even obsessed, with the ability to dream and with what those dreams might mean.

Humans aren't the only animals to dream. Apparently, nearly all mammals experience dreams of some sort, and anyone who owns a pet cat or dog has probably watched, fascinated, as the lips, whiskers and paws twitch in tune to the tiny flickers of the eyelids that speak of activity beneath, and little yelps and whimpers escape from the sleeping animal. Of course, at present we have no way of knowing *what* animals dream, only that they appear to do so.

The situation is quite different in humans. The vast majority of people consciously remember at least some of their dreams: some individuals are able to control their dreams, while others find themselves experiencing apparently prophetic or precognitive dreams. Some creatively talented people, indeed, are able to take their dreams and turn them into works of art or literature. But what, exactly, is a dream, and what does dreaming involve? Scientifically speaking, dreaming is the result of electrical activity in the brain – but there is, obviously, a great deal more to dreaming than that!

The Mechanics of Dreaming

It wasn't until the very beginning of the 1950s that the actual physical processes of dreaming were explored. It started with an observation.

Eugene Aserinsky, a graduate physiology student at the University of Chicago, was studying sleep cycles in babies when he noticed that the infants' eyes continued to move, under their eyelids, once they were asleep. Thinking that the movements might be an indicator of periods of light and deep sleep, he reported his data to his professor, Nathaniel Kleitman, and together they commenced a two-year study that combined and coordinated research into what came to be known as REM (for "rapid eye movement") sleep, electrical activity in the brain, and the responses of the body to different types and levels of sleep.

Prior to the publication of their results, in 1953, sleep had been generally thought of as part of a continuum of consciousness, with highly-alert mental states at one end and deep sleep at the other. Dreams were considered nothing more than random events, tending to occur a short while before the sleeper awoke. Now, however, it became apparent that sleep, and dreaming, were far more complicated processes than had been previously thought.

More research has been done over the years, using more and more sophisticated equipment, particularly the electroencephalograph (fortunately usually abbreviated to ECG), which, through electrodes attached to the scalp, measures the electrical activity of the brain. This has been categorized into a variety of brainwaves (patterns of electrical activity), each with its own particular pattern and meaning. It is now known that the sleep cycle falls into several distinct stages.

During the transitional phase between waking and sleeping, known as the hypnagogic stage, muscles relax, the body prepares for sleep, the individual may experience sensations of floating or drifting, and see vivid mental images such as landscapes, abstract forms, a montage of faces, or hear music, voices or jumbled sounds – exactly what sort of images or sounds are seen and heard depends on the individual. (The sudden jerk or spasm that can disturb this state and waken the sleeper, and with which many people will be familiar, is called a hypnagogic startle.)

From the hypnagogic state, the individual slips into the first stage of sleep. This is characterized by alpha waves, which are revealed as rapid, spiky patterns on the ECG, and which typify a relaxed but still wakeful brain. Alpha waves give way to the more regular, slower theta waves which represent light sleep, from which the sleeper can be easily awoken.

The first stage of sleep is usually short, lasting from just a few seconds to about ten minutes. It is followed by a second phase where two different sorts of brain waves are combined: spindles (groups of sharp spikes) which exhibit fast bursts of activity within the brain, and K-complexes (more regular waves with steep peaks and troughs). While this phase is generally considered to be true sleep, individuals waking from it may remember their actual thoughts during the period, or even deny having fallen asleep. (Anyone who has ever "dropped off" after going without sleep for any length of time, then been woken after only a minute or so, will be familiar with the thoughts and sensations associated with this state!)

The third stage occurs fifteen minutes to half an hour after falling asleep, and is characterized by increasingly prevalent large, slow delta waves, and the decrease of spindles and K-complexes. (This phase, often called stage three-four, is frequently divided into two, known as stages three and four, where stage four is marked by even greater delta wave activity and a further decrease in spindle and K-complexes.) It is the deepest level of sleep, when the brain is at its least active, and waking is difficult: disorientation, grogginess and an almost insurmountable need to go back to sleep characterize stage three-four.

Up until this stage the individual has been experiencing non-REM sleep, that is, sleep without dreams. About an hour and half after falling asleep, however, the spindles and K-complexes briefly surge again, triggering true REM sleep, and the dreaming starts.

REM sleep is so different from either wakefulness or non-dreaming sleep that it has been suggested it should be considered a different state of existence. The blood pressure and heart rate both increase, the eyes start making their characteristic rapid movements, and the activity within the brain approaches that of an alert and thoroughly awake mind. At the same time, the body is practically paralysed, with the exception of the eyes, the facial muscles, fingers and toes.

It has been suggested that this paralysis evolved to prevent the animal (the same thing appears to happen to all other mammals believed capable of dreaming) from acting out the activities in the dream and thereby causing harm to itself. The nerve centres that control the paralysis are located within the most primitive and ancient part of the brain, the brainstem. This evolved more than 500 million years ago, and is similar to the entire brain of present-day reptiles, which accounts for its other name, the "reptilian brain". Brainstem activity also determines such vegetative processes as breathing, blood pressure and heart rate. (It has been suggested that some individuals claiming alien abduction are actually suffering from an extended period of paralysis, coupled with disorientation and feelings of paranoia.)

The first period of REM sleep lasts only ten to fifteen minutes, but this increases as the night progresses: the final period can be up to an hour long, which means that most actual dreaming takes place during the last couple of hours of sleep. After each period of REM sleep the brain returns to the second stage and the cycle normally starts again, although stage three-four may be skipped as the night goes on. The cycle takes around an hour and a half to complete.

Brain activity during normal, primarily visual dreaming is centred in the visual cortex of the frontal lobes (one of the latest parts of the brain to evolve), while nightmares, on the other hand, produce activity in the limbic system, the second most ancient part of the brain, and that which deals with "primitive" matters such as the sex drive, the "fight or flight" response, and where emotions are generated (though not actually felt; that happens in the frontal lobes).

Infants spend a great deal of sleep time in the REM state. The proportion of REM sleep declines as we grow up, until reaching young adulthood, when it can make up around 20 per cent of an average adult's sleeping time – meaning we spend about four years dreaming, and can experience 150,000 dreams in a lifetime!

Dreaming has been shown to be vitally important for health. Volunteers in sleep experiments who were woken when their rapid eye movements revealed they had started to dream experienced, amongst other symptoms, stress, irritability, inability to concentrate, and physical symptoms such as high blood pressure, sweating, and bouts of dizziness. (If allowed to go on too long, the dream-deprived individual may even begin to perform acts of violence or display psychotic tendencies, which suggests that such tendencies are dealt with during REM sleep: dreams allow the dreamer to become a little insane while asleep, and act out those primitive emotions in the safety of his own dreaming mind.) When the volunteers were allowed to resume normal sleep, they tended to experience far more REM sleep than normal, as if the brain was trying to make up for the deprivation. Other mammals have been shown to be affected by the lack of REM sleep as well. Experiments with cats have shown that after a period of time (rather longer than for a human) without dreaming, their characters changed: while some became listless, others showed a marked reluctance to take care of themselves in matters such as cleaning and washing.

Why Dream?

So dreaming is of great importance to our health, both mental and physical. Everyone dreams, whether they remember doing so or not. But are dreams significant in and of themselves?

They appear to be so. But different schools of thought have different opinions about the meaning of dreaming. There are those who believe that dreams represent the mind classifying and categorizing the day's experiences, storing anything of importance into the memory and expunging everything else, much like reformatting a computer disk ready to receive the next lot of data. Others – echoing Freud – suggest that dreams are windows into the individual's psyche and represent unfulfilled (and sometimes unrecognized) desires: remembering and interpreting such dreams can give a deep insight into the self. Some people regard dreams as wish fulfilment, finding satisfaction, while asleep, in doing those things they desire but are unable to accomplish while awake. Yet others believe that dreams supply the answers to personal problems or dilemmas, or are messages from something outside the individual dreamer. Ancient cultures, including those of Greece and Egypt, and primitive peoples often believe that dreams are messages sent from the gods to the sleepers, as warnings, or for guidance. Those who believe strongly in the paranormal often consider dreaming as the mental record of astral travel, or see a particular sort of dream as prophetic or precognitive. Artistic people may find their dreams a rich source of creative inspiration. And there are those who believe that the life they live in their dreams is at least as real as that lived in their waking lives.

In general, most people believe that dreams originate from within our minds, are an intimate part of ourselves, reflecting both our inner worlds and how we perceive the external world. More significantly, dreams can help the dreamer to solve problems, especially personal dilemmas, not by "tapping into" any outside source, but by bringing to the surface clues and solutions resolved in the unconscious mind,

which is more sensitive to the subtleties and sublim-
inal messages we encounter in our day to day life. (For
example, an ambiguous relationship with a colleague,
where one is uncertain of the other person's real
feelings, may be made clear in a dream: the unconscious mind picking up on pheromones and body
language not noticed by the conscious mind.)

We can learn a great deal about ourselves from
studying our own dreams, solve some of our personal
problems, and enjoy ourselves along the way. A good
dream can be a source of pleasure and inspiration for a
lifetime!

Memorable Dreams

In the fourth century BC a Chinese philosopher slept
soundly, dreaming that he was a butterfly . . .

Chuang Chou's dream – or rather, the new perspective the dream engendered – has passed down in to
modern folklore. The philosopher, when he awoke,
was unsure of whether it was his human self who had
dreamed he was a butterfly, or whether he was a
butterfly, dreaming it was Chuang Chou. His dream
raises profound questions about the nature of reality.
We perceive all things through our senses, and our
senses can be mistaken or deceived, even if the mind
receiving the stimuli is rational, well ordered and
healthy. After all, strictly speaking, we have no solid
proof that anything exists outside our minds!

One very well-known dream, and its interpretation,
is detailed in the Bible. Genesis 41, 15–37, tells the story
of the Egyptian pharaoh's disturbing dreams. He had
dreamed that, as he stood on the banks of the Nile and
watched, seven fat cows came up out of the water to
graze, only to be followed minutes later by seven

emaciated cows, which proceeded to entirely devour the first group. The dream woke him, but he returned to sleep and a little later had a second dream: seven withered ears of grain devoured seven fruitful and healthy ears of grain. The pharaoh's wise men had been unable to explain his dreams, but Joseph, son of Jacob, imprisoned after being sold into slavery by his brothers and already with a small reputation as an interpreter of dreams, was able to explain to the pharaoh that each cow and ear of grain represented one year: the fat and healthy cows and grain symbolized seven years of good harvest, while the withered betokened seven years of famine. Forearmed with this knowledge, the pharaoh made sure his people took advantage of the good years to store up reserves against the famine.

Another significant biblical dream is recounted in the New Testament. After the birth of Christ, Joseph (husband of Mary, Christ's human mother) was warned in a dream that Herod the Great, king of Judaea at the time, having been visited by wise men who advised him of the birth of Christ, was intent on the destruction of the new king. Heeding the warning, he fled to Egypt with Mary and the newborn, thus escaping what later became known as the Massacre of the Innocents, the slaughter of all male children under two years of age in Bethlehem, in an attempt to kill Christ. Without that warning dream, the Christian faith would never have become reality.

Dreams have often played a part in religion. There are many scattered throughout the Bible, and significant events in other religions are frequently presaged by a dream. Buddha's mother, Maya, dreamed of her son's future greatness before he was even born, and according to Islamic teaching, the first chapter of the Koran was delivered in a dream to the prophet Muhammad, the faith's founder, by the archangel Gabriel.

One particularly significant dream was the basis for a new insight into the human psyche. Jung dreamed he travelled through a grand and imposing two-storey mansion. The upper two floors were handsomely decorated, filled with good, contemporary furniture and fittings, and although he had never visited the house before, he felt at home there, that the house belonged to him. He moved down to the underground parts of the house, which were much older than those above ground. The first level was seemingly medieval in character and the second appeared to be Roman, with a stone-flagged floor. One of the slabs had an iron ring embedded in it. Jung lifted the slab and found himself descending a flight of narrow, stone steps. At the bottom he found himself in a cave, where, amongst scraps of bone and broken pottery, he found two ancient human skulls.

On waking, and after much thought, Jung decided that the mansion symbolized the human psyche. The upper floors, clean, tidy, and well organized, represented the conscious mind; the lower levels, going further back in time the deeper they went, represented the mysterious realms of the unconscious; while the cave at the bottom symbolized the primitive man, the first human. This part of the human psyche, he believed, was filled with a savage energy and psychic potential. He used the insights revealed by the dream to formulate his theory of the collective unconscious.

In 1869 Dmitry Mendeleyev, a professor of chemistry at St Petersburg technological institute, found in a dream the answer he had been seeking for some years. He had been trying to find a way to classify the known chemical elements, according to their atomic weights, into some sort of plan that would not only facilitate ease of use, but also allow him to predict the existence of as yet unknown elements. In his dream he saw what is now known as the Periodic Table of Elements: on waking he carefully and concisely recorded what had been revealed in his dream, only finding one error. (And remarkably, a couple of years later, he was able to correctly predict and assign the properties of three new elements – elements that weren't actually discovered until many years afterwards.) A contemporary fellow scientist, the German chemist, Friedrich von Stradonitz, dreamed that he saw a snake with its tail in its mouth (an *Ouroboros* – see *Common Dreams*). With a flash of uncommon insight, the dream inspired him to run laboratory tests in which he discovered that the atoms in the benzene molecule formed a ring, rather than a straight-line arrangement as had been previously believed. (Given that benzene derivatives are used in the manufacture of everything from painkillers to insecticides and from photographic developing fluids to explosives, this is a more important discovery than might at first appear to the non-scientist!)

Writers and artists have also found dreams to be fertile sources of inspiration. Robert Louis Stevenson believed strongly in the "Little People" (brownies, elves and other faerie folk), and credited them with delivering many of his stories to him, complete, in dreams – a claim that could be viewed either as misplaced modesty or as a way to allocate blame to an external force should his tales not prove successful. Mozart, Schumann and Wagner (amongst others) claimed to have first heard a number of their own compositions while dreaming, which they then wrote down upon waking.

Finally, one notorious historical dream is that claimed by a twenty-eight-year-old corporal in the German army, at the Somme in November 1917, during World War I. The rest of his exhausted company were asleep in their bunker during a lull in the artillery bombardment, but he was restless. Eventually he did fall asleep, but was jolted awake soon after by a nightmare in which he was buried alive under earth and molten iron, bleeding and trapped with no way to escape. Shaken, he left the bunker and, as if still dreaming, walked into the area separating the German army from the French (the shell-pocked stretch of land known as no-man's-land). Brought to his senses by a burst of gunfire, he turned to rush back to safety – only to see that an artillery shell had scored a direct hit on the bunker, caving in the ground and burying his companions under tons of earth and rubble. The dream, apparently, had saved his life. Of course, it is possible that the watchers on the French side, seeing the lone figure appear from nowhere, had made the logical assumption that there was a bunker nearby and acted accordingly. Nevertheless, whether the dream saved his own life, or actually caused the death of his fellows, the young man survived. His name was Adolf Hitler, and he went on to become one of the most hated and infamous figures in recent history.

Psychoanalysis and Dreams

Two well-known and, in their time, innovative individuals come immediately to mind when considering the impact the concept of dreaming has had on the relatively new science of psychoanalysis. Although both were generally in agreement on the subject, eventually they came to promote quite opposite theories. It is a subject for speculation as to how much their very different childhood backgrounds influenced them in their later work!

Freud

Sigmund Freud was born into a middle-class Jewish family on 6 May 1856, at Freiberg in Moravia, the adored first son of Amalie and Jacob (a wool merchant.) Ambitious, intelligent and studious even as a child, Freud's parents encouraged his education, later sacrificing their own comfort to send him to the University of Vienna (in 1873), where he trained as a neurologist. From 1885 until 1886 he studied at the Salpêtrière, the Parisian hospital for nervous diseases, under Charcot: it was during this time that he first became interested in hysterical "ailments" (previously thought to have physical origins), and the way in which hypnosis could be used to explore the workings of the mind.

Eventually Freud developed the ideas inherent in hypnosis (that the subject should be persuaded to remember traumatic events or occurrences that had resulted in their conditions) into his own theory of free association. Although most people nowadays are familiar with the notion of having a subject say whatever comes into his mind, at the time it was novel and perhaps even a little alarming, since it was able to provide profound insights into the human mind. After a while, however, Freud found that the subject seemed to come up against a barrier, preventing the individual from continuing with the exercise. The conscious mind effectively comes up against the unconscious, which operates entirely differently to the controlled, well-ordered (in the main) conscious mind.

Using his own dreams as source material, and employing the research of Karl Scherner (who considered that dreams communicate in symbols) and Dr Radestock (a proponent of behavioural research), Freud gradually developed his own theories about the nature of the human psyche. He divided it into three unequal parts: the id (the uncoordinated unconscious), the ego (the organized, realistic, conscious mind) and the super-ego (the moralistic, critical, controlling force of the modern mind, that which, in Freud's view, made the individual a responsible, moral being able to function in society). Freud believed that the human psyche found sexual urges repugnant, and the super-ego existed to keep them under control. The id he saw as a negative, frightening force, which should be kept tightly restrained. The unconscious contents of the mind, contained in the id, consist of desires and wishes, primarily sexual in nature, which derived their potency from basic physical instincts. And sex, to the vast majority of Western people in Freud's time, was something dangerous, taboo and not to be discussed.

Dreams – and the symptoms of insanity in its various phases – were seen as manifestations of repressed desires, which were nearly always sexual in nature. Freud's inquiry into the nature of dreams led him to conclude that they are the product of the conflict between the instinctive unconscious impulses and the controlled conscious motivations. By analyzing the dreams of his patients, he was able to determine the causes of their neuroses. He also discovered that the unconscious has no organizational ability: impulses and desires are uninfluenced by each other, and opposite desires can exist side by side.

Freud is perhaps best remembered for his formulation of the Oedipal theory, which states, in brief, that every male child has a deeply buried desire to kill his father and mate with his mother. (A more recent companion theory, the Electra complex, proposes that the female child desires to kill her mother and mate with her father. It is known that his mother was Freud's inspiration for the Oedipal complex.) He was also responsible for determining that all human beings have sexual impulses, from newborn infants onwards, a suggestion that would have been quite shocking in the restrictive atmosphere of his day!

Jung

Jung was born in 1875 in Switzerland, into a family of psychics. His mother had frequent premonitions, his relatives held séances, and glass in the family home shattered for no reason. As a child, Jung was fascinated by the paranormal, and started having vivid, intense and profoundly moving dreams, which lasted into his adult life. He became a student of Sigmund Freud around 1906, although he had been fascinated by the man's work and theories since reading his *Interpretation of Dreams* in 1900. For a while, he adhered to Freud's theories of psychoanalysis, but gradually, between 1910 and 1913, he began to have serious misgivings about some elements of Freud's work. At the same time he continued to develop his own theories, a process helped immeasurably by the profound insight revealed to him in a dream (see *Memorable Dreams*).

Jung believed that dreams are messages from the subconscious to the conscious mind, a relatively painless way for the mind to deal with unpleasant past experiences, resolve problems in the present, and solve inner conflicts, and that dreams communicate in a fairly uncomplicated manner. He also considered that dreams may be the mind's way of exploring life's mysteries. Dreams are glimpses into a commonly shared heritage – known as the Collective Unconscious, in which all humankind participates.

The theory has much to recommend it. It explains, for example, why certain symbols seem to have a global meaning (the circle, for example, symbolizing wholeness and completion world-wide). It is also far more flexible than Freudian analysis. Using Freud's method, practically everything is reduced to a sexual symbol: tall upright objects, no matter what they might actually mean to the dreamer, were phallic symbols; climbing a ladder, flying or even playing a piano represented sexual excitement and the sensations and rhythms of sexual intercourse. Jung advised that objects and activities in dreams should be interpreted according to the dream's meaning for the dreamer (which meaning may, or may not, have sexual content). Sometimes the object might simply be just that, a familiar object with no hidden meaning. An open mind was absolutely essential when approaching dream-analysis: Jung himself said:

"Never forget even for a moment that, in dream-analysis, we walk on treacherous ground – nothing is certain except uncertainty. An apt warning for the dream-interpreter – despite its paradoxical nature – would be: 'do anything you like. Just don't try to understand!' "

Of course, this theory not only removed much of the unrelieved negativity with which Freud, himself apparently sexually repressed, imbued the unconscious mind: Jung agreed that it could be destructive but that, more importantly, the unconscious was also the source of artistic creativity, and was the driving force behind humanity's urge towards reaching its true potential. Jung's ideas also directly attacked Freud's fundamental theory of the human psyche as divided into id, ego and super-ego. To Jung, there was no need for a controlling, moralistic "warden" to ensure that the individual behaved correctly and responsibly in daily life: when balanced, the conscious and unconscious minds worked together in harmony to enhance the individual's drive to achieve wholeness. If they are not working in equilibrium, the unconscious will make it quite clear to the conscious mind, in dreams, what is going wrong, sometimes by inducing neuroses.

To achieve a state of wholeness, it may be necessary to face some startling – and possibly unpalatable – truths. Jung considered that the psyche of every human contains male (the *animus*) and female (the *anima*) halves, which need to be accepted and integrated into the character. If they aren't, they will make their presence known in dreams, significant female figures symbolizing the *anima* and significant male figures the *animus*. (These are not necessarily restricted to the opposite sex, incidentally. A woman trying too hard to behave like her male colleagues, to the extent that she denies much of her femaleness, may be subject to dreams centred around a powerful female figure, her *anima*. In much the same way, a man who is subjected to continual criticism and denigration, in circumstances in which he cannot fight back, may find his dreams focused on a strong male figure, his *animus*, pointing out that he needs to do something to redress the balance.)

Jung thought it likely that humans actually dream all the time, but that the noise and concerns of our waking lives drown out the sounds and images produced from the unconscious. Current research into the science of dreaming has shown this to be inaccurate, in the literal sense in any case, although anyone who has ever experienced daydreaming – and knows how easy it is to slip into that consciously dreamlike state – may feel that perhaps Jung was right, after all!

How far Jung's unconventional and surprisingly tolerant (for the time, anyway) perception of the human psyche was influenced by his upbringing is a fascinating topic, especially if compared with the way in which Freud's upbringing biased his own theories.

Common Dreams
There are some archetypal dreams common to all people, regardless of their origin or lifestyle. While the individual's reaction to them may be slightly different, depending on the culture in which they have been raised, nevertheless these dreams touch something very primitive in everyone.

Falling
A dream of falling can be very frightening. Usually the dreamer wakes before hitting the ground, coming

awake with a jerk and usually an uncomfortable adrenaline rush. The fear of falling is a primal one. It has been suggested that it may stem from the experiences of the human species' very ancient, tree-dwelling simian ancestors and reflect a fear of falling to one's death from the trees, or possibly from those first few steps as a baby, when the act of learning to walk marks a momentous change from being dependent to becoming independent. Then again, falling – or rather, the landing after falling – is most often painful, if not actually injurious, which makes it something to be avoided!

Falling has other connotations, less physical but no less real. Falling and failing are often seen as symbols for each other, and as most people know, the knowledge that one has failed is an unpleasant sensation, regardless of the circumstances. A dream of falling frequently symbolizes insecurity.

Freud suggested two interpretations of falling in dreams. The first may be seen as a wish for someone else to take responsibility for a while; falling represents a desire to return to infancy, when the child who fell was picked up, comforted and carried (though to be honest, given the sensations of sheer fear that normally accompany such a dream this seems a little unlikely!). The other interpretation is that a dream of falling may suggest that the dreamer feels he himself has fallen, and this could be morally, or in status, or in some important physical activity. As with all things, the final interpretation must be left to the individual dreamer.

There is a (hopefully!) apocryphal tradition that if the dreamer should hit the ground when dreaming of falling, they will die in reality.

Flying

In direct contrast to dreams of falling are dreams of flying. Very much the opposite of the fear inherent in a falling dream, flying in a dream is usually an intensely pleasurable experience, bringing with it feelings of success and competence, especially if the dreamer has full control over the flight.

There are a number of different interpretations of dreams of flying. Freud, of course, saw it as a symbol of sexual prowess. One of Freud's students, Wilhelm Steckel, linked it with thoughts of death (apparently because ghosts and angels, both associated with death, also flew). It has been perceived as a longing to impose one's will on others, and Jung saw dreams of flying as a desire to break free of limitations, overcome problems, or to attain freedom.

Generally speaking, Jung's interpretation is most readily accepted these days, and the notion of escaping from private problems by simply flying away and leaving them behind, is a very attractive one. It quite often happens that the answers to personal problems are suddenly made clear during dreams of flying, almost as if soaring above the ground has allowed the dreamer a more comprehensive view of the obstacle and the way it may be resolved or avoided. There is a school of thought that equates flying dreams with out-of-body experiences (OOBEs or OBEs: see the section *Taking Control*, later), particularly with what is generally known as astral travel.

Public Nakedness

Naturally, in cultures where physical nudity is the norm such a dream will have far less force (although it may still be meaningful since even in such cultures there is usually some form of habitual bodily adornment – tattoos, jewellery, hairstyling – without which the individual may feel naked).

Generally speaking, dreams of being naked in public reveal a fear of being exposed, though whether such exposure is of something one has done, or said, or actually *is*, may be very much up to individual interpretation. The individual's response to the situation is also important. If being naked produces strong feelings of shame, embarrassment or fear, this will obviously colour the interpretation: the dreamer may feel ashamed of themselves, vulnerable that something they feel guilty about ha be discovered by others. On the other the nakedness can indicate a shedding final or happy acceptance of something changed, or a wish to drop all pretence the real person.

Fleeing

Possibly the most frightening dream running for one's life while being chase someone or something, often only half all the more terrifying because it cannot be clearly seen. The meanings of such a dream can range from the simple fear of being attacked while walking alone (not unusual if such an attack has actually happened in the past), through a morbid fear of a life-threatening illness such as cancer (again, not unusual if friends or family members have already been touched by the disease), to the overpowering presence of past deeds threatening to overtake the dreamer's present life.

The sort of dread this kind of dream evokes easily carries over into waking life, and if at all possible, and especially if the dream keeps recurring, the dreamer should try to interpret the dream in order to resolve and thereby overcome whatever is shaping the situation in the first place.

Uncommon Dreams

Some dreams can be, quite simply, bizarre. Without actually qualifying as nightmares, some can be alarming in the extreme: others may be hysterically funny, while yet others may be highly creative.

Killing
Why should a happy, peace-loving young woman dream, vividly and in great detail, that she took a handgun and a rifle, hunted down two complete strangers, and shot them in cold blood and with a sense of enormous satisfaction? In waking life, she liked meeting strangers, and had a healthy curiosity about other people, other cultures, and life in general. She had no physical, emotional, work-related or mental problems at the time of the dream, in fact she was very happy with her life. Yet she thoroughly enjoyed the dream, and regretted not being able to return to it a second time.

Possibly it was simply a desire for change, for a little excitement in her life. Possibly it symbolized some deep-seated resentment against some hidden part of her own psyche, which she resolved by violence. She has never been able to explain the dream to her own satisfaction.

Dreaming a Song

It had to be one of the most frustrating dreams ever. She heard the music, saw the words written on the lyric sheet, sang along with the others around the campfire. It was a terrific Country and Western song, and in true C&W style it recounted the adventures, and romances, of a free-living cowboy as he rode leisurely from state to state. As the song ended she awoke, immediately grabbing for pencil and paper to write down the words before she forgot them. But as she finished scribbling down the second line, she found, to her distress, that the words and the tune were fading. Within moments they were entirely gone, and she has never been able to recapture them.

Some Common Symbols

Just as there are a few seminal dreams that are common to all humans, regardless of their culture or race, there are also a few highly significant symbols shared by the entire human species. One of the most important of these is the snake.

The snake, or serpent or dragon, appears in all cultures worldwide. Originally, the snake was a potent symbol of the Mother Goddess (see *Witchcraft – the Old Religion* for more details about the Mother Goddess) and therefore of fertility and the power of creation. At the same time, snakes are strange and magical creatures: they have no legs, yet they can move with great swiftness across the earth and under it, making the animal dual-natured, both a symbol of the familiar, nurturing Earth itself and the mysterious, fascinating depths of the unknown.

In the main, the snake as symbol is a strong, positive image. In India, snakes are often viewed as spiritual guides and in America snakes were revered, especially that most powerful of snake forms, Quetzalcoatl (the Feathered Serpent). Quetzalcoatl was the god of the wind, the master of life, who both created and civilized man; he was also the patron of all the arts, and the inventor of the art and skill of metallurgy. For the Greeks, the snake possessed healing powers (partly, perhaps, because of its ability to slough its skin without harm to the animal beneath), an attribute still seen today in the *caduceus*, the snake-entwined staff which is the symbol of the medical profession. The ability to slough its skin grants the snake a further level of meaning as a symbol: that of renewal, both spiritual and physical, and hence reincarnation and rebirth. The *Ouroboros*, pictured as a snake with its tail in its mouth (sometimes believed to be swallowing itself) takes this one step further and symbolizes eternity.

Some snakes, of course are poisonous, and large constrictors are quite capable of crushing a human to death, so snakes should, as a general principle, be treated with caution. Nevertheless, and despite the misunderstandings its dual nature occasionally causes, in symbolic terms the snake is a potent and positive image. Unfortunately the biblical image of the snake as a symbol of darkness and evil has become firmly entrenched in the public consciousness, at least in the West, at one and the same time denying its positive aspects and disparaging the wholesome, female-centred religion of which it was an emblem. Freud, of course, given his preoccupation with sex, saw the snake as a phallic symbol; alternatively (and perhaps more significantly) the dual nature of the

The Ouroboros is an ancient totem for seekers of self-understanding.

snake can be seen as representing the merging of the "above ground" conscious mind with the "underground" unconscious, signalling a developing harmony and maturity.

Another potent common symbol is that of water. Life began in the oceans, and without water life is impossible. Water refreshes, relieves thirst, and makes crops grow and animals thrive. It cleanses, purifies, comforts and heals. Yet at the same time it can destroy. Storms, hurricanes, tidal waves, whirlpools – all of these symbolize the destructive power of water.

Water, in both elemental and symbolic terms, very often symbolizes emotion. In dreams, water can represent many familiar feelings or emotions. Calm water and a comforting or comforted feeling suggest security, or a return to the womb with its protective, trouble-free embrace. An expanse of water, with a suggestion of mystery in its depths, often symbolizes the unconscious; calm water suggests that the dreamer is untroubled by the thought of what may lurk below, while a stormy expanse can indicate fear of what may be found in the depths of the dreamer's psyche. A stormy sea often symbolizes the dreamer's sense of helplessness in the face of personal problems which may seem too difficult for one person to deal with; alternatively, it may indicate that the dreamer feels unable to cope with the demands of his own physical or emotional urges. Diving into water may symbolize a search – for meaning, for the solution to problems that may go beyond the exigencies of ordinary day to day life, or to explore the deeper reaches of one's own psyche. Travelling across water often indicates a metamorphosis from one state of being to another, or at least the awareness that such a transformation is possible. And paddling at the water's edge? Slightly fearful curiosity about what lies beyond, perhaps ...

Fire is probably the least ambiguous of the common symbols. It certainly has the capacity to be the most obviously destructive. Yet fire is also, though more subtly, creative.

The sun is the first and most evident representation of fire. Without the sun there would be no warmth, no seasons, no life on the planet. Too little sun makes for a land in the grip of a freezing cold, where living things shrivel and die; yet too much brings drought, sickness and a dry and barren land. While it is possible to control water to some extent (for example with irrigation where there is too little water, or terracing where there is too much), there can be no such control over the sun.

The smaller fires the human race creates on earth have the same kind of power. Fire provides warmth, light and comfort, heat for cooking and, significantly, for forging metal into tools and weapons to make life easier. Fire *transforms* things, changes one thing into another, even if that change is only to cause something that was alive to become dead. But in doing so, fire can also purify.

In dreams, the significance of fire depends very much on both the context and the dreamer's perception of the element. A small fire can symbolize comfort and security, while a large one may indicate passion, possibly a desire that the dreamer fears may burn out of control. A real conflagration may mean that the individual feels he has no control over an external force that may prove life-threatening – or at least life-changing – and of which he is desperately afraid.

Mythologically speaking, fire is very often stolen

from the gods and given to man by a hero figure, who often suffers because of his generosity – the gods being notoriously jealous of their powers. Dreaming of fire, at this deeper level, often indicates a revelation in the mind of the dreamer; it's very much a rite of passage, and as all such changes are, it brings a certain amount of trepidation, as well as elation, in its wake.

Each of these symbols has a dual nature, they can be seen as both creative and destructive. Perhaps they appeal to the human species precisely *because* of this duality which echoes what humans instinctively know about themselves.

The Ancient World and the Interpretation of Dreams

> "A dream not interpreted is like an unread letter
> to the Self."
>
> (The Talmud)

Since time immemorial the human species has recorded, puzzled over and tried to interpret its dreams.

In the case of the aborigines of Australia, it was the land itself that was dreaming, and in dreaming created all the things that live upon it, including the human species itself. (This period of creation is known as the Dreamtime, or the Dreaming: the aborigines still believe that they belong to the land, not the land to them, a healthy and respectful attitude to take towards the homeworld . . .) There are still some cultures which make little or no distinction between "reality" and dreams, including the Ashanti people of west Africa, the Kai of New Guinea, and the Pokomam of Guatemala, while the San of southern Africa consider that they are a dream being dreamed by some greater force.

In the West, in earlier times, it seems most likely that all dreams were believed to be messages from the gods, often giving advice or warnings of problems that could arise if the wrong actions were taken. The ancient Assyrians, Babylonians and Egyptians, amongst others, used professional dream-interpreters to decipher their dreams, and their ideas were disseminated through trade and intermarriage.

The Egyptians of the Middle Kingdom (2000 to 1785 BC) had lists of dream interpretations to assist them in deciphering what their dreams actually meant. Interestingly, Merikare (who ruled around 2070 BC) apparently believed that a dream of disaster presaged exactly the opposite, and *vice versa*, a notion that still prevails today, as anyone who has ever glanced into a dream dictionary will know! (Why this should be so is somewhat unclear. Perhaps it is a form of wish fulfilment or perhaps, by taking note of the negative dream and working to avert the bad fortune, one can ensure it doesn't come about. By that token, presumably a dream of good fortune would inspire complacency, which could overturn any benefit to be gained from future opportunities.) A papyrus from the Ramesside Period (1292–1075 BC) gives detailed interpretations of over 200 dreams, including:

"If you see yourself killing an ox yourself, it betokens killing your enemy – a good dream."

"Eating crocodile flesh betokens being given authority over people – a good dream."

"Burying an old man is a good omen – it betokens that you will prosper."

"Seeing your face reflected in a mirror is unfortunate – it betokens a second wife."

"Being submerged in the river [Nile] is fortunate – it betokens purification."

"Working as a stone mason in your own house is a good dream – it betokens stability and domestic security."

"Wearing white sandals in a dream is unfortunate – the dreamer will roam the earth, with nowhere to call his home."

"Copulating with a woman betokens a period of mourning."

"Being bitten by a dog betokens being afflicted by evil magic."

"Looking at a snake is fortunate – it betokens abundance."

"Dreaming of your bed catching fire is bad – it betokens driving away your wife."

Most ancient Greeks believed that dreams were sent into their sleeping minds by the gods – particularly Hypnos, the god of sleep, and his son Morpheus, the god of dreams. Quite naturally, they were anxious to understand the meaning of these messages, and dream interpretation became a thriving business. One famous interpreter, Artemidorus Daldianus (2nd century AD), actually published a five-volume treatise, the *Oneirocritica* (The Interpretation of Dreams) containing the interpretations of over three thousand dreams. Artemidorus was perhaps the first person to classify dreams into categories, certainly he appears to have been the first actually to commit them to a permanent record. He identified five types of dreams –

symbolic, prophetic, fantasy, nightmare, and daydreams – and, unusually amongst his contemporaries, asserted that while he could provide a basic interpretation for the actions and images in the dream, to be fully understood they must be considered in context and, more significantly, the dreamer's own perception must be taken into account (different images symbolizing different things to different people).

To some extent, Artemidorus acted as a bridge between the accepted belief of dreams as divine messages and the views of Plato and Aristotle who, pre-dating psychoanalysis by many centuries, believed that dreams came from within: "Within us all is a lawless, primitive, wild beast nature that is set free when we sleep" (Plato).

That dreams were considered vitally important is reflected in the fact that most cultures with the ability to record information created books of dream interpretations. Beside Artimedorus's volumes, there were ancient books of dream lore in Hebrew, Latin, Arabic, Russian, German, French, Italian, the Indian languages and Chinese scripts. To some people, however, dreams don't just require interpretation: the dreams shape their entire lives.

Most American Indians believed that their dreams were the foundation and source of their spiritual life, which was, if anything, even more important to them than their physical existence. Dreams and visions shaped the life of the tribe, telling its people where and when to hunt or fish, what songs to make or dances to dance, when to make war. On an individual level, personal dreams gave instructions on choosing a life's work, discovering and adopting a personal totem and selecting symbols, foods, garments or decoration that provided spiritual energy and power. These often came in the form of visual images that were then carved or painted onto personal or tribal artifacts.

Not all dreams were special or powerful, of course, but those that were were eagerly pursued. Many tribes developed "vision quest" rituals, designed to foster spiritually potent dreams: such rituals included fasting, depriving oneself of sleep (which in itself would promote more intense dreaming when sleep was finally allowed), isolation and meditation. Rituals such as the vision quest were also a common part of the Indian rite of passage from childhood to adulthood, and were frequently open to both girls and boys.

Over the last century or so, "dream dictionaries" have become readily available to the buying public. Many of them are simply lists of objects, such as flowers, animals, foodstuffs etc. – or situations – being on board ship, in a garden, climbing a ladder etc., with relatively simple (and sometimes downright spurious!) interpretations allocated to them. (For example, one dictionary suggests that the appearance of a giraffe in a dream is a warning not to meddle in other people's affairs. Quite where this interpretation came from is open to debate, unless it is a visual pun on not "sticking your neck out" . . .) The value of such dictionaries is questionable, not so much because of their content, which can be very useful in suggesting possible meanings for some of the more familiar images and symbols in dreams, but because they are unable, by their nature, to deal with the context and personal meanings of dream-images. Of course, dreaming of consulting an A–Z dictionary of dreams might indicate the search for simple answers to complex problems!

To properly interpret dreams, it's essential to know what each image means to the dreamer. Even the fairly simple image of a bird is fraught with complications. A bird may be a symbol of flight and freedom, or an object of fear, an image of loneliness or bad luck, like a single magpie, for example, or of motherhood and the nesting instinct, or of clear-sightedness and broad-mindedness, or of the struggle for success, or a symbol of frailty and insecurity, or . . . You get the general idea! And all the images, feelings and situations within the dream must be considered as a whole, in context, in order to achieve a comprehensive understanding of the dream in its entirety. The best way to start is by keeping a dream diary.

Taking Control

The keeping of a dream diary requires nothing more than determination and self-discipline. That being said, forcing yourself to lie for a moment after first waking, and run through your dream(s) in your mind before writing them down in as much detail as you can, is hardly the easiest of things to do first thing in the morning (or whenever is your usual rising time), especially if you have to get to work and/or feed a family prior to their making their way to school or employment. Nevertheless, it is a prerequisite for learning to interpret, and even more excitingly, take control of your dreams.

The act of regularly keeping the diary automatically prompts the brain into gradually remembering more and more of your dreams: telling yourself, just as you feel yourself slipping into sleep, that you *will* remember what you dream also helps and after a while your brain starts cooperating. As the diary grows, a number of symbols may recur: it's a good idea to make a special note of these, as they may be highly significant. Try considering what your dream images and situations mean to you: although it may sound paradoxical, the best way to do this is to avoid thinking too hard about them, but just idly to think around the symbols and see what associated images, feelings or emotions are linked to the original. Many people find themselves re-visiting the same dream place, or situations over and over again and, after a while, finding your way around your own "dreamscape" becomes not just easy, but satisfying, and often a positive pleasure. (It's even possible, eventually, to draw maps of your own dream world.) Once you are familiar with your inner world, you can start interpreting what happens there.

Knowing what your dreams mean can be of enormous help in your waking life. Since everything we say, do or think during the day is held in our consciousness and influences, to a greater or lesser degree, what happens in our minds when we sleep, it is quite possible for the unconscious to devise solutions to problems we encounter in our daily life, and not just with regard to our emotional problems or our relationships with other people. Physical ailments and complaints can also be dealt with in dreams, something that was recognized by our ancient ancestors but which has been rather overlooked since the advent of the specialized medical profession. (Of course, serious illnesses should be dealt with professionally.) However, our own bodies often know, instinctively, what they need to cure simple problems, so if you have been feeling under par and your dreams suggest you try eating a lot of honey, forget the diet for a while and see what effect including nature's sweetener with your food can have on your health!

Nightmares can be very nasty, but they can also act to enlighten the dreamer. Nightmares stem from the limbic system, the second most primitive part of the human brain, and are generally concerned with very basic, fundamental fears, although they may be couched in quite sophisticated imagery. The limbic system generates sexual impulses and the "fight or flight" response to perceived threats. Analyzing your nightmares can at the very least reveal deep-seated personal fears – and their sources – which can then be dealt with by your conscious, self-aware mind.

There is an interesting and comparatively rare state of consciousness called *lucid dreaming*. In a lucid dream, the dreamer is not only fully aware that he *is* dreaming, but is also able to affect the dream, which is usually extremely vivid and very realistic. A lucid dreamer interacts with the dream, changing its tone, characters, events, even its location, in effect directing the dream. It's a fascinating experience, and very useful for exploring situations which are not open to the dreamer in waking life (although it's not a great deal of use for problem solving since most dream solutions come unbidden from the unconscious). It is also very effective when dealing with nightmares, since the dreamer can control both the situation and outcome of the dream.

Lucid dreaming is extremely difficult to learn, not least because the dreamer's usual response to the realization that he is aware of dreaming is to wake up with a jerk! Nevertheless, routinely keeping the dream diary can be of assistance, since it helps the brain to be more disciplined while the body is resting, and instructing the mind to dream lucidly before falling asleep may also help. It's certainly worth trying, at any rate.

The notion of prophetic or precognitive dreams is viewed with considerable scepticism by the scientific fraternity. Yet such dreams do happen. Often called psychic dreams, they very often act to warn the dreamer against taking a particular action, or portray events that will happen in the future (or are happening at the present moment but in a location far removed from the dreamer). Such dreams can be frightening: dreaming about the death of a friend or relative is bad enough, but to find out later that they actually *did* die around the time of the dream can be terrifying.

Sometimes, however, a precognitive dream can actually save lives. There have been many instances of individuals who, dreaming of train or plane crashes in which they were involved, have postponed the trip or changed their plans, only to discover later that the vehicle was, in fact, involved in the kind of accident they had dreamed about. By not being on board they had saved their own lives. (To be fair, there are, no doubt, at least an equal number of cases where such a dream did not come true, and the dreamer did nothing more than cause himself inconvenience. This does not change the fact, however, that some people have avoided a lot of pain, mutilation and even death by paying attention to their dreams. Which can't be bad . . .)

Perhaps the best-known case of precognitive dreaming concerns the tragedy of the *Titanic*. Declared unsinkable by her owners, the ship was nevertheless in collision with an iceberg on the night of 14 April 1912 and sank, taking over 1500 people to their deaths. At least one booked passenger, dreaming of the disaster the week before it happened, postponed his trip, and there were at least nineteen other cases of individuals who had dreamed of the tragedy before it happened.

An even more scientifically dubious concept is that of astral travel (sometimes also known as out-of-body experience, OOBE or OBE), but it would be unjust to leave the subject of dreaming without at least touching on the subject.

Astral travel relies on the assumption that humans possess both a physical body and another, insubstantial but nonetheless entirely real "astral" or "etheric" body. This intangible and invisible body, which contains the human soul or spirit (or essential life-force – there are many terms to describe the fundamental "Self" that makes us each unique) is capable of leaving the physical body, travelling under its own power, and returning to the physical body at a later time.

Many, many people through the ages have reported OBEs, sometimes when close to death (after being in a serious accident, for example), sometimes when caught up in religious ecstasy, sometimes due to the use or abuse of various drugs, and sometimes while sleeping. The sensation is said to be something like floating or flying, very pleasant, enjoyable and non-threatening (astral travel of this kind is akin to lucid dreaming). Returning to the physical body is accomplished by simply deciding to do so and willing it to happen (except in the case of OBEs associated with near-death experiences, when the ministrations of the medical staff are usually the recall factor).

It is possible – and can be quite fun – to try a simple experiment in astral travel. Agree to "meet" a friend at a mutually-known location (ideally somewhere you are both very familiar with) on a specific night. Concentrate on the meeting as you fall asleep: if you feel enthusiastic about the rendezvous the chances of success are higher. As soon as you wake, write down your dreams, and meet up with the friend later in the day to compare notes.

It's more than likely that you will need to try this several times before you achieve any valid result, and you may never manage to meet your friend at all. Then again, you might find that you did meet, and talked, and your accounts of the meeting agree. If such is the case, you could always try continuing with the experiment. If nothing else, you will have proved to your own satisfaction that there really may be more to life than is dreamed of by the scientific community . . .

Happy dreaming!

THE unXPLAINED

A great
new series of
six volumes on the
UnXplained. Essential reading
for all fans of curious facts and
strange phenomena.

MIND'S SECRETS

Discover the secrets of the Mind

Explore the most complicated and mysterious phenomenon of all: the human mind.

Mysteries investigated in this volume:

- Hidden Powers of the Mind
- Mystical and Forbidden Knowledge
- Reincarnation
- Mysteries of the Human Body
- Fate, Destiny and Coincidence
- Unknown Forces
- Jinxes and Curses
- Shadows of Death

STRANGE PEOPLE

Discover the private worlds of People

Find out about the inner thoughts and beliefs of some of the World's strangest people.

Mysteries investigated in this volume:

- Vanishings
- A World of Luck
- Hoaxes and Deceptions
- Crimes and Punishments
- Odd and Eccentric People
- All the Rage
- Manias and Delusions

VISIONARIES AND MYSTICS

Discover the secrets of Visionaries and Mystics

For centuries visionaries have explored the hidden pathways of fate. Learn about their discoveries.

Mysteries investigated in this volume:

- Mystic Places
- Visions and Prophecies
- Mystic Quests
- The Mystic Year
- Eastern Mysteries
- Search for the Soul
- Utopian Visions

STRANGE ENCOUNTERS

Discover the world of the UnXplained

Find out the truth behind the strangest phenomena ever witnessed.

Mysteries investigated in this volume:

- UFO Phenomena
- Mysterious Creatures
- Mysterious Lands and Peoples
- Alien Encounters
- Time and Space
- Hauntings
- Phantom Encounters

DREAMS AND MAGIC
Discover the secret world of Dreams and Magic
Find out about the power of dreams and magic.
Mysteries investigated in this volume:

- Ancient Wisdom and Secret Sects
- Powers of Healing
- Dreams and Dreaming
- Witches and Witchcraft
- Magical Arts
- Earth Energies
- Transformations

PSYCHIC POWERS
Discover the world of the Psychic
Find out about the inner recesses of the mind and the power of the psychic.
Mysteries investigated in this volume:

- Psychic Powers
- Psychic Voyages
- Cosmic Connections
- Spirit Summonings
- The Mind and Beyond
- Search for Immortality
- Psychics
- Mind over Matter